WITHOUT PREJUDICE

WITHOUT PREJUDICE

MY LIFE AS A GAY JUDGE

HARVEY BROWNSTONE

Published by ECW Press
665 Gerrard Street East
Toronto, Ontario, Canada M4M 1Y2
416-694-3348 / info@ecwpress.com

Cover design: David Drummond
Photo of author: Adam Sokoloski | mediaUP

To the best of his abilities, the author has related experiences, places, people, and organizations from his memories of them. In order to protect the privacy of others, he has, in some instances, changed the names of certain people and details of events and places.

LIBRARY AND ARCHIVES CANADA CATALOGUING IN PUBLICATION

Title: Without prejudice : my life as a gay judge / Harvey Brownstone.

Names: Brownstone, Harvey, author

Identifiers: Canadiana (print) 20260121797 | Canadiana (ebook) 20260121819

ISBN 978-1-77041-878-3 (softcover)
ISBN 978-1-77852-576-6 (PDF)
ISBN 978-1-77852-575-9 (ePub)

Subjects: LCSH: Brownstone, Harvey. | LCSH: Judges—Ontario—Biography. | LCSH: Gay men—Ontario—Biography. | LCGFT: Autobiographies.

Classification: LCC KE416.B76 A3 2026 | LCC KF345.Z9 B76 2026 kfmod | DDC 347/.014092—dc23

This book is funded in part by the Government of Canada. *Ce livre est financé en partie par le gouvernement du Canada.* We acknowledge the support of the Canada Council for the Arts. *Nous remercions le Conseil des arts du Canada de son soutien.* We would like to acknowledge the funding support of the Ontario Arts Council (OAC) and the Government of Ontario for their support. We also acknowledge the support of the Government of Ontario through the Ontario Book Publishing Tax Credit, and through Ontario Creates.

Canada Council for the Arts | Conseil des arts du Canada

ONTARIO ARTS COUNCIL
CONSEIL DES ARTS DE L'ONTARIO
an Ontario government agency
un organisme du gouvernement de l'Ontario

PRINTED AND BOUND IN CANADA

PRINTING: MARQUIS 5 4 3 2 1

This book is dedicated to the blessed memory of my beloved parents, Odette and Sam Brownstone, who raised me with love and gave me the greatest gift parents can give a child: self-esteem.

And to my partner and best friend, Steve Silver, whose unconditional love, support, and belief in me has given me wings to soar.

And to all my guardian angels: Mrs. Barbara Jarrett, Mr. John Reynolds, Justice Rosalie Abella, Chief Judge Ted Andrews, Julian Schlossberg. Without your belief in me and your constant encouragement, support, and friendship, my life story would not have been worth telling.

And finally, to everyone along the way who told me I would never make anything of myself in life, thank you for teaching me that success is the best revenge.

CONTENTS

INTRODUCTION

It was April 4, 1995, a cool, cloudy day. My parents and I stood gazing at the historic, grandiose edifice of Old City Hall, the central courthouse in downtown Toronto. We entered and, approaching the security officers guarding the foyer, I explained that I was the new judge being sworn in. The two officers gave each other a look of bewilderment, one of them remarking, "You look way too young to be a judge."

I was thirty-eight and thought to myself, *How many more times will I hear that comment before I'm old enough to look like a real judge?*

My mother, bristling at what she felt was an implied insult, rose to her son's defence, like a bear defending its cub. "That's my son! Yes, he's young, but that's because the government couldn't wait to make him a judge. Why wait till he's old? In a few years, he'll be running this whole place!"

I loved that I was making her so proud of me but at the same time felt that old, familiar twinge of embarrassment I'd experienced countless times when my mother's exuberant praise for her son erupted without any hint of humility.

I recalled the time several years earlier when I'd brought my parents to my office at the Ministry of the Attorney General to show them where I worked. I'd just been promoted to the position of acting director of the Ontario government's child support enforcement agency and had moved into my new corner office.

I introduced my parents to my secretary, Jackie, who gushed, "Oh, Mr. and Mrs. Brownstone, your son is just wonderful — so brilliant, accomplished, beloved, and such a great boss."

Without hesitation, my mother, in her inimitable way, replied, "Of course he is. And why wouldn't he be? Who do you think raised him?"

Mortified, I quickly ushered my parents into my office and shut the door. That was Mom. She was incapable of simply replying, "Thank you," and leaving it at that. There was always an edge to everything she said.

And here we were on the day of my swearing-in as a judge of the Ontario Court of Justice. After satisfying the officers that I was indeed the new judge being sworn in, and having passed through the screening station without setting off any alarms, we were admitted into the courthouse. In front of us stretched the stately, ornate front lobby, which was graced by a massive grey-and-white marble staircase, flanked by thick marble balustrades; after a few steps, the staircase split into two, each leading to the second-floor atrium off which the hallways led to the courtrooms.

Courtroom 121 was the largest, most ornate, and by far most imposing chamber. Always used for swearing-in ceremonies, it was awe-inspiring, panelled in gleaming dark oak with intricately carved wainscotting and tracery above the dais and steeped in history and reverence. Above the judge's heavy oak, green-upholstered, throne-like chair hung the coat of arms of the province of Ontario, reminding everyone entering of the significance and dignity of the institution.

A secretary from the regional senior judge's office greeted us and ushered my parents into the courtroom. She then led me to one of the courtrooms being used as a robing room, where the male judges changed into their robes, while the female judges dressed in the next courtroom. All the judges then assembled in an anteroom off the entrance to Courtroom 121.

It was the first time I'd met my new colleagues as one of the "inner circle." They gathered around me, welcoming me into the fold, saying how happy they were for me. As a lawyer who had appeared in front of them (which, I must say, hadn't always been a pleasant experience), I knew many of them. I'd endured homophobic comments like "Tell me, Mr. Brownstone, do you ride sidesaddle?" to which I responded, "Well, Your Honour, that depends on the horse!"

There'd been less-than-subtle admonitions like "Counsel, could you possibly make your arguments in a less effete manner?" which drew a response of "Oh, I'm sorry, Your Honour, I flunked Macho 101 in law school."

One time I had a car accident on my way to court, which made me late for a trial. I ran into court out of breath, looked up at the none-too-pleased judge, and said, "I'm sorry I'm late, Your Honour, but I was rear-ended on my way here." Furrowing his brow, the judge dryly said, "Well, Mr. Brownstone, I hope there was a *car* involved." Without missing a beat, I replied, "Oh yes, Your Honour, it was one of those Italian imports. Compact, but it gave me quite a — jolt."

A notoriously bigoted judge once asked, "Counsel, are you trying to show contempt for this court?" Borrowing a line from Mae West, I coyly responded, "No, Your Honour, I'm doing my best to *hide* it."

I always had a ready answer whenever a judge tried to poke fun at me, and because I did it with humour and a twinkle in my eye rather than with abrasive militancy, I always won over those old geezers. I wish more lawyers and judges understood that, used prudently and tastefully, a touch of levity can be a very effective tool in cooling heated exchanges in the courtroom.

And now, here they were, these last bastions of the "old boys' club," my new colleagues, treating me like a friend and telling me to call them by their first names, despite my instinct to still call them "Your Honour." One of them said to me, "Well, Harvey, you opened our eyes to a new world when you were a lawyer, and now you'll shake us up and bring our court into the twentieth century as a judge. It had to happen eventually, and you're the best one to do it." I resisted the urge to remind him it was almost the twenty-*first*.

Another one remarked, "When you appeared in my court, there was never a dull moment. You brought so much passion and animation to the proceedings. I can't wait to see how you reinvent yourself as a judge with that big personality of yours."

One of my new colleagues, known for his sour and humourless demeanour, came up to me and murmured, "Enjoy this day, kid. Your swearing-in will be the best day of your judicial career. Getting the job is the best part about being a judge. It's all downhill from here."

I smiled politely and thought, *You judges have been living in your ivory towers for so long that you have no idea how most people live. If you think being a judge, with all the perks that come with the job, is "downhill," you've completely lost touch with reality.*

That's exactly what I had a good mind to say, but knowing better than to offend a colleague, I simply smiled and replied, "Well, I think the best part about being a judge will be getting to work with you and all these great colleagues." When you're dealing with people with supersized egos, flattery is a very effective tool.

As I drew the robe over my shoulders for the first time, I suddenly became aware of the weight — not of the robe itself, but of the responsibility for which it stood, and which I was assuming. It was a deeply emotional, reverential moment. I was awestruck by the sheer magnitude and majesty of the title "Judge" and felt a fusion of excitement, pride, and trepidation. The thought of becoming a member of the court, a fundamental institution at the cornerstone of our democracy, was overwhelming. I took several deep breaths and then it was off to the anteroom to begin the ceremony.

The clerk of the court began the swearing-in ceremony with a loud command: "Order. Please rise." Then, led by Chief Justice Sidney Linden and Toronto Regional Senior Justice Bernard Kelly, the procession of judges entered the courtroom. Then it was my turn, followed by dozens of judges and Justices of the Peace.

As I stepped into the courtroom, my vision narrowed, becoming focused on the dais ahead, the great coat of arms above it, and the two senior judges looking down at me as I entered. Despite this being mid-April, the room, given its massive dimensions, was surprisingly warm. I slowly became aware of the crowd and, as I took my seat, quickly scanned the packed courtroom.

Amongst the throng of people attending, including my mother's sister and cousins from France, my father's brothers, and all my friends, I saw my parents seated in the front row, faces beaming, tears welling in their eyes with pride and love. Dozens of former colleagues were also in the crowd. How many of them had told me I was wasting my time to apply for a judicial position? How many times had I been told by supposedly well-meaning people, "Harvey, you're openly gay. No government in their right mind would appoint an openly gay judge, no matter how good a lawyer you are. If you really wanted to be a judge, you should have stayed in the closet." As I proudly took my seat at my swearing-in ceremony, looking out at all those naysayers, I'm sure my facial expression conveyed at least a slight "I told you so" smugness. I had defied all the odds, and I was on top of the world.

Was I the first gay judge ever appointed in Canada? Absolutely not. During my time as a lawyer, I knew at least five or six lesbians and gay men on the Bench, all deeply closeted. Their family and close friends knew they were gay, but none had ever been open about it in the way I had been. I'd worked for the government for six years and brought my partner to parties, never trying to hide who I was. Did I pay a price for my openness in terms of career advancement? Yes, and you'll read about that in the coming chapters. Did I ever, or do I now, regret living my life openly as an out, proud gay man? Never. Not for a single moment. Did I ever think I would be appointed a judge? Honestly, no. But I've always believed in destiny, that some things in life are preordained, and on that momentous day, let me tell you, it made quite a splash in my life.

The ceremony was conducted by the chief justice and the Toronto regional senior judge. As I took my oath of office, my hand on the bible, it was a transformative moment. No longer was I just Harvey. In that moment I became "Mr. Justice Brownstone," with all the gravity and responsibility the title encompassed. Former Chief Judge Ted Andrews, a man I had known, admired, and loved, all the way back to my days at Queen's University, gently and proudly affixed the sash of my new office to my shoulders and warmly shook my hand.

Members of the legal profession, Crown attorney's office, and Law Society of Ontario gave speeches. The Attorney General of Ontario, Marion Boyd, whom I had briefed many times when I was director of the Child Support Enforcement Program, kept her promise to me and attended the ceremony, an extremely rare occurrence. The Attorney General is almost always represented at swearing-in ceremonies by a senior Crown attorney. She made a truly moving speech, commenting on what a historic day this was for the administration of justice and the people of Ontario.

I'd worked on my speech for days, wanting to strike just the right tone of gratitude and reverence for the importance of the day in terms of what it represented for the judicial system, the LGBTQ+ community in Canada, and especially my parents. When it came time to address them, I took a deep breath, fought back the tears, and said, "Mom and Dad, you and I have surmounted more obstacles than most families, and I want you to know how grateful I am for everything you have done to bring me to this momentous day. I love you very much, and I'm so happy you're proud of me."

All I could see as I looked out over the packed courtroom was my parents, beaming, tears streaming down my mother's face.

In that instant, a decade of torrential tears, hysteria, arguments, insults, threats, recriminations, and shame evaporated. I'd waited a lifetime to see that expression of pure love, pride, and joy on my mother's face. It was a powerful moment of redemption, catharsis, and immense healing beyond description. And in that moment, I realized without question that everything I'd been through had been worth it and had happened so that I would turn out to be the person I had become. But what a tempestuous, tumultuous, and turbulent journey it had been.

CHAPTER 1

THE FRENCH CONNECTION

It's a cold, bleak, grey October morning in 1959. I'm three years old and my mother and I are sitting in a hallway outside a nondescript office at the Montreal airport, waiting to be seen by an immigration official. We've just arrived from France to begin a new life. My mother's crying hysterically, and although I have no idea where we are or why she's so despondent, I'm trying my best to reassure her. "Don't worry, Mommy. Everything will be okay. Please don't cry."

Between my mother's sobs and the PA system's constant announcements of arrivals and departures, mostly in a language as foreign to me as Swahili, it's all very confusing and frightening.

That's my earliest memory. A single mother who didn't speak English, with a toddler in her arms and no money, sitting in an airport waiting for a uniformed official to stamp our passports and admit us into Canada, a country about which she knew nothing. I didn't know it but we were heading to a city called Hamilton, a city of unknowns, a city of strangers, and yet, a city of hope. My mother's sister, whom she hadn't seen in years, lived there and had convinced Mom that moving there was the answer to all her problems.

Waiting to meet with the immigration official, Mom sobbed uncontrollably. How had her life come to this? Was she doing the right thing, leaving her native country behind, having no idea how she was going to survive or make a living? The courage and determination it must have taken for her to act so decisively is unimaginable.

My mother's upbringing had been difficult and traumatic. She and her family were originally from France, and in 1940, when the Nazis invaded, being Jewish became unspeakably dangerous. One year before the invasion, to escape the coming Nazi brutality, my mother's parents, who had foreseen the coming storm, packed up their eight children and moved to Oran, Algeria, which was then a French colonial city. They were relatively safe. For the moment. The country wasn't directly occupied by Nazi Germany, but it was controlled by the Vichy French government, a collaborationist regime under the thumb of the Nazis. However, being overwhelmingly populated by Arabs and under the Vichy government, Algeria wasn't a friendly place for Jews.

I never learned many details about my mother's childhood, but it wasn't for lack of trying. Whenever I attempted to broach the subject, she'd get visibly agitated, declaring, "I don't want to think about those days. It was a long time ago and that part of my life is dead and buried. You don't need to know what I went through." To this day, I'm not sure if she was trying to forget or to protect me from the horrors she'd survived. Maybe it was a bit of both.

I knew better than to press the issue. My mother had an explosive temper that, believe me, was best left untriggered. But she did give me some key information, and over the years her sisters in France, my dear aunts, fleshed out more details for me, although they too had to be prodded into revisiting the painful memories of their childhoods.

My mother had good reason to want to obliterate her youth from memory. Her father was blind and received a meagre disability pension from the French government. There were eight children to support, so to make ends meet he helped his brother, who had a fruit-and-vegetable stand at the local market. Her mother was a severe woman, a strict disciplinarian without humour or affection, overwhelmed by the task of providing the necessities of life to a house full of rambunctious children while also caring for a blind husband. Clearly, this woman had reached the limit of her patience and tolerance.

One day, soon after the Nazis occupied France and the Vichy government had been installed in Algeria, my mother's uncle was walking home from Shabbat service at the synagogue when he was brutally attacked and murdered by one of the many antisemitic mobs that routinely terrorized the Jewish community. Not satisfied with simply killing the poor man, the enraged mob cut off his head, stuck it on a pole in the town square for all to see, and hung a sign beneath it with the words "Sale Juif," meaning "Dirty Jew." His name, along with the names of many of my mother's relatives who perished in the Holocaust, is engraved on one of the memorial walls at the Mémorial de la Shoah museum in Paris.

After that horrific event, with rumours circulating that the Nazis were deporting and killing Jews in every country they occupied, and being advised by the local authorities that it was only a matter of time before the Nazis occupied the entire region, my grandparents were jolted into grasping just how precarious their situation had become. They realized they had to do something to protect their children. It was a desperate time filled with terrifying uncertainty and overwhelming, crushing anxiety.

My grandparents heard, through the grapevine, that there were Catholic convents willing to take in and hide Jewish children. After many attempts and failures, and close to their breaking point, they finally found a convent in Algiers. The nuns, putting their own lives at great risk, agreed to hide my mother and her sisters, who lived with them for two years. Mom had one brother, but unfortunately (yet understandably) the nuns refused to take any Jewish boys because they were circumcised, making it easy for the Gestapo to identify and deport them. Fortunately, my grandparents were able to find a non-Jewish family who, for a hefty monthly fee, hid their son.

Mom spoke positively and with great warmth whenever she mentioned her time with the nuns. In fact, although she never specifically said so, I sensed that she liked the nuns more than she liked her own mother. She described them as kind, compassionate, and affectionate — words she never used to describe her mother. And I understand why. I met my maternal grandmother several times when I went to Paris with Mom. She was a real hard nut to crack, definitely lacking warmth and kindness.

My mother's gratitude to the Catholic Church, and in particular the nuns who saved her and her siblings, was immense, and it impacted me in a very unusual way. When the war was over and as she left the convent, Mom told the nuns she would never be able to thank them enough for what they'd done for her.

According to Mom, the Mother Superior responded by saying, "My dear Odette, the best way for you to express your gratitude, to us and to God, would be to raise your first-born child as a Catholic." Mom immediately promised she'd do it. Explaining it to me much later, she said she didn't consider the request that unusual as the nuns had taught her that Jesus was Jewish, and so my Mom reasoned that in truth we were all part of one religion.

Because of that promise, my mother paid a lovely elderly Catholic woman, whom I called "Gram," to take me to the French-Canadian Catholic Church until I was seven years old. Every Sunday we faithfully attended Église Notre-Dame du Perpétuel-Secours, where I learned the catechism and to recite the rosary. Then, when my mother was sure I was sufficiently well rehearsed in the recitations in French, she took me to see the nuns who had saved her. Three of the nuns were living in a convent in Paris at that time. They seemed ancient to me, but I'll never forget their beautiful, warm smiles and all-embracing hugs.

The nuns were thrilled to see her and hear about the new life she'd made for herself in Canada. And then came the moment for which I'd been so well prepared. The nuns sat huddled together in a small group, hushed and intensely focused on me. Standing before them, I delivered the performance of a lifetime, reciting the ancient prayers that formed the very cornerstone of the Catholic Church: the Apostles' Creed, the Our Father, the Hail Marys, the Glory Be, and the Hail Holy Queen, all the while making the sign of the cross as I'd been so well taught.

I still remember, as if it were yesterday, the emotional reaction of those nuns. They wept uncontrollably and smothered me repeatedly with hugs and kisses, telling my mother that seeing a little Jewish boy — the offspring of a Jewish child they'd saved — reciting those Catholic prayers with such enthusiasm (I was a ham, even back then) was the best thanks they could ever have wished for. They took me to the priest, who blessed me and gave me one of the warmest hugs I've ever received.

That event is forever seared into my memory, my consciousness, and my very soul. I learned to respect and appreciate other religions. And I will always remember my mother explaining, "When you make a solemn promise to do something, you must always keep that promise, no matter the cost or effort involved."

As I watched her tearfully express her thanks and appreciation to those sweet, beautiful women, I learned the meaning and importance of true gratitude. Those lessons have served me well throughout my life.

I truly enjoyed going to church and loved the beautiful hymns and Christmas carols ("Jesus Loves Me" and "Angels We Have Heard on High" were my favourites). However, on our return from France, my Catholic education abruptly ended. Having fulfilled her promise to the nuns, my mother decided it was time for her Jewish son to be raised as a Jew.

I promptly began attending synagogue and Hebrew school, but to this day, the Catholic Church occupies a permanent place of warmth in my heart. And when I enter a Catholic church, I have an instant feeling of comfort and familiarity. I think the nuns were right: We are all part of one big religion.

But let's get back to 1959, when my mother and I first arrived in Canada. What drove her to travel with her toddler son to a place an ocean away from everything she ever knew?

After World War II, she and her family left Algeria and moved to Paris. Like most non-Arab French nationals in postwar North Africa, they could see it was only a matter of time before Morocco, Algeria, and Tunisia would break away from France and become independent countries. My mother's family was part of the massive exodus of North African French nationals to France, becoming known by the pejorative term "pied-noir," literally meaning "black foot." I am very proud to be the descendant of a "pied-noir."

Life in Paris wasn't easy. Racism against the "pieds-noirs" was rampant, and my mother's family was poverty stricken, doing their best to survive on my grandfather's paltry disability pension. There was only one solution: to marry off the children at the first opportunity.

My mother married a much older man, a dentist with whom she had absolutely nothing in common. It wasn't a happy marriage, and although brief, it was long enough to produce me. They divorced soon after my birth and my mother was forced to support the two of us on her meagre salary as a secretary at a printing company.

My mother's sister, Jeanine, married a man who'd gotten a job at International Harvester in Hamilton, Ontario. They'd been living in Canada for two years when Jeanine persuaded Mom that life in Canada was good and that she should move there. And that's how my mother and I ended up in Hamilton. Throughout my life, many people have asked how a child born in Paris, France, ended up in the unglamorous, industrial city of Hamilton, Ontario. I have my aunt Jeanine to thank for that, and my gratitude to her is immense, because moving to Canada — and specifically Hamilton — was the best decision my mother ever made.

Now living in Canada, my mother knew she had to find a way to make a living. Over a period of a few days, strolling through downtown Hamilton, she quickly realized no stores were selling ladies' wear from France. There *were* ladies' wear stores, but none had the designs, styles, and elegance of the dresses, suits, blouses, and coats designed and produced in France. Somehow, Mom instinctively knew there was a market for such clothing in Hamilton and, there and then, she decided to open a French fashion boutique.

My aunt and uncle introduced her to a French-Canadian lawyer, Ryan Paquette, who was immediately captivated by Mom's enthusiasm and drive. He took her to a French-speaking bank manager, who, equally mesmerized by Mom's effervescent charm, agreed to give her a small loan — just enough to rent a vacant store and buy some inventory. Et voilà, Odette de Paris, Hamilton's first French fashion boutique, was established.

Although my Mom never made it past Grade 6 and had no training in fashion or any other kind of business, and had only the most rudimentary English-language skills, she built a small empire using her razor-sharp instincts, street smarts, intuitive people skills, and incomparable salesmanship, laced with her irresistible French accent and unique Gallic charisma. Over the years, her business grew from a retail storefront operation in a seedy neighbourhood in Hamilton's east end to an exclusive "by appointment only" boutique operated from home, which she opened in order to be more present in my life as I was growing up. I was so proud of her, because, of all the kids I knew, I was the only one with a mom who had a career beyond being a homemaker.

Mom's retail store was immensely successful, attracting a wealthy, sophisticated clientele. But my irrepressible mother wasn't satisfied. So, in 1979, she decided to step out of her comfort zone and kick it up a notch. She travelled to Paris and convinced one of her suppliers, the prestigious Devernois fashion house, to grant her the exclusive right to represent, import, and sell their line of clothing to other ladies' wear boutiques across Canada. And, as they say, the rest is history. As could only happen with Odette, her drive, determination, and charisma created and grew a spectacularly successful wholesale business.

My mother was a true force of nature and a formidable presence in the fashion community. I've been privileged throughout my life to know some brilliant people, but there is absolutely no question my mother was the smartest human being I've ever known.

She was also the walking definition of a "tough cookie" — irrepressible and relentless in her determination to do things her way. The hardships she'd encountered early in life made her strong, resilient, driven, straight-talking — a person with no filter who didn't mince words. If someone said to her, "Odette, you look gorgeous in that outfit," she'd bluntly respond, as if speaking to an idiot, "Well of course I do. Why do you think I wore it?" I always joke that when I took her to Marineland, she took one look at the sharks and asked, "Do they come with fries?" (I'm kidding, but you get the point.)

Mom sometimes lacked empathy, and when people ask me to describe my mother, I always relate this story. On the day Princess Diana died, I said, "Mom, did you hear the news? Princess Diana just died. Isn't that terrible?" Without skipping a beat, Mom replied, "Better her than me. Pass the salt."

That, in a nutshell, tells you everything you need to know about Odette Brownstone.

As a kid, I'd sometimes cringe at her tough-as-nails interactions with other people. But she passed a lot of that toughness on to me. I couldn't have known back then just how much I would soon need to draw upon that strength and resilience to face the enormous challenges awaiting me . . . many of them because of her.

CHAPTER 2

FINDING A FATHER

My mother's sister Jeanine, her husband Roger, and their three children lived in a compact two-bedroom bungalow on Ferguson Avenue, in the north end of Hamilton, with barely enough room for them all. Once we'd immigrated to Canada, they invited us to live with them (as did many families of Holocaust survivors), making room for us in that modest home. With seven of us sharing not much more than eight hundred square feet — and only one bathroom — it was tight, but we made it work.

And then something miraculous happened, something that would forever change both our lives.

One bright October morning my aunt and uncle took my mom on a tour of Hamilton. They wanted to show her that life in Canada for Jews was nothing like it was back in France, where many Jews, still traumatized by the horrors of the Holocaust, lived very much "under the radar" and did everything possible to conceal their Jewishness. They wanted my mother to see that in Canada, Jews could live openly, in peace and security.

Along the way they showed her the three synagogues in Hamilton, and then took her to the Hamilton Jewish Community Centre — a large building housing a gym, auditorium, Hebrew school, nursery school, summer day camp, seniors day program, programs for teenagers, and many recreational and social activities such as concerts, lecture series, dance classes, pottery classes, cooking classes, and much more. She was stunned. Here was a building where Jews from all different walks of life could openly congregate, play, and learn and not have to fear acts of hatred, violence, or oppression. It was overwhelming.

When these three French people entered the community centre, the receptionist, following her regular routine when newcomers showed up, called the director, Sam Brownstone, to come to the front lobby to greet them. Sam was a handsome, athletic, and charming single man in his early thirties who was instantly smitten by the beautiful, equally charming French woman standing before him. He spent the rest of the afternoon proudly shepherding them around the facility. By the time the tour ended, he asked my mother out on a date, and she readily accepted. I've never understood how they communicated. Sam didn't speak French and Mom didn't speak much English. But without question, a palpable chemistry compensated for those deficits.

Sam had been briefly married to a woman who clearly didn't love him. One day, he came home from work to find her in bed with another man. That was the end of their marriage. Although they had two children, Sam was certain that at least one of them, if not both, was not biologically his. His ex-wife ended up marrying the man she'd had an affair with, and that man raised both children as their father. I've never met them and have no recollection of my dad ever seeing them or even talking about them after he married my mother. In fact, it was only when I was an adult that my father told me about his past. Until then, I'd had no idea he'd been married before meeting Mom.

It didn't take long after that chance meeting at the Jewish community centre for Sam and Odette to realize they were made for each other. They'd each come out of unhappy marriages and were lonely and looking for companionship. Sam was a dignified, gracious, introverted, and serious young man who exemplified the word "gentleman." He had the looks of a matinée idol and exuded kindness in everything he said and did. He was beloved by the Hamilton Jewish community because he could always be counted on to help anyone in need. Odette was a passionate, exuberant, glamorous, and confident young woman oozing with more charisma and joie de vivre than anyone in the quiet, sedate city of Hamilton had ever seen. They found each other irresistible from the moment they met. It was love at first sight.

They had a whirlwind romance and married just three months after they'd met. My dad always said it was my fault they'd married so quickly. He said he'd fallen in love with Mom's French accent, and mine too, when she'd introduced us before going out on their first date. He insisted on including me on all their outings. He took us to drive-in movies and I'd fall asleep in the back seat. He taught me to speak English and enrolled me in the nursery school at the Jewish community centre. Before long I was calling him "Daddy," raising more than a few eyebrows among the centre's staff, who began to believe that I really was his son. Dad was hooked, and I thank God every day that this wonderful man always treated me as his own son.

Having come from a society that made Jews the object of virulent hatred and persecution, my mother was comforted and reassured to be living in Canada. This led her and my father to make a decision when I was four years old that I now fully understand, but at the time caused me great pain and discomfort.

Like many Jewish women in postwar Europe who gave birth to boys, my mother chose not to have me circumcised, since circumcision was the way in which the Nazis identified Jewish boys. She was so traumatized by the stories she'd heard of the Gestapo making little boys drop their pants, and then taking away all the circumcised ones, that she adamantly refused to risk the same thing happening to her son should the Nazis ever regain power.

However, after she married my dad, he convinced her that I should be circumcised, in keeping with Jewish tradition and so I would fit in with all the other Jewish boys, especially at summer camp where we would be changing into our bathing suits to go swimming. Besides, as he explained to her, at that time in North America almost every boy was circumcised at birth regardless of religion, it being considered more hygienic. Attitudes towards circumcision have evolved significantly since then, but at that time it was a routine procedure.

I was four years old, and yet I still remember my trip to the hospital. In the car, Mom cooed reassuringly, "The doctor is just going to do something very quick and simple, and we'll be back home in no time. Don't worry, you won't even feel it."

I've always maintained that my mother was the ultimate salesperson, but nothing could have been further from the truth than what she was trying to sell that day. I don't know how much babies feel when they're circumcised, but when you're four years old, believe me, you definitely feel it. Of course, I was anaesthetized during the surgery, but I will never forget the first time I had to urinate after the operation. It felt like I was peeing razor blades. I almost hit the roof! But after that, I was perfectly fine. I'm not unhappy to have been circumcised, but man oh man, I wish it had been done at birth and not when I was four years old.

Finding Sam Brownstone was the best thing my mother ever did for me. He was an exemplary father. Although his job as "mayor of Hamilton's Jewish community" kept him extremely busy, he never missed an opportunity to spend time with me when he could. He got me up every morning, made my breakfast, and got me to school. He helped me with my homework, always found time to attend every event and activity in which I ever participated, and enthusiastically encouraged me to pursue whatever I expressed interest in — music, theatre, pop culture, stamp collecting, and of course our beautiful cat Suzette and our dog Aimée.

There was never any doubt in my mind that Sam was my real father. I had no memory of my biological father, and since Sam married my mom when I was three, I'd known no other father. And although I never had the movie star looks that Sam had, I resembled him just enough to believe that he was my real father. But, when I was nine years old, my world suddenly came crashing down around me.

I was visiting the home of a schoolmate when my friend's mother suddenly remarked, "Harvey, you look so much like your dad. Isn't that amazing?" I didn't understand what she meant, so I asked, "What do you mean? He's my dad. Why wouldn't I look like him?"

She promptly replied, "Well, no, Harvey, actually he's not your *real* dad. Your mother brought you here from France and *then* she married your father."

I was stunned and couldn't believe what she was saying. My chest felt as though someone had dropped a weight on it. I couldn't seem to catch my breath.

I immediately ran home and confronted my parents with what this woman had just told me. I'll never forget the look my parents gave each other and, in that instant, I knew that what she'd said was true. There were no denials and no reassurances that I'd been misinformed. Instead, my mother exploded in a volcanic fury rivalling that of Mount St. Helens. She screamed, at the top of her lungs, "How could that bitch do such a thing? What business is it of hers? Sam, go get her and bring her here. I'm going to kill her!" My dad stood there in a stupor, too shocked to even react.

In the midst of this tirade, the doorbell rang. It was my friend's mother. I suppose that when she saw how upset I'd been at what she'd revealed, she immediately realized she'd disclosed a well-kept secret. To her credit, she'd come over to our house and faced my mother's towering wrath, bursting into tears and apologizing profusely. I don't know how Mom, given her ferocious rage, restrained herself from violently attacking that poor woman, but I remember standing there, watching this highly volatile scene play out and desperately wishing the woman would go home so that I could ask my parents the questions burning inside me: Who was my real father? Where was he? Why hadn't they told me Sam was not my biological father? And when, if ever, were they planning to tell me the truth?

My friend's mother finally went home, a crumpled, broken woman, tears streaming down her cheeks. My parents then sat me down and told me the truth, that my mom had been married and divorced in France, that she and I had immigrated to Canada when I was three years old, and that very soon thereafter, she had met and married Sam, who'd then adopted me. I took the news well because I loved my dad very much. But I remain firmly convinced that, had my friend's mother not spilled the beans, my parents would have never told me the truth about who my real father was.

I've been asked many times whether I've ever had any curiosity about my biological father, and whether I've made any efforts to find him. The answer to both questions is no. I never asked my mother about him and have never even seen a picture of him. Sam Brownstone is the only father I've ever known, and the only one I would ever want. There was no room and no need in my heart for another father.

One day, when I was in my mid-thirties, I received a letter from a notary in France explaining that my mother's first husband, my biological father, had passed away. In France, a parent is not allowed to disinherit their child, and the letter advised that I was entitled to a small sum of money from his estate. I respectfully declined.

My experiences in family court taught me that the words "mother" and "father" are not just nouns. They're verbs. Being a mother or father is not simply a title, or a crown one wears. It's what you *do* that makes you a parent. And my father, Sam Brownstone, one of the most beloved men in Hamilton's Jewish community, honoured me by choosing to be the father I wanted and needed. I believe the reason I started calling him "Daddy" almost immediately is because my heart and soul knew he was the right father for me.

At the age of fifty-six, Dad was diagnosed with Parkinson's disease, and a decade later, the diagnosis evolved to Lewy body dementia. The neurologist said the illness likely resulted from all the blows to the head he'd endured playing football for the Winnipeg Blue Bombers during the 1947–48 season. He endured his illness with no complaints and with the dignity and serenity he'd demonstrated his whole life. And Mom made sure all his needs were met, in their home, with a live-in caregiver to help them. He died peacefully at the age of eighty-eight, and I miss him every day.

I know I got my extroverted, high-energy personality from my mother, as well as my drive, determination, and ambition. But I inherited my compassion, warmth, sincerity, and desire to make a positive difference in the world from my dad. I am immensely grateful that destiny brought him into my life.

CHAPTER 3

LESSONS ONLY BULLIES CAN TEACH

I don't know exactly when I knew I was different from other children. But I just knew. Sports didn't interest me at all, and neither did playing "cops and robbers" or "cowboys and Indians" with toy guns like the other boys on my street. All I really wanted was to watch sitcoms, memorizing the dialogue. To this day, I can still recite episodes of *I Love Lucy* by heart. I also loved being at my mom's ladies' wear store, watching the customers try on the beautiful dresses.

At age eight, I went to Camp Kadimah in Hamilton. My counsellor, a handsome sixteen-year-old, had a warm smile and a kind disposition. I had a mad crush on him. It wasn't sexual; I didn't know anything about sex. But I was infatuated with him and fascinated by his rugged good looks, athletic build, and magnetic smile. It was complete hero worship, which, of course, many boys develop at that age, but for me there was something else attached to it, a need for attention and maybe even a little affection from him. I had an inkling that my attraction, and the way I interacted with him, wasn't the same as the way the other boys related to him, but I didn't spend much time thinking about it. I just knew, deep down inside, that I was, in some inexplicable way, different from other boys my age.

I was an only child, not growing up with a lot of other kids around me, except at school. Grade 4 was a watershed moment in my life. I was nine and my world degenerated into a living nightmare. Suddenly, I began attracting the attention of the meanest kids at school. I was quickly labelled a "faggot," a "sissy," and a "queer": words I'd never heard before and didn't understand. When I asked one of the bullies what a "faggot" was, he pointed a finger at me and laughed, "*You're* a faggot. A girly boy."

I couldn't understand what he meant. I was clearly a boy, not a girl, and had no desire to be a girl. I was confused, embarrassed, and hurt by the name-calling; whatever those words meant, it was painfully clear from how they were being hurled at me that they meant something horribly vile and despicable.

Children can be incredibly cruel. They zero in on any aspect of a person's personality or physical features different from their own. My classmates became obsessed with taunting, ridiculing, and tormenting me verbally and physically every single day. They were relentless, and there were a lot of them. I tried my very best to be invisible, but to no avail. The bullying continued mercilessly from Grade 4 through Grade 8 — five years of a living nightmare. My only objective every day was to get into the school building in the morning and get back home again in the afternoon without getting beaten up. Unfortunately, most of the time I failed miserably.

The first time I was beaten up, I told my parents. They were horrified and furious. My mother was incandescent with rage. They marched into the school principal's office the next day and read him the riot act. In fact, the secretary had to leave the office due to the volume of my mother's invective. Summoned to the office along with the offending boys, I stood there listening, mortified, as the principal, rather than taking the bullies to task and punishing them, meekly said, "Now children, you've all got to learn to get along. We can't have you fighting with each other."

The perpetrators were instructed to apologize to me and shake my hand. Each of them complied, murmuring, "I'm sorry" and giving my hand the most perfunctory shake imaginable. And that was it. Or so I thought. My parents left and we all went back to class. As the bullies and I walked down the hallway back to class, one of them whispered venomously, "Brownstone, you fucking faggot, just wait. You're dead meat." I was petrified and wanted to crawl into a hole and die.

In those days, school bullies weren't disciplined or suspended. Parents weren't called, nor were the police. Thankfully, schools today have "zero tolerance" policies when bullying and assaults occur, and there are severe consequences, including criminal charges (I dealt with many as a judge), suspension, and sometimes even expulsion from the school. But back then, bullies were simply told to apologize and not do it again. I knew instinctively my parents had accomplished nothing by complaining to the principal. But I was wrong. They had indeed accomplished something — they'd made the situation *much worse*.

You can guess what happened next. The bullies retaliated tenfold. Instead of beating me up on school property, which would have put them in further trouble, they'd wait until I stepped off the school grounds and beat me up in the street. So, I learned the hard way that if I reported the bullying, they'd only make my life infinitely worse. I never complained to my parents again.

For some reason, which I still struggle to understand, my parents never again asked me about the bullying, despite having gone to see the school principal about it. They never commented on the frequent bruises, bumps, scratches, and torn clothing that were impossible to miss. Throughout my elementary school years, there was an "elephant in the room" about which we never spoke: the fact that I was mercilessly victimized, regularly, by my schoolmates.

On only one occasion did I come close to mentioning the bullying to my dad. After a particularly difficult time trying to get home from school in one piece, I casually asked him whether it might be a good idea for me to learn judo, karate, or some other form of martial arts. He didn't ask why I was asking, and I didn't offer any explanation. He simply said, "Harvey, you can't beat the hate out of people." And that was that.

I'm positive now that my parents understood, at some level, what I was going through, but they must have felt powerless to do anything about it. They likely believed that if I wasn't making a big deal out of it (and I wasn't, because of their one failed attempt to help), they shouldn't draw attention to it either, since doing so would only make matters worse. And, in those days, it was generally believed that learning to deal with schoolyard bullies was par for the course, the norm for every child and a rite of passage we all had to overcome. Bullying wasn't really seen as a big deal then.

We lived in a non-Jewish neighbourhood, and I was the only Jewish kid in my school. One day, during the Christmas season, I made the foolish mistake of speaking up and telling the teacher I was Jewish, and that we celebrated Hanukkah, not Christmas. From that day on, I wasn't just the "faggot," the "queer," the "sissy," and the "girly boy." I was the "dirty Jew."

Because of that, the worst beating I ever received was shortly after, in Grade 5. It was the day before Good Friday, and I was surrounded by four boys in the schoolyard who had been taught that the Jews killed Jesus. As I was the only Jew they'd ever met, and therefore the quintessential representative of the Jewish people in their eyes, these morons felt it was their solemn obligation and divine right to punish me as brutally as possible. As they started taunting, threatening, and hitting me, I pleaded, "No guys, you've got it wrong. The Pope said the Jews didn't kill Jesus. The Romans did. My dad saw it on TV."

The bullies were having none of it and kept punching and kicking me. Desperate to end the beating, I got a bright idea and suggested, "Wait a minute. Why don't we go see Miss Parkhouse. She'll clear this up and explain that it was the Romans who killed Jesus, *not* the Jews."

Miss Parkhouse was one of those teachers who was respected by everyone. She was considered to be the authority on all things, so the bullies agreed this was a good idea, and off we went to see her.

I exclaimed desperately through my tears, "Miss Parkhouse! Miss Parkhouse! These guys are saying the Jews killed Jesus. Can you please tell them it's not true?"

She could clearly see I was being ganged up on by four rabidly enraged boys and was crying, panicked, and obviously dishevelled from being beaten up. And yet, this cruel, heartless, despicable excuse for a human being stood there smugly and pompously proclaimed, baring the most evil smile I'd ever seen, "But Harvey, it *is* true. The Jews *did* kill Jesus."

You can guess how those bullies related to this confirmation of their beliefs. They dragged me back to the playground and gave me the worst beating of my life. All I could do was curl up on the ground, cover my head, and wait for the kicking, punching, and spitting to stop. I remember one of them saying, "I think he might be dead. We'd better go." So they left and the ordeal ended. Thanks, Miss Parkhouse. You were some help.

Miss Parkhouse was my homeroom teacher the next year and, within a few days, it was painfully obvious she had an intense dislike for me. On my report card she'd written, "Harvey is excessively talkative and domineering. His personality is off-putting." My dad, who had sized Miss Parkhouse up correctly at the parent-teacher interview, got a red pen and wrote underneath her comments, "Like teacher, like pupil," and sent the report card back to her. This was so out of character for him because he was a gracious and non-confrontational person. You can imagine how that went over with her. Suffice it to say, my year in Miss Parkhouse's class was less than enjoyable.

I had just one friend in elementary school when I was ten years old, a classmate named Jamie. He invited me to his home one day after school for milk and cookies, and I met his parents. The next day he completely avoided me, so I went to him and asked why he was ignoring me. He replied, "My dad says you're a faggot and told me to have nothing more to do with you." He didn't speak to me after that. I was crushed and, once again, couldn't understand what it was about me that made everyone hate me so much.

Several years ago, I received a Facebook friend request from Jamie, and we reconnected. He fleshed out the story a bit more. It turned out that when we were ten years old, he'd written, "I love Harvey" a bunch of times on a piece of paper, and when his father found it on his bedroom nightstand, he exploded. Jamie turned out to be gay and, as you might expect, was totally rejected by his father.

Although most of my elementary school teachers were oblivious to schoolyard bullying, I was extremely fortunate to have had one teacher who was the exception. In Grade 6 I met my first guardian angel, Mrs. Barbara Jarrett. She made it her business to protect me. She'd pretend to scold me in class, fabricate a reason to give me a detention, and make me stay late so that I could leave the building after all the bullies had gone home. On other days, she'd send me off to mail a letter or do some other errand for her, ten minutes before school was to let out, so that I could get away from the building before the bullies got out of school. But this woman's kindness and compassion didn't extend only to me. If she ever heard a student say something unkind about anyone, she'd make the student stand up in front of the class and explain, in detail, why they thought they were better than the person they'd criticized. That was a very effective tool in deterring bullies. She was truly an angel.

On the last day of school in Grade 6, I disconsolately said to my beloved teacher, "Mrs. Jarrett, you've been so good to me. What am I going to do without you next year?" She looked at me with a big, beautiful, warm smile and twinkling eyes and replied, "Harvey, I've gotten myself transferred to Grade 7. I'll be your homeroom teacher again next year." I will never forget the overwhelming surge of happiness and gratitude flowing through me at that moment. I was able to enjoy a great summer holiday and not spend every day dreading my return to school in September, because I knew Mrs. Jarrett would be there to take care of me.

Mrs. Jarrett literally saved my life by doing many extraordinary things to protect me from the bullies. In Grade 8, she persuaded me to run for president of the student council. Imagine my reaction. Me? Student council president? I adamantly refused, but she said I should just trust her and everything would be all right. So, with great reluctance, I agreed. I simply didn't have the nerve to disobey her. But the two students against whom I was running were so much more popular than I could ever hope to be. How could I possibly win?

The election was held by secret ballot and the votes were counted by the principal. To everyone's utter amazement, I won the election by a landslide. The most bullied student in the school was now student council president! When the bullies realized I had so much more support from the student body than anyone could have imagined, they began to back off. Interestingly, no one was prepared to admit they'd voted for me, but there it was: I'd won the election!

Many years later, Mrs. Jarrett and I were sitting in a restaurant having lunch when I asked her, "Do you remember when I was in Grade 8 and you told me to run for student council president?" to which she replied, "Yes, of course I remember that."

"How could you be so sure I would win?" I asked. "Had I lost, I would have been even more bullied than I already was."

Shining a coy, all-knowing smile, she responded, "Oh Harvey, you should know me better than that. You were such a good student. The principal really liked you and knew you'd make an excellent president. It was easy to persuade him that if you won the election, this would convey an important lesson to the students about merit winning out over bullying." She then winked at me and continued, "Besides, you came very close to winning anyway."

My eyes welled up with tears. How many teachers would ever have thought of doing such a thing to give a bullied kid a much-needed victory? Yes, of course it was a case of election rigging, and in retrospect, there are obvious ethical issues arising from what she and the principal did. But when I look back at the lengths to which my schoolteacher went to turn me from a victim to a hero, my heart overflows with awe, gratitude, and love.

Mrs. Jarrett and I have remained dear friends for over sixty years, and she is now approaching ninety years old. We see each other frequently, and I have always considered her to be a substitute mother. She's been present at every major milestone in my life — school graduations, my book launch, award ceremonies — and she was there to console me at the funerals of my parents. When I was sworn in as a judge, she gave a highly memorable speech that brought tears to everyone's eyes. She said, "Harvey, you were the best student I ever had. I always knew you would become a great success, and I'm so happy, proud, and grateful that you made it happen while I'm still on this Earth to share your joy." None of my colleagues could believe I'd kept in touch with one of my elementary school teachers all those years. And after Mrs. Jarrett's speech at my swearing-in ceremony, the Attorney General came up to her and said, "Mrs. Jarrett, you've redeemed my faith in the public education system." It sure isn't easy to find teachers like her anymore.

By the time I got to high school, the bullying ended. By then, those boys were far more interested in pursuing girls than bothering me. Except during gym class, which was always a nightmare because I was so hopelessly klutzy. I was always the last kid picked for baseball or football teams, for good reason. During a soccer game, I once kicked the ball into my own team's net, scoring a goal for the other team. No one had told me we were supposed to kick the ball into the *opposing* team's net. Oops! Definitely not one of my proudest moments.

But even in gym class, I got lucky. I had a very special phys. ed. teacher named Mr. Fairley, whose wife was my music teacher. One day in gym class, we were told to perform three manoeuvres on the parallel bars. I was nonplussed and had no idea what to do. When it came to my turn, I climbed on (which in itself was a minor miracle), moved my hands forward a few paces, and jumped down. Mr. Fairley said, "Harvey, what were your three manoeuvres?" I said, "Sir, my first manoeuvre was to get up on the bars, my second was to manage not to fall off and break my face, and my third was figuring out how to get off that contraption." The entire class roared with laughter.

Mr. Fairley turned to the other boys and, pointing a finger at them, said emphatically, "Gentlemen, you're laughing at Harvey right now, but mark my words. One day he'll accomplish more than *all of you* put together." Then he winked at me and smiled. I was dumbfounded and left the class with my dignity intact. Mr. Fairley instinctively understood that the measure of a great gym teacher is not how he treats the best athlete in the class, but how he treats the worst — and that was definitely me.

Although I was deeply traumatized by the bullying I'd endured as a child, I gained some important lessons from it. Firstly, I learned the value of humour. By the end of Grade 8, I'd developed a quick wit and realized that if I could make people laugh *with* me instead of *at* me, they'd lose interest in attacking me. Making people laugh made me not only feel safe, it made me feel *accepted*. Secondly, I learned that likeability was not necessarily an innate personality characteristic; it could be an acquired skill. For the first time, I was able to use my newfound talent to become popular. Those abilities — humour and likeability — became invaluable and have served me well, not only in my legal career but also in my post-retirement career as a celebrity interviewer.

One day in 1999, I received a call from Mrs. Jarrett. "Harvey, I saw an ad in the newspaper announcing a class reunion party at your high school for the grads of 1974. That's the year you graduated. I think you should go."

I replied, "Mrs. Jarrett, I didn't keep in touch with any of my high school classmates, and I've got no interest in seeing those guys who were so mean to me. I never want to see them again."

"Harvey, you're a well-known judge now," she responded. "You're one of the few students who really made something of himself. I know many of your teachers will be there and they'd love to see you. We're all so proud of you. I want you to go to the party and I'm going with you."

I couldn't bring myself to say no to Mrs. Jarrett, so I reluctantly agreed to go. It turned out to be a life-altering experience.

As the day of the party approached, I became increasingly apprehensive. Which of my classmates would be there? How many of them would I even recognize? How many would remember me? How many of the bullies would be there and, most importantly, did I really want to give them the satisfaction of finding out they'd been right all along, that I *did* turn out to be gay? Part of me hated to admit that those kids who'd labelled me as "faggot" and "queer" had been correct in somehow picking up on my true nature, long before I'd realized it myself.

I arrived at the event a nervous wreck, trying to look confident and self-assured, hoping to conceal my anxiety and apprehension. It was wonderful seeing many of my high school teachers, now retired, who told me how proud they were of my career accomplishments. And many classmates came up to me to say the same thing. I was particularly gratified when so many people said, "Harvey, we always knew you were special and that you'd grow up to be successful in whatever field you chose to pursue."

Back in high school, I certainly hadn't seen myself as "special" or one of those students "most likely to succeed." Far from it. I was amazed and deeply touched that even back then, unbeknownst to me, I'd demonstrated something resembling the seeds of future success.

And then it happened. I came face to face with two of the bullies. They hadn't aged well. Both were overweight, unattractive, and poorly dressed. They appeared to have had more than their share of challenges in life — divorces, unstable work histories, and criminal records for drunk driving and domestic assaults. One of them snidely remarked, "Well, well, well, Harvey Brownstone. Look at you. Mr. Big Shot. A judge now. What's the world coming to? And what's it like being a judge?"

Without missing a beat I declared, "It's great, because I get to send bullies like *you* to jail."

They both stood there wide-eyed, mouths gaping, speechless. And suddenly, a wave of applause and cheering erupted. I hadn't noticed the small group of classmates surrounding us, listening attentively to every word. The two bullies slunk out of sight, and I later learned they both left the event immediately after that awkward exchange.

It's hard to express how cathartic, redemptive, and healing that encounter was for me. The experience brought a sense of closure I hadn't even realized I needed. And I learned one of the most important lessons of my entire life: Success is the best revenge.

A few years ago, I was visiting my beloved Mrs. Jarrett at her retirement home when she remarked animatedly, "Harvey, you won't believe who I just met in the dining room. I was seated at the same table with a woman who introduced herself as Marilyn Bower. She looked familiar to me, so I asked if, by chance, she had any children who'd attended Adelaide Hoodless school. She told me she had three kids who'd attended that school — Jerry, Gary, and Debbie. I realized I'd taught all three of them."

I could feel the blood draining from my face and thought I was going to be ill. Jerry had been the most vicious, relentless bully I'd ever known and had sadistically terrorized me and made my childhood a living hell. He hadn't attended the class reunion, and I hadn't seen or heard anything about him after graduating from high school. And now I found out that his mother was living in the same retirement home as Mrs. Jarrett.

I knew I had to meet this woman. She had to know what her son had put me through. And I was curious to know what had become of him. I told Mrs. Jarrett to be sure to sit with Jerry's mother that night at dinner, and I would show up.

For the next few hours I rehearsed exactly what I was going to say to the mother of the boy who'd so horribly victimized me. I was going to tell her what a monster her son was, and chastise her for her obviously appalling parenting skills. And I was going to make sure she told Jerry that I'd turned out to be successful despite all the terrible things he'd said and done to me.

Feeling confident, with a fire in my belly, I showed up in the dining room at dinnertime. Mrs. Jarrett was seated at a table with a frail-looking, withered, and hunched elderly woman whose lank grey hair hung in strands like wet spaghetti. Her pinched, pale face wore an expression of dejection and defeat. My heart sank. I couldn't reconcile the pathetic-looking woman before me with the image I'd conjured in my mind.

After joining them at the table, Mrs. Jarrett introduced me. "Marilyn, this is Harvey Brownstone, who was in your son Jerry's class at Adelaide Hoodless. I was their teacher."

Mrs. Bower looked at me quizzically and asked, "Harvey Brownstone? I remember that name. Jerry used to talk about you."

I replied, "Well, that doesn't surprise me because he bullied me terribly all through school. He beat me up more times than I can remember. He ruined my childhood."

Without pause, she looked me right in the eye and, with an expressionless face, replied, "Well, what would you expect? That's exactly what he saw his father doing to me every day."

My heart wept for this woman. My carefully rehearsed script went out the window, and all I could bring myself to say was, "How's Jerry now? What's he up to?"

With a look of sadness and frustration, she spat out, "I have no idea. Haven't seen him in years. The last I heard, he got fired for drinking on the job. He's an alcoholic, his wife left him, and I heard he went to jail for beating her up."

Yet again, I felt vindicated. But this time, now understanding *why* Jerry had behaved as he had, my feelings were tempered with empathy, something I would never have expected to feel for the boy who'd tyrannized me so terribly. And in that moment, I was truly healed.

CHAPTER 4

COMING OUT: TIMING IS EVERYTHING

When the schoolyard bullies called me "faggot" and "queer," I had no idea what those words meant. But, by my adolescence, I completely understood, and I knew the bullies had seen something in me that I hadn't. I was physically and emotionally attracted to other men.

I was, without doubt, a homosexual.

At first I tried to convince myself that it was just a phase that would vanish when the right girl came along. But by fourteen, my attractions were intensifying, not diminishing. They were a part of who I was and I couldn't repress those feelings, despite my best efforts.

In the early '70s, as far as I knew, homosexuality was never represented in the media, on TV, or in the movies until Billy Crystal portrayed the first gay character in a sitcom called *Soap*, which premiered in 1977. I'd never heard anyone (except the bullies) talk about homosexuality, and I'd never met anyone who was openly gay. In fact, I'd never even heard the word "gay" until I got to university. As a kid, I remember seeing Liberace on TV and thinking, *He's so outrageous and effeminate, he must be queer like me. But I don't have any desire to wear flamboyant clothes or prance around the way he does. So maybe*

I'm not really queer. It was confusing and perplexing, and there was no one I could talk to about it.

During my high school years, I did what many gay kids of my generation did and suppressed any thoughts of acting on my sexual interests. Unlike some young adolescent and teenaged boys who "experimented" with other boys, I'd had no sexual encounters of any sort before coming out in university when I was nineteen. I kept busy with school, summer camp, watching those wonderful '70s sitcoms and variety shows on TV, participating in community theatre productions, and working at part-time jobs babysitting, delivering newspapers, and taking phone orders for home delivery at a local pizzeria.

When girls expressed interest in going out with me, which thankfully only occurred a few times, I was friendly but always insisted on going out with friends in a group, because I knew there was safety in numbers. And any girl who was hoping for more than simple friendship would be rebuffed with "You're just like a sister to me." That always did the trick.

Being an only child, I was extremely overprotected by my mom, who displayed the typical anxieties manifested by most Holocaust survivors. She wanted to know where I was every minute of the day. If I went out with friends, she'd smell my breath and my hair when I got home to see if I'd consumed alcohol or smoked cigarettes, which I never did.

As I got older, I felt smothered and, like all young adults, longed for my independence. By the time I was nineteen and ready to attend university, I dearly craved the experience of living away from home. So, when my application was accepted by one of Canada's "Ivy League" schools, Queen's University in Kingston, my parents agreed I should attend. And naturally, they agreed to pay for my tuition, residence, books, and living expenses, without which I would never have been able to afford attending university away from home.

And so, in September 1975, at the age of nineteen, I moved into Gordon-Brockington House, the men's residence at Queen's University, to begin my undergraduate studies in French and political science. Thanks to my parents' support, I wouldn't need to apply for a student loan, grants, or scholarships. I was feeling confident and optimistic about my future. And I certainly felt financially secure.

Campus life was exciting, and I loved being away from home, but I was also very lonely. The other young men with whom I lived in residence had only one thing on their minds: sex, with as many girls as possible and as often as possible. It was the mid-'70s and, thanks to the birth control pill, the sexual revolution was in full swing. I had absolutely nothing in common with the other guys, and we ignored each other. I began to feel sorry for myself, resenting that all these guys were partying and getting laid non-stop, while I sat in my room alone every night, frustrated as hell. When would it be *my* turn to have fun? And how would I find other guys like me? I had no clue, and the loneliness and feelings of isolation grew stronger daily.

Several weeks after starting school, I noticed a tiny ad in the student newspaper announcing the weekly meeting of the "Queen's Homophile Association." I had no clue what "homophile" meant; looking it up in the dictionary, I discovered I was, indeed, a homophile. I was intrigued by such a group existing so openly, as well as more than a little curious and excited at the prospect of meeting other young men like me. Would they be effeminate and flamboyant like Liberace? Would any of them be masculine-acting, fit, and handsome? Would there be anyone who might be attracted to me? So with some trepidation, not knowing what to expect, I decided to attend the meeting, which took place at a house on campus called "the Grey House" — condescendingly termed "the Gay House" — which was used as a social centre. Still very afraid of anyone discovering I was gay, I made sure no one saw me entering or leaving the building.

My first meeting at the Queen's Homophile Association was a life-changing event. For the first time, I realized I wasn't alone. There were about twenty people at the meeting, roughly equal numbers of women and men, who were seated in a circle and included students, faculty, and even some members of the general Kingston community. Everyone looked "normal," and I remember thinking to myself, *If I saw any of these people on the street, I wouldn't have a clue any of them were gay.* Certainly no one looked like Liberace. There were no "flaming queens" or "bull dykes" or any of the other queer stereotypes sometimes referred to by ignorant bigots. I'd never met a lesbian before and was impressed by how similar they were to so many of the other girls I'd known. The room felt warm and comforting, and it was obvious that everyone was happy to be there in the company of like-minded people.

The meeting began and everyone introduced themselves. All I could croak out was, "My name is Harvey. I'm a first-year student from Hamilton. And I think I might be gay." I noticed everyone looking at each other with that knowing glance that only another gay person who's gone through what I was experiencing could understand. I was one of a few people there for the first time, and I was the only one who'd never (knowingly) met another gay person.

The group was very welcoming. They explained terms like "coming out," "gay liberation," and "homophobia." They told me about the 1969 Stonewall riots in New York City, led by the courageous Greenwich Village drag queens who'd had their fill of police brutality and discrimination and decided they were going to revolt. They spoke about the need to be more visible and stand up for our right to be treated with fairness, equality, and dignity in employment and housing.

Dan, the president of the group, spoke about the need to decriminalize gay sex. I wondered what he meant by "decriminalize" — was it illegal for two consenting adults of the same sex to have sex? I got my courage up and asked, "I haven't even had sex yet, but when I do, does it mean I could go to jail?"

Dan replied, "That depends where you have it. Homosexuality was decriminalized in Canada in 1969, but it's still illegal in many countries, including the USA. And even here in Canada, sex in gay bathhouses is illegal."

And then I learned that "bathhouses" were places with facilities like showers, saunas, steam rooms, hot tubs, and swimming pools where gay men congregated to meet each other and, if they rented a private cubicle, have sex. (This conversation took place in 1975, six years before the notorious 1981 Toronto bathhouse raids that so viciously persecuted the gay community.)

Dan went on to explain that the Immigration Act prohibited homosexuals from entering Canada (a prohibition repealed in 1978). Gays and lesbians were prohibited from serving in the military (the ban was lifted in 1992), and no protection for gay people existed in the Canadian Bill of Rights or any of the provincial human rights acts. It was completely legal to fire an employee for being gay, eject a tenant for being gay, or refuse to provide goods or services to gay people. As Dan spoke, a feeling of dread and despair grew in the pit of my stomach as what it meant to be gay in 1975 sank in.

There was one burning question I wanted to ask everyone that night. Had any of them told their parents they were gay, and if so, how had it gone? One by one, they told me their coming-out stories. Surprisingly, *all* of them had told their parents — not one had chosen to keep their sexuality a secret from their family. In some cases, the parents weren't surprised, as they'd already figured out the truth and were relieved the issue was finally out in the open. And for some people, especially those from strict religious backgrounds, their parents had disowned them. I remember feeling relieved when I heard that, because my parents weren't orthodox, so I didn't think their religious convictions would be an obstacle to accepting my sexual orientation.

Everyone at the meeting was extremely warm and kind to me, and they knew from personal experience that I was in the midst of self-discovery and turmoil. I asked for advice about how to handle my parents. I explained that we had always been very close and that I'd always confided in them and hated the idea of keeping such a big secret from them. I was sure that, eventually, I'd have a boyfriend and other gay friends. My parents had always known who my friends were, and the idea of hiding such a huge part of my life from them was repugnant. And the entirely dishonest idea of finding a girlfriend, only so that I could pretend to be straight and ward off any suspicions that I might be gay, militated against every fibre of my being.

After listening carefully to everything I'd just said, one of the guy's at the meeting responded, "Harvey, I think you've just answered your own question. You've explained why you'd find it impossible to live a lie and keep such a big secret from your folks." I knew he was right and spent several days ruminating over the conversations I'd had that evening and all that I'd learned from those who'd shared their life experiences and perspectives. I made the difficult decision to go home that weekend and tell my parents the truth, that I was gay. I was going to "come out."

It's said that timing is everything in life. I learned that lesson the hard way. The fact that telling my parents I was gay was the right thing to do didn't mean I had to tell them right away. But I've never been a procrastinator.

And I had absolutely no inkling that I was about to be confronted with a reaction and a series of consequences more negative, hostile, and devastating than I could ever have possibly imagined. My life was about to be turned upside down in every way.

On the bus ride from Kingston to Hamilton, I was in a state of heightened anxiety, my chest pounding as I repeatedly rehearsed and revised the exact words I was going to use to make my announcement to my parents. I must have changed the script at least a dozen times, trying to anticipate the various ways in which they might react, and trying to come up with answers to any questions they might have. I felt so alone and wondered whether I should have invited someone from the Queen's Homophile Association to accompany me, perhaps someone who had been openly gay for a long time and knew more about the gay world than me. I wished I had a sibling who could have been there for support.

There were even some brief moments during that long bus ride when I nearly talked myself out of telling my parents, thinking maybe it was too soon, or maybe it would be better to just lie about myself. But by the time the bus arrived in Hamilton, I'd convinced myself that honesty was always the best policy, that I needed to get this off my chest, and that I had to be strong and speak from my heart. I persuaded myself I had nothing to fear from the two people whom I loved more than anyone in the world, and who loved me just as much. How naïve I was.

It was late on a cool, blustery Friday afternoon when I arrived home. After unpacking, I sat my parents down, took a deep breath, and said, "Mom and Dad, I have something to tell you."

They looked at each other and then at me with great consternation. I took another deep breath and quickly declared, "I'm gay."

My mother replied, "Well of course you are. You've always been a happy, cheerful child. What's wrong with that?"

Shaking my head, I responded, "No, Mom. That's not what I mean. Do you know what a homosexual is?"

Her answer? "Of course. It's people who have sex at home."

Now I knew I was in trouble. She wasn't getting it at all. But my dad came to my rescue. He interjected, "What Harvey is trying to tell us is that he's sexually attracted to men. He's what they call in Yiddish a 'feigele.'"

My mother's mouth flew open. She stared at me for a few seconds that felt like an hour and let out the most bloodcurdling scream I'd ever heard in my life. She then burst into tears, screeching, "What? Nooooo!! *Nooooo!!* You are not a pédé!! You can't be. That's impossible. Not my son!!" (The word "pédé" is a pejorative slang word in French, derived from the word "pedophile.")

My mother was inconsolable. She went on a rampage, spewing myriad rapid-fire statements at a fever pitch, louder than I had ever heard her yell, screaming with such force that I could feel her breath. Through her wild sobs, she shrieked, "Who did this to you? Did someone molest you? Pédés are child molesters! You've been brainwashed! You've joined a cult! You're sick! You need to see a psychiatrist right away. You have to be cured. What did I do in my life to deserve this? This is the thanks I get for being such a good mother? How could you do this to me? Why do you hate me? Are you saying you're never going to get married, and I'm never going to have grandchildren? Who else have you told about this? I don't want anyone to know. What would people think? They'll say I caused this. It's always the mother's fault."

Over and over again, bawling uncontrollably, she screamed, "This can't be happening! God, what's happened to my son! Oh God, don't let this happen to me! Please, God, you have to help me!" She went on like that incessantly for hours.

And my father's reaction? Stunned silence. He had a social work background and was the kindest, most generous, and least judgmental person I've ever known. He told me many years later that he wasn't at all upset or disappointed that I was gay, and that all he ever wanted was my happiness. That weekend, however, he had no visible reaction whatsoever to my announcement. But I know what he was thinking: "A bomb has been dropped on my life. My wife is losing her mind. How am I ever going to deal with my hysterical wife?"

Mom's out-of-control behaviour was all he could focus on, and that was perfectly understandable, because it was all I could focus on as well. My poor dad never got the opportunity to say anything because my mother didn't shut up long enough to give him that chance.

As the weekend progressed, my mother's level of agitation, anger, and panic got worse. Everything I tried to say just backfired. When I said, "But, Mom, I was born this way. It's not a choice I made," she replied, "So you're saying it's my fault. I must have done something wrong when I was pregnant."

When I said, "Mom, I'm exactly the same person I've always been. It's just that you now know the truth about who I am," she said, "I don't want you to be like that. You are not the son I raised. I want my *real* son back!"

When I said, "Mom, there are millions of people all over the world just like me. I'm not the only one," she responded, "What do I care about other people? There are millions of people who are criminals too. Should I care about *them*?"

When I said, "Mom, there are books you can read and experts you can talk to, so you can learn more about homosexuality and dispel all the myths you have in your mind about it," she replied, "Oh, it's not bad enough that *you're* gay. Now you want to make *me* gay too?"

When I said, "Mom, you're not the only parent who's been through this. There's a support group called PFLAG (Parents and Friends of Lesbians and Gays), made up of other parents just like you, and they can really help you deal with this," she responded, "It's bad enough you're putting me through this hell. Now you want me to mix with a bunch of other losers who have raised perverts and child molesters? Are you crazy?"

I was at a complete loss and had no idea what to do.

The last thing my mother said on Saturday night was, "I would rather die than have a gay son. In fact, we should both die. That's the best thing to do." The comment really frightened me, but I went to bed hoping that if Mom had a good night's sleep, she'd calm down and feel better about it in the morning.

A little while after I'd gone to bed, my father came rushing into my bedroom in a panic. "Harvey," he said, "your mom has tried to commit suicide. I've called an ambulance."

I couldn't believe it. Mom had swallowed a bunch of pills (what turned out to be a few Aspirins) and told my dad she was ending her life. I ran to her bedside and asked, "Mom, what have you done? Why are you doing this?"

Gasping with every ounce of dramatic flair she could muster, she murmured, "My son, my son, you've killed me. I can't go on living like this. I want to die. I hope one day you can forgive yourself for what you've done to me."

Not even Greta Garbo's death scene in *Camille* could compare to the Oscar-worthy performance my mother was delivering, and her manipulative behaviour began to anger me.

I said, "Mom, I really doubt you can kill yourself by taking a few Aspirins. And trying to make me feel guilty isn't going to change anything. I've done nothing wrong by just being myself. *You're* the one making this situation so terrible by refusing to accept me." Mom continued to moan, groan, gasp, and sob.

The ambulance attendants arrived. Mom yelled, "I'm dying, I'm dying, my son has just killed me."

The two medics shot me a glance of mixed severity and perplexity. I rolled my eyes and said, "Yes, that's right, she thinks she's going to die because I just told her I'm gay. Should we call the police? Do you think I should be arrested?"

Mom said, "Shut up, you! Does the whole world have to know? This isn't a joke. I know my own body. I can feel myself dying." She then turned to the medics, shrieking, "Are you just going to stand there? Can't you see I'm almost dead? *Do something!*"

The medics sprang into action, putting Mom on a stretcher and loading her into the ambulance. I rode with her in the ambulance out of self-protection. I had no idea what other ridiculous accusations she might decide to hurl at me in the presence of those two attendants, and I had to do damage control by being there to defend myself.

As I was getting in the ambulance with Mom, and expecting Dad to join us, he surprised me by saying, "I'm staying home. Call me when they discharge her and I'll come get you." I didn't ask him why he wasn't coming to the hospital, but I think he was exasperated and exhausted by his wife's behaviour, and he knew as well as I did that she was in no danger whatsoever of dying. I also think he wanted to save himself the embarrassment of what he was sure would transpire at the hospital. Boy, was he right.

Throughout the registration process at the hospital's emergency department, Mom kept repeating, "My son, my son, you've put a knife in my heart. You've killed me. How could you do this to your own mother?"

You can imagine how humiliated and distressed I was in front of the medics and nurses, who glared at me like I was a serial killer. But within minutes after our arrival, I was sure the nurses could clearly tell there was nothing wrong with Mom.

It was obvious my mother was loving all the attention she was receiving. As the crowd around her grew bigger, her performance intensified — gasping, coughing, whimpering, and throwing her head back with great dramatic flair, determined to make everyone believe she was about to heave her last breath. I could tell no one was buying it. The nurses just looked at each other, eyebrows raised, eyes rolling, shoulders shrugged, faint smiles on their faces.

The highlight of the evening came when the emergency room doctor — a handsome, dignified, bespectacled man with clipboard in hand who appeared to be in his late forties — abruptly asked her in a sterile tone why she'd taken so many Aspirins. She sat bolt upright and snapped at him at the top of her lungs, "What do you want from me? They were the only pills we had in the house. Did you expect me to go out and buy real drugs from some criminal just so I could make my son feel guilty? What kind of a woman do you think I am? Do you think I really wanted to die before saving my son from a terrible life?"

I'll never forget the expression of stunned disbelief on the doctor's face, and I swear I noticed him slightly biting his lower lip to keep from laughing. The two nurses who witnessed all this turned to each other, and then to me, with a look of astonished bewilderment, as if they had just watched an incomprehensible scene in a movie. I just shrugged my shoulders, smiled faintly, and gave them a look that said, "Welcome to my world."

While the nurses took my mother to the treatment room for some medication to counteract the effect of the Aspirins, the doctor motioned me over to him and asked, "What's going on here? Why do you think your mother took those pills?"

I explained that she was reacting very badly to my revelation that I was gay. He replied, "What? That's what this is all about? Your mother is trying to manipulate you into feeling guilty by faking a suicide attempt so you'll decide to be straight? This is ridiculous, and with your permission, I intend to tell her so."

I replied, "Doctor, you don't know my mother. She's high-strung and volatile, to put it mildly."

He chuckled and said, "Believe me, you have no idea what I've seen in this emergency room. I can handle her. You'll see."

I thought to myself, *Yeah? You think so? This I gotta see.*

A few hours later, my mother emerged from the treatment room, ready to be discharged. The nurse took me aside and said, "This is the first suicide attempt I've ever seen where the patient insisted on having her hair brushed and makeup applied before even getting treatment. Your mother is unbelievable."

I snickered. "Trust me, you ain't seen nothin' yet."

Just then the doctor appeared, took her aside, and stated, "Look Mrs. Brownstone, suicide is very serious, and you should not be threatening such a thing just to manipulate your son. If he's gay, then that's the way he is and it can't be changed. You're just going to have to accept it."

Mom hissed at him and burst into tears, saying, "Oh, really? Well you've never been a mother. Can't you see my son is sick and needs to be cured? You think it's okay for him to be a homosexual?"

The doctor responded, "No he is *not* sick, and there's *nothing* to cure. He is what he is and you're going to have to come to terms with that."

Mom then turned to me and said in French, "Just my luck. He's probably gay too. The whole damn world has gone crazy. Get me out of this fucking place! Do you realize I could have died in this dump? And it's all your fault!"

And that's how we spent our Saturday night. I shuddered to think what was in store for me on Sunday, my last day before returning to school. It turned out to be one of the worst days of my life.

On Sunday morning, my mother got the bright idea of calling my father's brother-in-law, Stan, a psychiatrist in Calgary. My parents had never been close with my father's sister and her husband, and I don't think I'd met him more than once or twice at family functions. We certainly didn't know each other. But my mother was desperate and was convinced that only a psychiatrist would know what to do about this situation. And since my uncle Stan was the only psychiatrist she'd ever met, it made perfect sense to her that this man, whom she barely knew, would have the solution she was looking for.

She called Stan. I stood there, able to hear only her side of the conversation. To this day I have no idea why I didn't go to one of the other phones in the house and listen in so that I could hear both sides of the conversation.

She began, "Stan, Stan, we need your help. Something horrible has happened. Our son Harvey just told us he thinks he's a homosexual. We're devastated. He's only nineteen, and he's about to ruin his life. We don't know what to do. You're a psychiatrist. What should we do?"

She listened intently while he spoke. I thought he was going to ask to speak with me, but he didn't. The next thing I heard my mom say was, "Really? You think that will work? Okay, we'll do it." And she hung up. That was it. The entire conversation lasted under two minutes.

The next thing I knew, my mother said, "We're throwing you out. Until you come to your senses and change your ways, we want nothing to do with you. Get out of this house."

I was beyond stunned and tried to reason with her, saying, "Mom, you can't be serious. Is that what Uncle Stan told you to do?"

"Yes, that's exactly what he said," she replied. "And he's a psychiatrist, so he knows what's best."

"Mom," I said, "you must have misunderstood him. Let's call him back. Let me speak to him."

She shook her head emphatically and replied, "No. He was clear. There's nothing more to discuss. It was embarrassing enough that I had to call him. Now he'll tell his wife. That bitch has always been jealous of me. She'll tell the whole family. Look what you've done to me."

I could feel tears welling up in my eyes. "But, Mom, this makes no sense. I'm your son. I love you and I know you love me. You're punishing me for something I have no control over. I didn't ask to be gay. It's no different than having brown eyes or being right-handed. You won't change anything by throwing me out."

Clenching her jaw into a monstrous expression, Mom then viciously spewed the most vile and unforgettable words I ever heard her say: "I can't believe I survived the Holocaust for this! You're having sex with other men? If I'd known you would turn out this way, I would have had an abortion. You've ruined my life. I wish you'd never been born."

Those soul-destroying words, uttered in a hysterical fit of volcanic rage, seared themselves into my heart and memory, permeating my consciousness with guilt, shame, and profound remorse for breaking my mother's heart. And those were the last words my mother said to me for five years.

Exhausted, exasperated, defeated, and angry, I knew there was no point saying anything more. And to be honest, after having endured her hysteria all weekend, not to mention the ordeal at the hospital the previous night, I was definitely ready to go back to school in Kingston. So I left.

My dad drove me to the bus depot. He sighed. "Harvey, don't worry. I'll talk with Mom. She'll calm down. She doesn't mean the things she said. You know what she's like. She has a hot temper, but eventually she always cools down. We'll work this out. Just go back to school and give her some time."

His words reassured me, and by the time I got back to school, I was feeling better. I figured the worst was over, and now I just had to give Mom some time to adjust. Everything would be all right.

I couldn't have been more wrong. I was about to find out that life can make you strong, or it can break you. And thank God, I was soon to discover that I had the fortitude to know that nothing would ever break me.

Why did I choose to tell my parents I was gay? The answer is simple: because I needed to. I wanted them to share in the relief I felt that I had finally figured out who and what I was. I needed the two most important people in my life, whom I loved so much and who I knew loved me just as much, to know the truth, because the idea of concealing such a major part of who I was, or being duplicitous and inauthentic, was anathema to me. I knew, without question, that I was constitutionally incapable of living a double life or keeping such a big secret.

The more difficult question is, why did I choose to tell my parents I was gay *at that time*, when I was totally financially dependent on them? That's a question I've asked myself a thousand times, and after thinking long and hard about it, the simple explanation is that I didn't, for a moment, anticipate the extent of my mother's volcanic reaction to the news.

I wasn't naïve. I knew my parents wouldn't be happy that I was gay, because even today most parents would prefer that their children not grow up as part of a minority that's still so very misunderstood and despised by a sizeable part of the world's population. Most parents want their children to have as few obstacles as possible to achieving success and happiness, and many parents perceive gay people as having a more difficult and challenging life than straight people. They don't want their children to be discriminated against or ridiculed, which still happens to many LGBTQ+ people today.

I also knew my parents would be terribly disappointed at the prospect of never having grandchildren (the notion of gay people becoming parents was unfathomable back then). And given that my parents were very well known in Hamilton, I knew they'd be embarrassed if people found out their son was gay because of the negative stigma attached to homosexuals. And yet, even considering all those factors that I knew would present a challenge to parental acceptance, I *still* didn't anticipate the horrific consequences that befell me when they got the news.

Over the years, many people have asked me how I could have so terribly underestimated my mother's reaction. Didn't I know her well enough to anticipate her explosion and the devastating aftermath that ensued? First of all, she was in the fashion business, which was dominated by gay men, many of whom were her friends. As a child I'd accompanied her to Paris on many buying trips, and even in my repressed adolescence, I easily suspected that many of the men she was dealing with were gay. She seemed so comfortable with them, clearly enjoying their company, that I thought my mother liked gay men. I wasn't wrong. She did. But not when it came to her own son.

Secondly, the topic of homosexuality had never come up in conversation with either of my parents, so I'd never heard them express any opinions about it one way or the other. Thirdly, I truly believed that my parents already knew, deep down, that I was gay. After all, if those schoolyard bullies were able to figure me out, how could my own parents have been so blind? I was in many ways the classic, stereotypical gay kid — sensitive, emotional, effeminate, theatrical, and I showed no interest in sports or any activities that other boys typically enjoyed. And most significantly, I'd never expressed any interest whatsoever in dating girls. How could they not have figured me out?

Finally, and perhaps most importantly, I was an only child and had been the centre of my parents' world. Everything revolved around me when I was growing up. My parents showered me with an overabundance of affection, acceptance, encouragement, and love throughout my childhood. I couldn't imagine, in my wildest dreams, that they would cut me out of their lives. But that's exactly what happened.

As for Uncle Stan, the psychiatrist who allegedly told my mother to throw me out, there's a fascinating postscript to that story. When I was in my final year of law school, I got a call from Uncle Stan. He was an alumnus of Queen's University and was coming to Kingston for homecoming weekend and wanted to meet with me. He was the last person I wanted to see, but I was curious about what he wanted, so I agreed to meet him at a restaurant so I could at least get a free meal out of him. I thought it was the least he could do after what he'd put me through. And besides, maybe he would explain why he'd told my parents to throw me out.

He began the conversation by immediately apologizing profusely for the role he'd played in my parental estrangement. He insisted there'd been a terrible misunderstanding. "Harvey," he said emphatically, "I did *not* tell your mother to throw you out. What I said to her was, 'Odette, what are you going to do? Throw him out?' I was trying to make the point to her that she had no choice but to accept you, as there really was no other option. Your mother totally misunderstood me."

I was flabbergasted and beyond dumbfounded. For a moment I thought I was going to faint. I couldn't believe what I was hearing and replied, "You mean, everything I've been through was the result of my mother misinterpreting what you told her? Do you have any idea how much I've suffered because of that misunderstanding?"

He said, "I only recently learned [from another relative] that your parents had thrown you out. I immediately called them and tried to reason with them, but your mother barely let me get a word in edgewise. There was no reasoning with her. She hung up on me. I feel terrible about the situation.

Believe me, Harvey, I would *never* tell a parent to kick out their child, and certainly not for being gay."

What a revelation that was. We had a pleasant visit, and he even gave me a hundred dollars, which he hoped would "give me a hand." That was the last time I saw Uncle Stan, as he passed away the following year.

Many years later, after my parents and I had reconciled, I confronted my mother with what Uncle Stan had told me at the restaurant in Kingston. Of course, Mom exploded. "What? Are you crazy? Do you think I'm so stupid that I didn't understand what he said? He definitely told me to throw you out. I know what I heard. And he never called me afterwards to try to change my mind. That son of a bitch was lying to you."

My mother was convinced that Uncle Stan was embarrassed for having given her such terrible advice, and that's why he lied to me and claimed it was Mom's fault for misunderstanding him.

Who do I believe? Well, that fateful phone conversation between Mom and Uncle Stan was very brief, no more than two minutes. Mom was hysterical at the time and may not have been listening attentively to him. And her English-language skills were never very good. So she may well have misunderstood him. I'll never know for sure who was telling me the truth, and frankly, at this point, it doesn't matter anymore. I believe destiny had a plan for me, and I was meant to go through everything I did so that I could learn important life lessons, which equipped me to achieve success.

CHAPTER 5

THE AFTERMATH

I arrived back at school exhausted and exasperated, yet clinging desperately to my father's reassuring words that echoed in my ears: "Don't worry, Harvey. Mom will calm down and everything will be okay. You'll see."

I spoke to some of my new friends at the Queen's Homophile Association, and they all agreed my mother's initial reaction to the news was not unusual and that I should just give her time to process her feelings. One of them summed it up perfectly by saying, "Listen, Harvey, you're an only child. You're all they've got. Do you really think they're going to erase the only child they have from their lives? It's extremely unlikely. Only religious fanatics disown their children, and your parents aren't ultra-orthodox. You'll probably hear from them in a few days, and life will go on as before. You did the right thing telling them the truth. Now there won't be any lying and you can be yourself."

Those words were comforting, and I tried to put that horrible weekend out of my mind.

A few weeks went by. I was enjoying school, making friends, and going to the Queen's Homophile Association for weekly meetings, where I finally met a few guys that I dated. I was feeling happy, confident, and at peace — except for one thing. Two weeks had passed, and I hadn't heard from my parents. I desperately wanted to call them, but the consensus among my friends was to give them time and space. Dan said, "Don't push them. Believe me, they haven't forgotten about you. They'll come around when they're ready." I took their advice and kept myself occupied in campus life, hoping for the best.

One day in early October, I was summoned to the office of the dean of the men's residence, Mr. Reynolds. He was a husky man who looked to be in his late fifties, with thin strands of grey hair barely covering his balding head, and he wasn't smiling. He asked me to sit down and, with a stern look on his face, inquired, "Harvey, are you having some sort of problem with your parents?"

I shuffled uncomfortably in my seat, totally perplexed, and replied, "Why are you asking?"

He responded, "Because your parents' cheque for October has been returned by the bank with a 'stop payment' — not 'insufficient funds,' a '*stop payment*.'"

My parents had given the university residence office a series of postdated cheques to cover my residence fees and meal plan, and they'd also given me postdated cheques for miscellaneous living expenses.

"Why would your parents deliberately refuse to pay your fees?" he asked. "What's going on?"

I thought I was going to faint. Or vomit. Or both. My heart began racing, my head was pounding, and my stomach felt like it had hit the floor. I could feel my legs trembling. I tried to open my mouth to speak, but no sound came out of me. Mr. Reynolds leaned in towards me and asked, "Harvey, are you okay? What's wrong?"

I burst into tears and told him the truth. "My parents kicked me out because I told them I'm gay. I didn't think they would really cut me off, but now it looks like they have. What am I going to do? I have no money, no other family, and no place to go. Does this mean you're going to throw me out of the residence? Will I have to quit school and get a job?"

I was sobbing uncontrollably and in such a heightened state of panic, fear, and desperation that I'm sure this very nice man was totally taken aback, wondering what in the world he was supposed to do in such a situation. He gave me a tissue to wipe my eyes, made me a cup of tea, and helped me to calm down, stating soothingly, "Harvey, let's see what we can do about this. I'm going to try to help you. Your parents shouldn't have cut you off like this no matter how upset they are. They're in the wrong, not you."

I said, "But what about the fact that I'm gay? I know that gay people have no rights, and you could throw me out of here if you wanted to."

He smiled and responded, "Harvey, we're not living in the Middle Ages. There are many gays and lesbians here at Queen's. Some of them are very highly respected professors. We would never throw anyone out for being gay. And as a parent of two young adults, I can tell you that if one of them were gay, I would certainly never throw them out. What your parents have done is wrong. Let me make a few phone calls and see what I can do. Come back in a few days, and try not to worry too much."

I left his office feeling terribly shaken by the knowledge that my parents had really done the unthinkable and cut me off. But somehow I trusted Mr. Reynolds and felt certain he'd find a way to help me. I soon came to see that this man, whom I'd never met before this, would turn out to be one of the many guardian angels that destiny has blessed me with throughout my life.

Two days later I was once again summoned to Mr. Reynolds's office.

"Harvey," he began, "I have good news." He'd arranged for me to receive a scholarship on the condition that I maintain an "A" average for as long as I attended Queen's University. The scholarship would pay for my tuition and books. Since my parents had already paid for my tuition and books for the first year, the scholarship would begin the following year.

Mr. Reynolds also gave me the forms I'd need to apply for a student loan. In those days, one's eligibility for a student loan depended on their parents' incomes. If your parents earned over a certain amount, they were deemed able to afford to finance your education and you weren't eligible for a student loan, *unless* your parents specifically refused in writing to support you. My parents' incomes were too high, making me ineligible for a student loan, so Mr. Reynolds sent them a form to sign that stated they were refusing to support me. In the meantime, until the loan could begin, he arranged for a "needy student grant" from the school to cover my meals and other expenses.

Ten days later I was again summoned to Mr. Reynolds's office. My parents had returned the student loan form unsigned, with a note from my mom saying, "We are *not* refusing to support Harvey. We will be happy to support him when he comes to his senses and stops being a homosexual. It's all up to him. You're supposed to be giving him a good education. Tell him to do the right thing."

Once again, I burst into tears. "Now what am I going to do?" I asked. "I can't even get a student loan. The grant you got for me isn't going to last much longer."

Mr. Reynolds gave me another tissue to wipe my eyes and responded, "Harvey, calm down. I'm going to call your parents right now. I'm sure I can talk some sense into them."

I countered, "I'm telling you, sir. You don't know my mother. She's extremely difficult to reason with. When she makes up her mind about something, no one can change it."

He replied, "Well, then I'll talk to your father."

My heart sank. I responded, "Sir, you don't understand. My dad is a good man, but he has absolutely no power in that relationship. I know he's on my side but he can't stand up to my mom. It's always been that way."

Mr. Reynolds picked up the phone and declared, "Well, I really feel I have to at least try to get them to sign that form. Let's see what happens. We have nothing to lose."

So I gave him my parents' phone number and said a silent prayer, hoping for the best.

Once again, I was sitting there listening to only one half of a telephone conversation. My mother answered the phone and Mr. Reynolds introduced himself, saying, "Mrs. Brownstone, Harvey has told me the whole situation, and I can understand how upset and disappointed you must be, but depriving your son of the support he needs to get an education is not the way to handle this." My mother spoke for a long time. I could tell she was yelling because Mr. Reynolds was cringing, holding the phone a few inches away from his ear to protect his poor eardrums. Finally, when her tirade ended, he said, “Mrs. Brownstone, I work in the university residence office. I’m not qualified to deal with this issue, but if you really believe your son needs to see a psychiatrist, I can talk to him about that. And if he does it, will you sign the form?” Mom talked for a few more minutes and the conversation ended.

I said, “Mr. Reynolds, what are you talking about? How could you expect me to go to a psychiatrist? I’m not sick, and I’m not unhappy or in any distress over being gay. It’s my *parents* who are having trouble accepting my gayness, not me. Shouldn’t *they* be the ones to see a therapist?”

He replied, “Harvey, I understand, and I don’t disagree with you. But here’s what I’m thinking. Let me send you to one of the best psychiatrists in the city. He teaches in our faculty of medicine. That way, you can appease your parents by going to see him, and when he writes a report that you’re perfectly fine and that homosexuality is not an illness, they’ll have no choice but to change their minds and either sign the form or resume supporting you, in which case you won’t need a student loan.”

How could I argue? He was the only person trying to help me, and his plan made sense. Besides, I did have some curiosity about what a psychiatrist would say about homosexuality. So, I agreed to the plan.

The next week, I went to see the psychiatrist at his office at the Kingston hospital. The appointment lasted less than five minutes. He asked, “So, Harvey, what seems to be the problem?” When I explained, “I’m gay,” he responded by asking, “Yes, but what seems to be the problem?” That was reassuring.

I continued, “Well, my parents don’t accept me and insisted that I see a psychiatrist who can make me straight, so that’s why I’m here.”

He replied, laughing, “That’s impossible. A person’s sexual orientation can’t be changed. But what I want to do is confirm whether or not you are truly gay, and I can do that by asking you only one question, which will tell me everything I need to know.”

I was intrigued and asked, “Okay, what’s the question?”

“When you masturbate, do you think about men or women?” he asked.

Startled by such an intensely personal question, I could feel my face flushing. For a split second I thought I should say, “Oh, Doctor, I never masturbate.” But by that age I’d already figured out that there are two types of people in the world: people who masturbate and liars. So I knew he'd never believe me if I denied it. And then I thought to myself, *Well, he's a doctor, and he must have a good reason for asking that question*. I fidgeted in my chair and replied lustfully, "Well, to be honest, I think about hunky, muscular, tall, dark, hot men with hairy chests like Burt Reynolds, preferably naked, like that centrefold he did for *Cosmopolitan* magazine."

Without skipping a beat, the doctor smiled knowingly. "Yup," he said. "No question about it, Harvey. You're definitely gay. And you have good taste in men too. My wife's also crazy about Burt Reynolds. I'm actually jealous of him. Now get out of here and go enjoy your life. Don't worry about your parents. I'll send them a letter."

I left his office feeling really good about myself. Hearing a psychiatrist tell me that homosexuality was a natural condition and not an illness, and couldn't be changed, was profoundly validating and reassuring. I was hopeful that by fulfilling my parents' demands and seeing a respected psychiatrist, I'd finally get them to understand that I was never going to change, and that it was time to accept me for who I was.

Five days later, my mother called me, even more agitated and furious than she had been when she spoke with Mr. Reynolds. They'd received the psychiatrist's letter. She said, "Oh, so you think we're stupid? You obviously chose a psychiatrist who's gay himself, or maybe he's not even a psychiatrist at all. How do we know what kind of person he is? No decent doctor would say that homosexuality is normal. We want you to go to a *real* psychiatrist who knows what he's talking about. There must be doctors who can fix this."

I couldn't believe what I was hearing. I said, "Mom, the doctor I saw is one of the top psychiatrists in the city, and he even teaches at the medical school. Call any psychiatrist and I'm sure they'll know who he is."

She barked, "I will never accept that you are normal. Having sex with another man can't be normal. We need to find you a doctor who knows how to make you want to have sex with women. Have you watched *Charlie's Angels*? Are you telling me that when you look at Farrah Fawcett, you're not attracted to her? How could any man not want to have sex with Farrah Fawcett?"

Laughing, I blurted out, "No, Mom, I'm too busy fantasizing about Paul Newman, Sean Connery, and Burt Reynolds!" She wasn't amused and spewed at least five of the most vile profanities in the French language.

That's when I put my foot down. I shouted, "Mom, I've had enough of this. I went to see a psychiatrist just like you wanted me to. He told you I'm gay, that it's not an illness, and it can't be changed. You're still not satisfied. I can see now that you'll never be satisfied. I'm not wasting any more time seeing more doctors when there's nothing wrong with me. If you don't want to pay my way through school, then I'll have to find a way to survive. But I can't deal with this anymore, otherwise I really *will* get sick. Goodbye." And I hung up.

I burst into tears, shaking. Now what was I going to do? Mr. Reynolds's plan had failed miserably, which shouldn't have surprised me, given Mom's very predictable attitudes and behaviour. And yet, I was shaken to my core. As I write these words, I'm transported back to that moment, and I'm once again trembling and tearful. That terrible sensation of being totally alone in the world, with no one who loves or cares about you, and no idea what to do, is profoundly traumatic and paralyzing, and it left such emotional scars that I can summon it from memory in a heartbeat. I now realize, for the first time, that contrary to what I believed before writing this chapter, I've never fully healed from that devastating moment.

After that last conversation with Mom, I experienced the worst night of my life. I lay in bed thinking, "This can't be happening. I'll never get through school without money. Mr. Reynolds will blame me for losing my cool with my parents and hanging up on them." My mind started racing. Yes, Mr. Reynolds had arranged a small one-time grant, but if I couldn't get a student loan, how many more grants would he be able to get me? How was I going to support myself as a full-time student? And what was the point of getting an education anyway? If I graduated, who was ever going to hire me, a gay person? Why bother trying to struggle my way through school? I've never, before or since, felt so despondent and alone.

And then, suddenly, the solution came to me. Why not just end it all? What was the point of living? Now that my parents were out of my life, there wasn't a single person in the world who loved me, and if I were to disappear, no one would even miss me or care that I was gone. I started thinking of the easiest and most painless way to end my life. And then, for some reason I still don't fully understand, I decided to look up "suicide" in the phone book and see if there was someone I could talk to. I found the number for the suicide prevention hotline and decided to call them. I mused to myself, *If the person at the other end of the line can give me one single reason why I shouldn't kill myself, I won't do it. Then at least I'll know that I thought this through before I end my life.*

I dialled the number. The person who answered said, "Suicide prevention, please hold." I said, "What? You want me to hold?" But they were already gone and I was listening to music! I sat there and waited, and waited, and waited. Several minutes passed. I felt myself starting to get annoyed. Here I was, terribly disconsolate and in need of urgent help, about to take my own life, reaching out for a lifeline as a last resort, and they put me on hold? Is this the way a person in my situation should be treated? After more than five minutes had elapsed, I was furious.

And then it hit me like a slap in the face. If I was so angry about being treated like this, did I really want to die? After all, if I truly wanted to kill myself, why would I even care whether or not I was put on hold? As I continued to clutch the phone, listening to that gawd-awful Muzak and getting angrier by the minute, it started to occur to me that, obviously, somewhere deep down inside, I still believed I deserved to be treated with dignity and respect. And if that was true, then in my heart of hearts I knew I must really have wanted to live.

I hung up without speaking to anyone. And from that day on, no matter what difficulties or misfortunes have befallen me, I've never again contemplated suicide. As Carrie Fisher wrote, "Sometimes the only way to find heaven is to back away from hell."

After I became a lawyer and began earning decent money, the first charitable donation I made was to the Kingston Suicide Prevention Organization. With my cheque, I included a note that stated, "This donation is from a grateful caller whose life was saved by being put on hold. I hope these funds help you acquire the necessary resources so no one else will be deprived of your services when they need you. And if you do need to put callers on hold, the least you can do is make sure the music they listen to is cheerful. I did not appreciate listening to depressing ballads like 'Lost Without Your Love,' 'Love Hurts' and 'Without You.'"

I went to bed that night knowing not only that I wanted to live, but that I needed to find some way to get through school. I knew I needed an education if I was ever going to make something of myself. I couldn't wait for morning to arrive so that I could make an appointment to see Mr. Reynolds. I prayed he'd find some way to help me stay in school.

I was estranged from my parents for five years, and clearly my mother caused it. But over the years, I've been asked many times, "Where was your father all that time?" The answer is that he remained mostly invisible. He was simply not capable of standing up to my mom, even though he told me repeatedly that he didn't agree with the way she'd treated me.

Many years later, long after my parents and I had reconciled, Dad and I had a frank conversation about our long estrangement. I needed to get a few things off my chest. I asked, "Dad, if you didn't agree with Mom's decision to cut me off, why didn't you stand up for me and defend me?"

"Son, you know what your mother's like," he answered. "I tried to tell her a few times that what we were doing to you wasn't right. But no one can talk any sense into her when she's got an idea in her head. Nothing I said made any difference. She really believed cutting you off was the best way to make you change your ways, and I was helpless to stop her. Her favourite expression during those years was 'tough love.'"

"But, Dad, you must have known that I was struggling financially," I replied. "Couldn't you have put some money in an envelope and mailed it to me without telling Mom?"

His answer floored me. "Mom handled all the finances. I barely ever had any cash in my pocket. You had part-time jobs and summer jobs. I'll bet you had way more cash than me." So there you have it.

Was I angry with my father? No. What he must have endured during those five years living with my mom would have been indescribable. She was desperately unhappy without her son, and as time passed and she realized her "tough love" strategy wasn't working, her unhappiness only intensified. Her severe depression, mercurial temper, and incessant fits of rage must have been nearly intolerable for a man who was much too gentle and soft-hearted to ever stand up to a force of nature like Mom. It must have been like living in a hurricane combined with a tornado trapped in a volcano in the midst of an earthquake during a tsunami. I'm grateful that my dad stuck with my mom during those dreadfully painful years to give her whatever support and comfort he could. And it means the world to me that he always accepted me unconditionally, exactly as I am.

CHAPTER 6

UNIVERSITY LIFE: BROTHER, CAN YOU SPARE A DIME?

It was the fall of 1975, I was a nineteen-year-old freshman, and it was now abundantly clear I was not getting a student loan. I finally understood, once and for all, that my parents were never going to accept me and that I was truly alone in the world. I was furious, livid, fuming. And then it happened — my moment of truth, one of those "aha" moments Oprah Winfrey loves to talk about.

I decided right there and then to harness and channel all my disappointment, pain, and anger into burning, driving, unceasing ambition. I wasn't only going to survive, I was going to thrive and be a huge success, a highly accomplished and respected professional, a force with which to be reckoned, a real "somebody" — in Yiddish, a "mensch," a person of integrity and honour — someone my parents would be proud of one day. Although I had no idea how I'd accomplish this, there was one thing I knew for sure. In order to be considered equal as a professional, I'd have to be three times better than everyone else. That's been the sad reality forever for women and members of all minority communities, but it didn't deter me. I was determined to do whatever it took to make my parents see they were wrong to be ashamed of me, and they'd one day regret how badly they'd treated me. And presto, just like that, Harvey Brownstone reinvented himself into a relentless overachiever. In the words of the philosopher Eric Hoffer, "We are told that talent creates its own opportunities. But sometimes, intense desire creates not only its own opportunities, but its own talents." Those words definitely applied to me.

I went to see Mr. Reynolds. He was as angry with my parents' reaction to the psychiatrist as I was, and I got the feeling he'd become emotionally invested in my struggle and was going to make it his mission to do whatever he could to help me complete my education, no matter what. We went to the cafeteria and he bought me lunch. What an angel he was.

"Harvey," he remarked, "before there were student loans, people somehow managed to get through school. If they could do it, so can you. You're young, healthy, strong, smart, and motivated to succeed. That's all you need in life. But, let me see what else I can do to help you."

God bless Mr. Reynolds. The next day he arranged for me to receive social assistance (commonly called "welfare"), which was just enough to pay for my residence. Things were looking up. Thanks to the scholarship, I knew my tuition and books would be paid for, and the welfare payments ensured I'd have a roof over my head. Now all I had to do was come up with money for food and the other necessaries of life. I'd need to get a part-time job.

I asked Mr. Reynolds if he knew of anyone needing a house cleaner. "Why don't you start by cleaning my house," he suggested, "and if you're any good, I'll spread the word."

Although I'd never cleaned a house in my life, I quickly got the hang of it, thanks to the ladies who cleaned the dorm rooms at the residence where I lived. I learned about the many uses of white vinegar (it makes windows sparkle, but should be diluted with an equal amount of water), the correct way to vacuum a carpet (set the vacuum's height to the highest setting to allow for easy gliding and minimal damage to the fibres), and the proper way to clean a toilet (start by spraying the inside of the bowl with a cleaner and letting it sit; then, use a toilet brush to scrub the entire bowl, paying special attention to the rim and any stains). Before I knew it, I had five customers whose homes I cleaned regularly for twenty-five dollars, which was a lot of money back then. They also often fed me lunch and gave me food to take home. I was extremely grateful for every bit of help I could get.

I soon found other ways to make money. Mr. Reynolds's secretary taught me how to type so I could type essays for fellow students for ten cents a page, using her typewriter. I house-sat for people on vacation (I did it for free if they let me raid their fridges and freezers). I worked at McDonald's cleaning tables, floors, and bathrooms. (Why do men have such terrible aim at urinals?) I also wasn't above dating men who were willing to feed me, including a few who were considerably older than me (the most generous were university professors, but I never dated any who taught me; that would have felt too creepy). When you're twenty years old, hungry, and driven to succeed, you do what you must to survive.

And you get inventive. I'd go to fast food outlets and take the little tinfoil packets of ketchup and the little plastic cups of coffee creamer. Add the ketchup to boiling water, and voilà, tomato soup! I'd buy a bag of potato chips, put them in a casserole dish, pour the coffee creamer over them, bake it in the oven, and presto, scalloped potatoes! I learned that if you looked hard enough, there was free food everywhere. Unfortunately, this was before the advent of stores that willingly hand out delicious free samples, but when I look back, I marvel at my ingenuity in getting fed for free.

I attended events and religious services at the Kingston synagogue, the Beth Israel Congregation, and was sometimes invited to people's homes for wonderful home-cooked meals. Not surprisingly, the couples with daughters my age were the most eager to invite me, in the hopes of making the perfect match — a "shidduch" in Yiddish. After a delicious meal, the parents would nudge each other, get up from the table, and leave the dining room, saying, "We'll leave you two young folks alone now so you can get to know each other better." That was always my cue to respond with "Oh, I'm so sorry but I have a big exam to study for" or "I'd love to but I have a major paper to write." Anything to get out of there. Too bad none of those couples ever had a son to introduce me to!

Another way I'd get free food was to show up at the kitchen door of restaurants right before closing time and ask for handouts of any unsold food they were planning to throw out. There was always day-old bread and leftover soups and salads, which they knew they couldn't use the next day. Eventually the kitchen staff got to know and like me, and they'd save food for me. I lost count of how many pizzas and containers of cannelloni I got from Lino's Italian Restaurant. And Morrison's had the most delicious Reuben sandwiches and home-fried potatoes.

I learned another great trick to get free breakfasts. Go to any nice hotel with conference facilities and you'll find there's always a coffee break for conference attendees around 10:30 a.m. The hallways right outside the conference rooms are lined with tables covered with coffee and tea urns next to muffins and assorted pastries. I could show up midmorning on any weekday at the nicest hotel in Kingston, wearing a suit, and slip into the crowd, nodding imperiously to anyone whose eye I happened to catch, then quickly help myself to a lovely assortment of goodies (throwing a few extra into the briefcase I always carried), and then slip away again as surreptitiously as I'd arrived. And, of course, there were great snacks for the midafternoon coffee break, which I feasted upon many times. Years later, when I regularly attended conferences as a lawyer and a judge, the coffee breaks always transported me back in time to those lean, hungry years, and I always had to stop myself from hoarding as many snacks as I could stuff into my mouth (or my briefcase). Some experiences stay with you forever.

The thing about struggling hard in life is that, at the time, you don't know how you'll ever get through it. You just have to keep putting one foot in front of the other and hoping that everything will turn out all right.

I spent five years at Queen's University. My marks were so good that I was accepted into law school after only two years of undergraduate studies, without being required to get a degree, something that was and remains almost unheard of. I was a diligent student and studied relentlessly to get top marks — not only to retain my scholarship, but to satisfy my ever-present need to be the best. Being an average student and getting "good enough" marks was acceptable for most of my classmates, but was out of the question for me. Harvey the overachiever had to prove to everyone, and most of all to himself, that he could be the best. Of course, deep down, everything I did was for the purpose of one day regaining parental love and acceptance.

I was openly gay in university. It's not that I ever made a big announcement telling the world I was gay. I was just being my authentic self, not hiding anything. If I was dating someone and got invited to a party, I brought my boyfriend with me. If I was with a group of friends and the subject turned to relationships, I spoke openly about mine in the same way they spoke about theirs. My friends at law school totally accepted my sexual orientation and were incredibly supportive and kind to me. They knew my parents had kicked me out because I was gay, and that I was frequently short of funds. Some of them helped me by inviting me for dinner, or paying for a haircut, or buying me a pair of shoes and a nice suit so that I could go to job interviews when it came time to look for an articling job. My law school classmates became my chosen family, and many of us have remained close to this day.

Was I the only gay student in my class? No. There were two others who'd confided in me that they were gay, but they were deeply closeted and begged me to keep their secret. Of course, I did. I've never agreed with "outing" a person who isn't ready to disclose something private about their life.

The two closeted classmates, Martin and Liz, didn't associate with me much in public for fear of "guilt by association," but we did get together privately. Early on in our friendship, Martin asked, "Harvey, why are you so open at school about being gay? There's so much homophobia out there. Aren't you worried about finding a job? Our classmates will be our colleagues one day, and they'll tell everyone you're gay. Who's going to hire an openly gay lawyer?"

I replied, "Look, my parents — the only two people in the world I ever cared about — have rejected me. If I can live with that, do you think I really care what anyone else thinks of me? I've paid a huge price to live my life openly and honestly. I lost my family. But it's the only way I know how to live. And if I can't get a job as a lawyer, then so be it. I'll get a job selling shoes if I have to, or I'll be a waiter or drive a taxi. I'm not afraid of hard work. I can always make a living doing something."

They looked at me in disbelief. Liz said, "But then why are you killing yourself trying to get top marks in law school? What's the point of getting a law degree if you're never going to be a lawyer? Why don't you just go and start selling shoes now?"

"Because I happen to believe there must be more people just like me in the legal profession. Maybe one of them will hire me. And besides, look at how friendly and open-minded our classmates are. I haven't experienced a single incident of homophobia here at school, and I don't believe any of our classmates would stab me in the back the way you're suggesting. Times are changing, and for the better."

And then I went in for the kill and said, "Besides, just how long do you think you're going to be able to keep *your* gayness a secret? How do you know there aren't people who already suspect you're gay? Do you want to spend the rest of your lives lying and looking over your shoulders? Aren't you worried about being blackmailed? Why would you want to live like that?"

My friends just didn't get it. I've thought about that conversation many times over the years. What was it that gave me the courage to be so open? Where did that fearlessness come from? I think that, as I developed coping mechanisms and practical solutions to manage the life I was living at that time, I acquired self-confidence. I knew, in my heart of hearts, that I was a survivor. And that made all the difference.

After graduating from law school, I kept in touch with Martin and Liz, and they both eventually came out in their own time. They're both successful lawyers and have wonderful partners and great lives. In fact, I can honestly say that I've never known any gay person who ever regretted coming out. Whenever I'm asked by a gay person whether they should come out, that's what I tell them.

There's one more story about my openness at law school that I believe says it all. On the last day of school, one of my professors took me aside and said, "Harvey, it's such a shame you chose to be openly gay. You were a great student and could have made a terrific lawyer. But the legal profession is a very conservative, 'status quo' world, and I can't imagine any firm offering you a job. I'm sure there were other gay students here, but they were smarter than you and kept it hidden. You should have done the same."

I responded by repeating exactly what I'd said to Martin and Liz and to anyone else who'd asked me why I'd come out. The professor shrugged his shoulders, gave me a look of exasperation, shook my hand, and wished me luck.

Fast-forward fifteen years to September 1995, five months after I was appointed a judge. The dean of Queen's Law School invited me to give a keynote address to the students. In introducing me to the audience, he congratulated me on being the first openly gay judge in Canada, as well as one of the youngest judges to be appointed, and of course he mentioned how proud everyone at Queen's Law was of my achievements.

At the reception following my speech, I was approached by the professor who had told me on the last day of school that I would never find a job, and he congratulated me warmly on my judicial appointment. I responded by saying, "Sir, do you remember what you said to me on the last day of school? You said I would never find a job because I was openly gay. You tried to break my spirit."

To my utter amazement, he replied, "Harvey, I do remember saying that. But you have to understand, it was a different time. I was only trying to protect you. I was obviously wrong and I'm truly sorry."

Protect me? How could his words have protected me? Law school was over, and everyone already knew I was gay. The bullet couldn't be put back in the gun. He wasn't trying to protect me. He was trying to discourage and dishearten me. There was no other way to interpret what he'd said. But what was I going to do — lash out at him and cause a scene, ruining a lovely reception at which I was being honoured? That would have been entirely inappropriate and would only have reflected poorly on me.

I simply replied, "Yes sir, I understand. Thank God times have changed, and I hope you're more encouraging to *all* your students now, whether or not they're gay."

His response shocked me. He sighed deeply, pulled me close to him, and whispered in my ear, "Harvey, here you are, thirty-eight years old, already a judge, with a whole career ahead of you. And I'm still here, trying to impress twenty-one-year-olds, with no place to go. You won."

What a moment. Yes, my friends, success *is* the best revenge.

In the summer of 1979, my final summer as a law student, I hit the jackpot. One of my classmates, Judi Ryan, was dating Ted Andrews, then chief judge of the Ontario provincial court (family division). Although his office was in Toronto, he came to Kingston on weekends and was amazingly accessible to Judi's classmates. I socialized with them a lot and had many conversations with him about family law and the justice system. Ted was impressed with my interest in family law and arranged a job for me as a law clerk at the Toronto family court for two hundred and fifty dollars a week. That was great money back then. I was assigned to a new, brilliant young judge by the name of Rosalie Abella, affectionately known by everyone as "Rosie."

My summer with Rosie was life-altering. Watching her preside in court every day was a revelation. She considered herself more of a problem solver than a scholar. She saw the law as a tool to make people's lives better, especially the lives of the parents and children appearing before her. She treated everyone who appeared in her courtroom — as well as her judicial colleagues, the court staff, and the general public — with great respect, dignity, and a generous helping of warmth. She was always patient and listened attentively to what everyone had to say. She had impeccable judgment and common sense. When I would tell her how impressed I was with her ability to maintain her composure during a highly volatile situation in court (which, in family court, was a regular occurrence), she would say, "Harvey, always remember: Those people don't work for us. We work for them." I was smitten.

What appealed to me most about Rosie was her personal philosophy of how a judge should dispense "justice." It was comprehensive, inclusive, practical — and, most of all, accessible. Unlike the other judges I'd seen in action, who spoke only to the lawyers in a case and basically ignored the litigants, Rosie believed strongly that true and meaningful access to justice required the judge to also communicate and interact directly with the parties themselves — parents who had come to family court to resolve disputes over custody, access, and child support, or to respond to allegations of child neglect and abuse brought against them by child protection agencies. She conveyed important messages to them about acting in the best interests of their children. She took the time to explain her decisions in plain language. I didn't realize it then, but I'd just found the role model upon whom I would fashion my own judicial style. My mantra when deciding cases in family court was always "What would Rosie do?"

Rosie soon picked up on my enthusiasm for the law, and for her unique judicial style, because I'd frequently ask her to explain her philosophy of family justice, her understanding of certain legal principles, and especially how she'd arrived at the decisions she'd made. We'd talk for hours.

Rosie was incredibly astute and perceptive about people. She could look in your eyes and somehow tell how you were feeling. One day, about a month after we'd begun working together, she said to me, "Harvey, you never talk about yourself — your family, your background, your life goals. Tell me something about who you are."

I think she'd picked up on the melancholy and anxiety I was feeling, knowing that I had only one more year of law school left, with absolutely no idea what I was going to do after that.

"Well," I said, "you may be sorry you asked, but if you really want to know, I'm gay, my parents kicked me out, I'm an only child with no family support, and I have no clue whether I'm ever going to find a job after I graduate."

Rosie's mouth flew open, she flashed that "double take" expression I'd seen so many times in court, and she said, "*What do you mean* your parents kicked you out? For being gay? Are you serious?"

I responded, "Well, my mom is from France and had a hard time during the war. As a Holocaust survivor, she feels her life wasn't worth saving if her only child is gay and she'll never have grandchildren. She told me that if she'd known I'd turn out to be gay, she'd have had an abortion." Tears started flowing down my cheeks.

Rosie's eyes almost exploded out of her head. Her voice went up several decibels as she exclaimed, "Now wait a minute. You're pushing all kinds of buttons here. Are you telling me that your mother actually *said that* to you?"

"Oh, you haven't heard the half of it," I replied. "You have no idea the things my mother said to me when I told her I was gay. She went ballistic."

Rosie couldn't remain seated. She stood up, began pacing the floor, and said, "Listen, Harvey. My parents are Holocaust survivors. They lost a child. They lost everything and everyone. I was born in a displaced persons camp in Germany, for God's sake. My parents would *never* say the things your mother did. Holocaust survivors know better than anyone how precious life is, and what really matters in life. Your mother's life was worth saving because *every* life is worth saving, whether or not they have children or grandchildren, and no matter what sexual orientation their offspring are. Give me your mother's phone number. I'm calling her right now."

My stomach rose to my throat, which I could feel constricting. I thought I might faint. I had to stop her. There was no telling what might come out of my mother's mouth, which I was sure would reflect terribly on me and make me lose one of the few allies I had in the world, this magnificent judge. In a panic-stricken voice I pleaded, "Oh Rosie, you don't know my mother. She's extremely hot-headed, she'll explode, and it won't do any good. Trust me, there's nothing you can say to get her to accept me. I really appreciate you wanting to help, but you have no idea who you're dealing with. She's tough as nails. She'll tell you off like you've never been told off before."

Rosie started chuckling and said, "Harvey, listen to me. I'm a judge. Don't you think I know how to handle difficult people? Besides, you've never met *my* mother. She's the toughest woman on Earth, believe me. Your mother is no match for what I've had to deal with all my life. Now give me your parents' number. I'm calling your mother. Trust me, it'll be okay."

What could I do? There was no talking her out of it. Rosie dialled my parents' number and Mom answered the phone. Rosie put the phone in speaker mode, so this time I was able to listen to both sides of the conversation. It felt surreal hearing my mother's voice, a voice entrenched in my soul, a voice I hadn't heard in almost five years.

"Hello, Mrs. Brownstone? This is Judge Abella of the Toronto family court. Your son Harvey is working here as a summer student, and he's a gifted young man with a brilliant future."

There were a few moments of silence at the other end, and then Mom said, "Yes, is there something wrong?"

Rosie said, "Harvey tells me that you and your husband cut him out of your life because he's gay. Is that correct?"

Mom exclaimed, "Is that what he's telling people? Well it's not true. We will be happy to take him back when he stops being gay. We've done the only thing a parent can do. A doctor told us this was the right thing to do. They call it tough love. We know he'll eventually come to his senses."

Rosie said, "Mrs. Brownstone, please listen to me. I understand you're disappointed that Harvey's a homosexual. But you need to learn more about it. He was *born* that way. It's not his fault and it can't be changed. If you love your son — and I'm sure you do — you're achieving nothing by keeping away from him."

That was all it took. Mom exploded, just as I'd predicted she would. "Listen, you judge, whoever you are. Don't you *dare* tell me how I should feel about my son. Of course I love my son. You have no idea what I've been through. I almost died over this. Are *you* a mother? Do *you* have children?"

Rosie replied, "Yes, as a matter of fact I have two sons. And let me tell you something, Mrs. Brownstone. You don't throw your children in the garbage, ever. No parent should ever do that."

Mom screamed at the top of her lungs, "Well let me tell *you* something, Miss Judge. It's easy for *you* to talk like that. *Your* child didn't break your heart. Just wait. It should only happen to *you*. I hope *your* kids turn out gay, and then let's see how *you* handle it." And then there was a click. Mom had hung up. The conversation had unfolded exactly as I'd thought it would. One thing about my mother, her behaviour was consistent and very predictable.

Rosie heaved a big sigh, hung up, looked down at her desk for a moment, raised her head up, heaved another sigh, and looked me right in the eye for a prolonged moment as I held my breath wondering what she was going to say. And then she came to me and gave me the biggest hug I'd ever had. It felt like that hug lasted an hour, even though I'm sure it was just a few seconds.

Again the tears poured out of me, and I could see her eyes welling up as well. She put both hands firmly on my shoulders and said exasperatedly, "Okay, Harvey, you win. Your mom is definitely a piece of work. I won't be nominating her for mother of the year." That made me smile. She went on, "But you listen to me and listen good. You don't need her. You don't need anyone. You're going to be a great lawyer. I know it. I'm never wrong about these things. You should go into family law. You have the right sensibilities for our clientele, and your heart understands family dynamics better than most people. And I'm telling you, Harvey, one day you'll be a judge. It's gonna happen. Just keep working hard and never stop believing in yourself the way I believe in you."

We hugged again, I thanked her profusely for taking the time to try to help me, and I left her office. My emotions were a torrential roller coaster of embarrassment, sorrow, anger, and gratitude. Thank God Rosie hadn't held my mother's venomous behaviour against me. And she'd said something I never in my wildest dreams thought I'd ever hear anyone say. She thought I had what it took to be a judge one day! Although I knew she was just being kind and trying to give a down-and-out kid some hope, I dared to tell myself, *She didn't have to go that far. She could just have said I'll be a good lawyer and that I should pursue a career in family law. She didn't have to say I'll be a judge one day. Maybe she really meant it!*

There I was, unsure if any law firm would hire an openly gay lawyer. That was enough of a stretch, but the thought that any government would ever appoint an openly gay judge seemed like an impossible dream. And yet, Rosie had put the idea in my head that I should aim high, and somewhere at my core I desperately wanted to prove her right and make her proud of me. I didn't know how I was going to do it, but I knew I wanted to try to reach for the stars.

I couldn't possibly have known on that fateful day that all Rosie's predictions would come true. But her words of support and encouragement were imprinted on my heart and helped me through some dark times to come. Rosie remained a dear friend, cheerleader, and mentor throughout my career, and when I became a judge, she screamed the biggest "I told you so" I've ever received.

From the day we met, I knew without question that Rosie was headed for superstardom. In 1992, she was appointed to the Ontario Court of Appeal, and in 2004 to the Supreme Court of Canada. After retiring from the Bench in 2021, she began teaching at Harvard Law School. I'm so very proud that the whole world has benefited from her brilliant mind and heart, and I will be forever grateful to the legendary Madam Justice Rosalie Abella for her wisdom, guidance, support, friendship, and love. I thank God every day that she's been one of my guardian angels.

Following my educational and eye-opening summer at the Toronto family court, I returned to Queen's to complete my final year of law school. And in May 1980, I was ready to graduate with a law degree. I'd earned top marks and received two prizes for high achievement, in evidence law and international law.

On my last day of school I went to see my beloved guardian angel, Mr. Reynolds, without whose help and support I would never have made it through school. He told me how proud of me he was and that he was certain I had a bright future. We hugged each other, and then he went over to his bookcase, selected a book of writings by Frederick Douglass, the great nineteenth-century African American civil rights leader, and handed it to me as a parting gift. He opened the book to a page with a bookmark sticking out of it and pointed to a sentence that had been highlighted in yellow: "You are not judged by the height you have risen, but from the depth you have climbed." He hugged me again, saying, "Harvey, never forget those words. They were written for you." I never saw Mr. Reynolds again. He passed away a few years later. But he lives on in my heart and soul forever.

As graduation day approached, there was one constant question permeating my brain. Should I invite my parents? My friends said, "Harvey, you've worked your ass off to become a lawyer. You owe it to yourself to let your parents know you made it despite their rejection. Invite them to the graduation. What have you got to lose? All they can say is no." I knew they were right.

I was afraid to call my parents on the phone and end up in a heated argument, so I wrote them a letter inviting them to the ceremony. I received no response at first, but then got one of the biggest shocks I've ever had in my life. On the morning of graduation day, my phone rang. It was my father calling from a phone booth at a gas station in Kingston. "Harvey, it's Dad. We're in Kingston. Where do we go for the graduation?" Once again, I thought I was going to faint.

The reunion with my parents was everything I'd hoped it would be. Mom and Dad kissed and hugged me repeatedly and told me how proud they were of "our son, the lawyer." There were no apologies, no explanations, no mention of me being gay. We were simply being in the moment, enjoying the beauty of being together, expressing love for each other, saying how much we'd missed each other, and sharing in the joy of my graduation. When I was called up on the stage to receive my diploma from the dean of law and shake his hand, I looked down at my parents, whose beaming smiles seemed to light up the entire auditorium.

Naturally, knowing my mother, there had to be a moment when she put me in yet another state of shock. It happened at the reception following the graduation ceremony. Many of my professors and classmates, who knew the struggles I'd endured, came up to my parents to say nice things about me. At one point Mom quipped, "Well let me tell you, you have no idea how much I sacrificed to get my son through law school. My son is my whole world and I'd do anything for him."

I thought I was going to pass out. Everyone who heard that jaw-dropping comment stared blankly at Mom, speechless, because they all knew only too well that what she'd just uttered was an outrageous fabrication. Then they looked at me, waiting to see if I was going to say something.

It definitely crossed my mind to say, *What? Are you kidding me? You did* nothing *to help me get through school. You stopped me from getting a student loan. Because of you I had to go on welfare and slave away cleaning people's toilets!* But did I say anything? No. I didn't need to. Everyone knew the truth, and I wasn't about to let anything or anyone ruin this beautiful day. Mom needed to save face, and this was her way of doing it. I just smiled, gave her a big hug, and said, "Oh Mom and Dad, thanks for everything." Believe me, the sardonic irony of those words were not lost on those present.

Although I wouldn't recommend it, I must confess that my professional success is a direct product of parental rejection — the gift that keeps on giving. Had I not been rejected by my parents, I would have gone on living an entitled, privileged, upper-middle-class life, and I probably would have settled for an average career. So in many ways, strange as it may seem, I'm grateful for the obstacles my parents put in my way, because those obstacles made me strong, resilient, focused, and determined to make something of myself.

In my post-retirement career as a talk-show host, I've interviewed hundreds of celebrities, and there's a common thread running through many of their lives. A great number of famous people got their burning drive, ambition, and desperate need to succeed from the pain of parental loss or rejection. Rejection is a powerful motivator.

Following my law school graduation, there was a slow and gradual process of reconciliation with my parents. We spoke regularly on the phone, and eventually I was invited to visit them. The visits increased in frequency over the next few years, but the topic of my homosexuality was never raised or discussed. They showed no interest in knowing about my relationships or friendships. Any conversation about me revolved around my career, which was fine with me. At least our interactions were pleasant and stress-free. We acted as if the five-year estrangement had never happened. And things remained that way for a decade.

My mother's attitude about me improved dramatically when I became a judge in 1995. Finally she was able to brag, "Well, anyone can have grandchildren, but not many people can say their son is a judge." She became so proud of me that I used to joke, "My mom has her own website, MySonIsAJudge.com."

I think that when Mom saw that the government was prepared to appoint an openly gay judge, she finally realized that homosexuality wasn't the terrible curse she'd thought it was and didn't carry the stigma it used to. She realized that times had changed for the better, and she no longer felt embarrassment or shame about her gay son. In fact, she became totally accepting and incredibly supportive of everything I did. We had a wonderfully loving relationship until she died in 2016.

I'm often asked how I was able to forgive Mom for what she put me through. The answer is easy: Forgiveness is something you do for yourself, not for the offending party. Mom came from an era where homosexuality was misunderstood, despised, and replete with terribly repugnant untruths and myths. She was a product of her generation, and she did the best she could, given her personal circumstances. And in her last twenty years she was extremely generous and loving, almost as if to make up for what she'd put me through.

A few days before she passed away, Mom said to me, "Harvey, before I die, I need to know something. Was I a good mother?" I took her in my arms, kissed her on both cheeks, held her for a long moment, and replied, with tears rolling down my cheeks, "Mom, you were the best mother in the world. I'm so grateful you were my mom and I wouldn't have changed anything about you." She gave me a big smile and said, "You were the best son in the world and I wouldn't have changed anything about *you.* Now I can go in peace." I knew that was her way of apologizing to me, and those words were immensely healing. Those were the last words she said to me. She died peacefully three days later, on April 21, 2016.

Three weeks after Mom passed away, I was at Queen's University to receive an award for distinguished alumni. Moments before the ceremony began, a law school secretary came up to me and pinned a rose to my lapel, saying, "Harvey, this rose is from your mother." Before I could react, she said, "A month ago she called to say she knew she wouldn't live long enough to see you get this award. She sent us money to buy you this rose so you'd know she's with you, and that she's extremely proud of you."

That's the person my mother turned out to be.

CHAPTER 7

CONFRONTING THE REAL WORLD: FINDING A JOB

Why did I decide to go to law school? Where did I get the idea to be a lawyer? What made me think I could ever do the job? Those were the questions I asked myself hundreds of times in law school during moments of self-doubt. We had no lawyers in our family and my parents had no friends who were lawyers. I didn't even know exactly what lawyers did, except for what I'd seen them do on TV shows like *Perry Mason* and in movies like *To Kill a Mockingbird*.

Perry Mason, portrayed by Raymond Burr, was the best criminal defence lawyer in the world and never lost a case. The courtroom scenes were dramatic, compelling, and irresistible to a kid like me with a theatrical flair for drama and catharsis. I learned many years later, much to my disappointment, that *Perry Mason* and all those other law-based TV shows bore no resemblance whatsoever to the real criminal justice system. But I probably picked up some useful tips from Raymond Burr in developing my advocacy style as a criminal defence lawyer.

My generation of Jewish kids was directed to become either lawyers or doctors — preferably doctors. No other professions were deemed good enough, at least not to my parents. Kids who couldn't stand the sight of blood, like me, were pushed to go to law school. So, from an early age, I knew I'd be pursuing a career in law. And it made sense, since I was frequently told by high school teachers, "Harvey, with that mouth of yours, you should be a lawyer." I wasn't sure if they were complimenting me — something tells me they weren't — but at least their advice was consistent with what I was hearing from my parents.

If you've seen the classic 1973 movie *The Paper Chase*, starring John Houseman and Timothy Bottoms (who appeared on my talk show and spoke about the movie), you have a pretty good idea of what law school was like. On the first day, all the first-year students were assembled in a lecture hall for the dean's "welcome" address. He began by stating, "I want you to look at the person to your left. Now look at the person to your right. By Christmas, one of them won't be here, and by the end of the year, the other one won't be here either. Good luck." Not exactly what one might call an encouraging message. His speech gave me what I like to call a "Depends™" moment.

The biggest secret, what they don't tell you, about law school is that you don't go there to learn the law. The law, meaning the legislation and case law, can easily be found online (or when I was a student, in books), so there's no need to memorize it. You just need to know where to find it. Besides, were you to memorize specific laws as a student, you'd quickly discover that, by the time you graduate, complete your one-year articling period, and write your bar exams, the laws would likely have changed significantly. The law is constantly evolving.

So what are you supposed to learn at law school? You learn how to *think* like a lawyer — how to understand foundational legal concepts, develop critical thinking and analytical skills, use logic in applying legal principles to fact situations, and master legal research and writing. And I loved it. I enjoyed the lectures and the reading, and I especially loved debating the law for hours with my classmates.

Following graduation, the process for becoming licensed as a lawyer requires a one-year period called "articling," during which the new graduate works under the supervision of a lawyer, followed by a series of bar exams.

When the time came to look for an articling job, I was both excited and apprehensive — excited because, as one of the top students in my class, I knew my transcript would guarantee me interviews at all the top law firms, often referred to as "the Bay Street firms" in Toronto. On the other hand, my apprehension stemmed from a fear of the impression I would create at an interview.

Ever since those schoolyard kids had instantly labelled me as "queer," I'd always known that, within a few minutes of meeting me, most people could tell I was gay. People have told me that all my life — not in a bad way, but just as a matter of fact. I suppose my tone of voice, mannerisms, and general comportment trigger people's "gaydar." Apart from my parents, I've never had to tell anyone I'm gay. They just seem to figure it out, which is fine with me now. But back in 1979, when I was looking for an articling job, I was terribly worried that my general demeanour would transmit a "gay vibe" and deter law firms from hiring me.

My classmates were sympathetic to my dilemma. There were several hilarious, alcohol-fuelled evenings when my straight male friends tried to give me a crash course in "Masculinity 101" — how to walk, lower my voice, sit without crossing my legs, adjust my crotch and transmit a virile vibe, how to talk about sports (a subject in which I had no interest), and especially how to give a firm handshake. It was like a scene out of *La Cage aux Folles*, and I'm afraid I failed the test as miserably as the drag queen in that movie did. I guess I'm not a very good actor. I just couldn't convincingly make myself someone I'm not.

I must have attended at least twenty interviews at the most prestigious law firms in Toronto. I was asked about everything . . . except the law. One lawyer looked me up and down within the first few minutes, pursed his lips, furrowed his brows, and said, "We have a baseball team at this firm. We play against the other law firms on summer weekends. You don't seem like the kind of guy who can pitch very well." I couldn't help myself. Without skipping a beat, I pouted, flashed him a coy smile, and said, "No, I'm much better at catching than pitching." The interview came to an abrupt end. I can't imagine why.

At another interview, the lawyer asked, "Do you play golf or squash?" I answered, "No, but I'm willing to learn if it will make me a good lawyer." He said, "Well, a lot of our business gets done on the golf course or at the squash court. And we don't have time to teach you." So ended that conversation.

At yet another interview, the lawyer said, "Let me be frank. You seem pleasant enough, but we do a lot of work in the construction industry. Our clients are tough, hard-talking, hard-drinking businessmen, not very sophisticated or genteel, and you'd have to know how to relate to them. You have to be a 'man's man' to work at this firm." Once again, I couldn't help myself. I flashed a devilish smile, batted my eyes, and quipped in my campiest voice, "Sir, believe me, I am the *very definition* of a man's man." To this day I don't even know if he caught my drift. Some straight guys are unbearably dense. That guy probably thinks a bisexual is someone who's had sex twice.

I thought my final interview was going well until the lawyer interviewing me said, "I'm just screening the candidates. The senior partner makes the decision. Let's go to his office."

We walked down the hall to a large, beautifully furnished corner office with glass walls overlooking the beautiful Toronto skyline. The senior partner, a grey-haired, distinguished-looking man who appeared to be in his late sixties, was sitting behind a battleship-sized oak desk and looked to be reading something. When we were introduced, he peered at me over his bifocals and inquired, "So tell me, son, what kind of a name is 'Brownstone'? Where's your family from?"

I responded, "Well, my dad's from Winnipeg and my mom's from France." Not quite the answer he was looking for. He then asked, "No, where are your *people* from, I mean *originally*?" Of course, I knew what he was getting at, so I replied, "From a shtetl in Eastern Europe." His face seemed to be losing colour.

"Hmm, I see. And what are your career goals?"

I replied, "Well, sir, I first want to learn as much as I can about how to be a good lawyer. I promise I'm a quick study. And then I hope to use my skills to enhance the delivery of legal services to your clients and be a valuable asset to your firm." That put a wisp of a smile back on his face.

Then he asked, "Tell me, young man, are you married? Do you have a wife?" I explained that I was single.

"Well son, we prefer *family* men here," he stated. "This is a *family* firm. We're all one big happy *family*. We socialize together. Our wives all know each other. I don't think you'd fit in here."

You guessed it. Once again, I couldn't restrain myself and retorted, "Gee, sir, that's a shame because my boyfriend Chuck would have loved hanging out with all the wives. He gives great fashion and decorating tips to all the girls!"

The poor man's eyes bugged so far out of his head that I thought we'd have to call 911. He swallowed hard, started choking, and softly mumbled, "Umm . . . okay then . . . thanks for coming in." Once again, I was escorted out of the firm with swift dispatch. And just for the record, I didn't even have a boyfriend.

One interview after another ended the same way. It was obvious I was a fish out of water at those fancy-schmancy law firms populated by Poindexter-like clones wearing the standard boring grey pinstriped suits. Those interviews were not about my legal aptitude. The interviewers already knew from my transcript that I had the brains to do the job. They were looking for people who would fit into their world, their ambience, their social circle. In other words, they wanted people who looked, acted, and thought just like them. When they used terms like "family values," that was a code for "exclusion."

My law professor appeared to have been right — the legal profession, judging by the lawyers I was meeting at those big Bay Street firms, was permeated by a "status quo" culture and a super-conservative mentality with no interest in diversity or inclusivity. It was painfully obvious by the questions they were asking that, regardless of my academic achievements, I wasn't what they were looking for and never would be.

And then I had another one of those "aha" moments. I asked myself, why do you want to work at those stuffy law firms anyway? They do high-stakes civil litigation, corporate commercial law, tax law, real estate law, and estates law. That isn't what you're interested in. You care about social justice, human rights, equality. Rosie taught you that the law can best be used to help improve people's lives. And besides, didn't you want to be the next Perry Mason? Why aren't you applying for jobs with family law or criminal lawyers?

Bingo. I immediately sent a flurry of job applications to family and criminal law firms. Unfortunately, all the family law positions in Toronto were filled and there were only a few jobs left at the criminal law firms. I began to worry that I really might have to get a job selling shoes at a department store. But, emboldened by the words of the nineteenth-century poet Albery Allson Whitman — "Adversity is the school of heroism, endurance the majesty of man, and hope the torch of high aspirations" — I sent out more applications. My perseverance paid off and I got some interviews.

Criminal lawyers are a breed unto themselves. They're generally extroverted and passionate performers, salespeople, public speakers, negotiators, and straight-talking deal makers — in other words, my kind of people. They have to be that way because their lives are spent advocating for clients by making deals with prosecutors, cross-examining police officers, persuading judges and juries to accept their arguments, and communicating with an extremely challenging and often very damaged clientele. I love criminal lawyers. They help the underdogs of society, a group with which I've always identified. (Can't imagine why.)

My interviews with criminal lawyers were the polar opposite of what I'd experienced on Bay Street — except for one arrogant he-man, who chuckled snidely at me and said, "Look fella, I gotta be honest. You seem kind of . . . umm . . . well . . . *soft* to me. My clients are really tough street kids, thugs, hoodlums, gangsters. These guys would chew you up and spit out the bones in a heartbeat. They'd never trust someone like you. I'd go out of business."

Me? Soft? With what I'd been through? My eyes saw red. I could feel my blood boiling. I stood up, looked him straight in the eye, channelled my best imitation of Joan Crawford in *Mildred Pierce*, and said, "Mister, you have *no idea* what I've been through to get this far. You obviously have the *worst* people instincts I've ever seen. And trust me, one day you're going to eat your words." And with that, I picked up my briefcase and marched out of his office before he could utter another word.

Flash forward two years. I was in criminal court representing a client charged with robbery. The evidence was complicated, and difficult legal arguments had to be made. And I won the case. As I was gathering up my papers following the trial, I felt a tap on my shoulder. It was the "he-man" himself. Smiling sheepishly, he extended his hand to me and I politely shook it, just as my law school classmates had taught me. He said, "Harvey, I owe you a big apology. I've seen you in court several times now, and you're anything but soft. I can't believe how wrong I was about you. I could kick myself for not hiring you. I really am sorry. You're terrific."

"Thank you so much," I replied. "That means the world to me. And listen, it's never too late. I just might have an opening for a junior lawyer, and I'll definitely keep you in mind." We both burst out laughing, hugged each other, and he ended up taking me out for lunch. He became a dear colleague and friend. When I became a judge, he told everyone at the reception, "Harvey was the best articling student I *never* had."

I got an articling job with two wonderful criminal lawyers, Leo Adler and William Gorewich. They were well known and well liked for their expertise and integrity. At the interview, Leo took one look at my transcript and said, "I can't believe you want to go into criminal law. With those marks, you should be making big bucks at one of those carriage-trade firms on Bay Street. What are you doing here?"

I thought to myself, *Man oh man, if you only knew what those firms put me through*. I replied, "Mr. Adler, those firms have no human clients. They represent corporations and big business and it's all about money. I'm not interested in any of that. I care about justice. I want to make a positive difference in the world helping people in trouble. I think I'd be good in court. I'm quick on my feet and know how to talk to people. Please give me a chance. I'm the hardest worker you'll ever meet, and I promise I won't let you down."

Leo and Bill looked at each other, nodded, and smiled. Bill said, "Well, Harvey, it looks like you've already mastered the art of making submissions. After *that* speech, I'm not only ready to hire you, I'm ready to put you in my will!" I was hired on the spot and earned three hundred dollars a week, which was more money than I'd ever seen. I was beyond thrilled.

Leo and Bill were excellent role models. They took me under their wings and taught me everything they knew about criminal law, legal research, advocacy, and dealing with clients, judges, and other lawyers. I never missed the chance to watch them in court, carefully observing every nuance of their advocacy and interpersonal skills, especially the way they interacted with the judges and how they addressed juries. I was immensely grateful to have the job and soaked up every bit of knowledge like a sponge. I was sent to court every day to address cases, and after court I would go to the jails to visit clients. I learned how to deal with prison staff, police officers, court staff, prosecutors, and the judiciary.

One day, several months after I started working, Bill said to me, "Harvey, you never talk about your personal life or your family. We really know nothing about you. You're like a human question mark. I want to know who Harvey Brownstone really is." I was a bit taken aback but figured maybe this was the time to open up a bit. After all, I knew they liked me and were happy with my work, so I wasn't taking a big risk.

I said, "Well, for one thing, I happen to be gay." Bill and Leo started laughing uncontrollably.

Leo said, "Oh really? Quelle surprise! Gee, Harvey, there's a shock. We had you figured out as soon as we met you. We're not stupid, for God's sakes!"

I replied, "Well, I never mentioned anything because I don't think my sexual orientation is relevant to my job. But since you asked about my life, yes, I'm gay. I was so happy and relieved when you guys hired me, because I was having trouble getting a job even though I had good marks. A lot of lawyers who interviewed me could tell I was gay and didn't feel comfortable around me."

Bill laughed and said, "Harvey, we represent crooks, wife beaters, drug dealers, murderers, child molesters, and con artists. Do you *really* think we'd be fazed by a gay person? Next to our clientele, you're a saint! Besides, there's nothing wrong with being gay and you have nothing to be ashamed of. We like you just the way you are." Can you imagine how that made me feel, to have my employers say that to me? I still have goosebumps as I write these words.

Leo and Bill treated me like a son, and even bought me lunch almost every day, which I so appreciated. I loved them both and we've remained good friends all these years. They were both at my swearing-in ceremony when I became a judge and it meant the world to me knowing they were proud of me.

CHAPTER 8

MOVE OVER, PERRY MASON: BEING A CRIMINAL DEFENCE LAWYER

Near the end of my one-year articling period, I was in court representing a highly emotional and disruptive client whom I'll call Joe. He'd been arrested for assaulting his girlfriend the previous night and was now in custody, clearly impaired, coming down from a drug-induced high, and screaming at me at the top of his lungs in open court, "Get me the fuck out of here, you fucking asshole! This is all bullshit! Those fucking cops are fucked up. I want my lawyer, not some fucking flunky. Who the fuck are you anyway?" That scenario is a typical daily occurrence in every criminal courtroom dealing with newly arrested individuals.

As was my usual practice in those situations, I requested a short recess and went to the cells to see the client. Every criminal courthouse has cubicles adjacent to the cells where lawyers can speak with their clients through a glass partition with tiny holes so they can hear each other.

Joe entered the cubicle, dishevelled and in handcuffs. No big surprise; he'd taken a swing at one of the court security officers and they'd had to restrain him.

Leaning close to the glass and speaking through the small holes, I gently said, "Listen to me, my friend [clients always calmed down when I called them friends]. I know you're feeling terrible, and I can see you've been through hell [clients always feel victimized, even when the "hell" they've been through is of their own making]. But look, if you wanna be properly represented by someone who knows what he's doing and can help you, then you have to trust me. I work with your lawyer. He sent me here to take care of you today. You've gotta shut up and let me do my job. Otherwise, you're gonna piss off the judge, which'll only hurt you. So the next time you open your mouth in court without my permission, I'm outta here and you can go it alone. And good luck with that. Got it?"

The threat of having to face the court on their own, after aggravating the judge, tends to help clients decide it's better to have you on their side than not. Joe agreed to behave himself and we returned to the courtroom.

Because I was an articling student and not yet a full-fledged lawyer, my job was to advise the court that our firm had been retained to represent the client and get an adjournment to the earliest available date on which Leo or Bill could attend court for a bail hearing. That seemed simple enough. That is, until Joe's girlfriend, the alleged victim of the assault, showed up in court, clearly inebriated and enraged. She had several large, red marks on her face and a swollen eye. She'd obviously suffered a brutal assault.

We were in the middle of scheduling the next court date when the girlfriend came up beside me, shouting, "Who the fuck are you? Where's Joe's lawyer? Where's Gorewich?"

Before I could explain that I worked for Bill and was there to schedule a bail hearing, she looked up at the judge, yelling and slurring, "Listen Judge, this was all my fault. Joe got jealous when he saw me at the bar with some guy I don't give a shit about. Some asshole called the cops without telling me. But I told the cops not to arrest him. Please, Judge, I don't want him in jail. I want him home *now*! Who's gonna pay my rent and support me if he's in jail? He'll lose his job if he can't get to work today. Please, Judge, just let him out. I promise it'll be okay."

Joe then chimed in with, "Ya see? I told you this is bullshit." He looked at his girlfriend tearfully, moaning, "You know I love ya, baby. You know it was an accident. I'm sorry, honey." Then he turned to the judge, pleading, "Hey, Judge, can't you see she needs me? She wants me back home. Why should I wait for my fuckin' lawyer to do a bail hearing? I need to get outta here *now*."

Before the judge could respond, I said (with a bit of a twinkle in my eye, hoping the judge would play along), "Well, Your Honour, the accused seems determined to represent himself today and *not* wait for Mr. Gorewich to conduct a bail hearing for him, even though he knows the prosecution is *definitely not* agreeing to his release on bail. So I guess there's nothing more for me to do here, and I wish the accused good luck. Thank you, Your Honour. May I please be excused?" I pretended to gather up my file as if I were about to leave.

Joe said, "What? Are you fuckin' crazy? Wait a fuckin' minute! I need my lawyer! Okay, okay, just give me the earliest date you've got."

The girlfriend was still standing, somewhat unsteadily, beside me. I whispered in her ear, "Don't say a word. I know what I'm doing. I'll explain everything out in the hallway."

The adjournment was ordered and the court appearance was over. Once out in the hallway, I explained to the girlfriend that Mr. Gorewich would be taking good care of Joe and pointed her in the direction of the victim witness office, where she could discuss the matter further with the counsellors.

Out of the corner of my eye, I noticed the director of Ontario Legal Aid's duty counsel program in Toronto, John Zado, watching me. Duty counsel, sometimes referred to as "public defenders," are lawyers who represent accused persons unable to hire their own lawyers. Mr. Zado frequently roamed the courthouse to scout for talented articling students he could recruit.

He approached me, introduced himself, and shook my hand. "Young man, that was quite impressive, considering you're still a student," he remarked. "You handled those people and the judge really well. I need duty counsel like you who know how to manage our clientele."

He handed me his business card and asked me to call him as soon as I finished my bar exams and was a licensed lawyer. I was thrilled, and as soon as I was admitted to the bar, he hired me. That's how I got my first job as a criminal defence lawyer.

I loved being a duty counsel in a busy inner-city criminal court. Every day brought a whirlwind of new adventures, representing accused persons charged with every imaginable offence in bail hearings, guilty pleas, fitness hearings to determine if an accused was mentally fit to stand trial, and in trials. Appearing in court every day, I became familiar with the judges, Crown attorneys, defence counsel, police, court staff, probation and parole officers, victim witness counsellors, Indigenous court workers, and volunteers from the Salvation Army, the John Howard Society, and the Elizabeth Fry Society, who worked so tirelessly to assist our clientele who were always in a state of crisis.

I took the time to get to know my clients and learned that no one is born bad. The vast majority of people living a criminal lifestyle have suffered great hardship and trauma in their youth, including poverty, homelessness, domestic violence, substance abuse, mental illness, neglect, and physical, sexual, and/or emotional abuse. Many grew up in foster homes and group homes. A significant number of people who engage in antisocial behaviour are suffering from post-traumatic stress disorder, or may be developmentally delayed or have other cognitive or emotional challenges stemming from fetal alcohol syndrome, attention deficit hyperactivity disorder, oppositional defiance disorder, or other mental health issues. In short, these are damaged people whose victimization of others, while certainly not excusable or acceptable, can largely be explained as resulting from the great misfortunes they've endured and are unable to overcome.

I found the work challenging and often heartbreaking, but also rewarding. The clients weren't always easy or pleasant to work with, but I quickly discovered that if I took the time to learn about their backgrounds, I'd develop great empathy for them (which they could sense and appreciate), which motivated me to advocate passionately for the services they needed to overcome their difficulties, such as alcohol and drug rehabilitation, mental health services, counselling, and access to housing.

Despite the inherent sadness of permeating criminal court, there were some remarkably amusing moments. One day, I was representing a lascivious, gregarious, and rather buxom young woman who'd been arrested for prostitution (thankfully, the law in Canada has evolved since then to make life somewhat easier for sex workers). After successfully advancing a defence of police entrapment, the charge was thrown out and my client released from the prisoner's box.

She ran right up to me, planted a passionate wet kiss on my lips, and cooed, "Thanks so much sweetie. Anytime you want a blow job, it's on the house!" She then turned to the judge, a sedate, grey-haired, humourless old codger, and yelled, "You, too, Judge! You sure look like you could use one." She then blew the judge a kiss and sashayed out of the courtroom. As I wiped my lips with my sleeve, I said to the judge, "Your Honour, that's one offer I know neither of us will be accepting." To my utter amazement, the judge flashed a devilish smile, winked at me, and said with a chortle, "Mr. Brownstone, speak for yourself." Everyone had a good laugh over that one.

Nowadays, such a comment would never be made by a judge. Humour in the courtroom is severely frowned upon and virtually non-existent in this age of political correctness, where even the slightest off-colour comment, however inadvertent, innocent, and well-intentioned, may well land a lawyer or judge in trouble. It seems there's always someone ready to take offence at anything you say. It's a shame people take themselves so seriously these days. I'm glad I got to be a lawyer during a more relaxed and easygoing time.

In 1981, the Toronto gay community was targeted for prosecution by the police. Five bathhouses were raided, and hundreds of men were arrested for committing an "indecent act," even though they were engaging in consensual sexual activity with other adults. These were victimless "crimes," as the activity within those premises constituted absolutely no danger to the public. Anyone who paid admittance to a gay bathhouse knew exactly what they could expect to see, and no one was forced to do anything they didn't want to do. Nevertheless, an enormous expenditure of public funds was used for the sole purpose of persecuting gay men, many of whom, for whatever reason, were closeted, and as a result the bathhouse was their only way of meeting other gay men. We were living in a society that forced homosexuals to live in hiding and then tyrannized them for living that way. It was infuriating, maddening, and, in some cases, fatal.

The newspapers gleefully published the names of the arrestees, effectively "outing" hundreds of men whose homosexuality (or in some cases, bisexuality) had previously been a deep, dark secret. The consequences for people who'd been living closeted double lives were horrendous. Marriages and family relationships came to a bitter end. Dozens of arrestees committed suicide. Some lost their jobs — schoolteachers, doctors, nurses, clergymen, and others who worked with children — as there was no human rights legislation protecting gay people at that time. Those who worked for banks and other companies requiring their employees to be bonded were at risk of being fired should they be given criminal records. Getting arrested is stressful enough in the best of cases, but for these men, it was catastrophic.

During my time as a duty counsel I represented dozens of these unfortunate arrestees. None of my clients had criminal records; all of them were employed and had been contributing in a positive and meaningful way to society. They all wanted to plead guilty, as at that time there was no legal defence, and they just wanted to get it over with and put this dreadful incident behind them. I could hardly blame them. Although I'd never been in the closet and couldn't totally relate to what it must have felt like to live a double life and then have your secret become public knowledge, my heart broke for these men. None of them deserved to be "outed" in such a brutal and humiliating manner. I was determined to do all I could to help them.

Because I'd taken the time to cultivate positive relationships with most of the prosecutors, and because many of them privately agreed that these prosecutions were nothing more than a witch hunt, I was able to obtain the best possible results for all of my clients. The key was to get them in front of the right judges — in other words, the ones who weren't homophobic. It's called "judge shopping," and it's one of the most important utensils in a criminal lawyer's toolbox.

The first rule of every litigation lawyer is "know thy judge." Despite the oft-quoted theory that "justice is blind," and the trite maxim that every case with the same facts should get the same results regardless of who the judge is, the reality is quite different. Judges are human beings with personal histories, opinions, preferences, predilections, and eccentricities. No two judges are alike, and it's a lawyer's job to be aware of each one's propensities and proclivities.

Listening to everything a judge says, and learning everything you can about their personal history, interests, and personality, and filing that information away for future reference, is an important job skill that can make the difference between winning and losing a case, and it was one of my strengths.

For example, if I was representing a client charged with drunk driving, I'd do everything possible to avoid a judge whose family member had been killed by a drunk driver. If I was representing a client who'd stolen someone's car, I'd avoid the judge whose own car had been stolen. And if I was representing someone charged with committing a homosexual act, I'd make sure *not* to have the case heard by a judge who was an active member of a religious denomination well known for its anti-homosexual tenets.

Technically, lawyers are not allowed to choose their judges. However, if a lawyer knows which judge will be presiding in which courtroom on a specific day, it's effectively possible to choose your judge by scheduling the case to be heard in their courtroom on that day. For criminal lawyers, knowing the judges' presiding schedules is as important as knowing the evidence in the case.

The Crown attorneys who were sympathetic to my clients' circumstances agreed to schedule my "bathhouse" cases before judges known to be tolerant and accepting. All of them agreed that, in return for pleading guilty, my clients would receive absolute discharges, which meant they wouldn't be saddled with criminal records. Although the judge always had the final say on the sentence, in almost every case they would endorse the agreement of the prosecution and defence and grant the accused an absolute discharge.

Unfortunately, not everything always went according to plan. In one case, the judge expected to preside that day was ill, and in his place sat one of the most despicable and reprehensible human beings ever to sit on the Bench, Judge Robert Dnieper. He was bitter, angry, vindictive, venomous, and sadistic, and he took great pleasure in torturing everyone who appeared before him. He was universally feared and despised. He was legendary for all the wrong reasons.

Although Judge Dnieper has been dead since 1993, every old-timer in Toronto's criminal justice community has at least one notorious horror story about appearing in his court.

I first encountered him several weeks after I began working for Leo and Bill as their articling student. I'd been sent to court for a simple matter: to have a case adjourned to another day, on consent of the prosecution. In front of any other judge, it would have been over and done in thirty seconds. But that wasn't how Judge Dnieper did things.

When my case was called, I stood up and said, "Good morning, Your Honour. My name is Harvey Brownstone and I'm a student in Mr. Adler's office. He's instructed me to respectfully request a one-week adjournment of this matter, and I'm advised that the prosecutor is consenting to the adjournment."

Judge Dnieper peered at me over his bifocals, started sucking his upper teeth (a disgusting habit that made a repulsive sound), and sneered, "Hmm, did you say your name is Brownstone?"

I responded, "Yes sir."

The judge said, "Oh, so *you're* the one my colleagues have been talking about. You really think you're something, don't you, prancing around this courthouse like you own it. Well, let me ask you a question. Do people call you 'Mister' Brownstone or 'Miss' Brownstone?"

I was beyond stunned and could feel my face turning beet red. I started feeling queasy and put my hand on the counsel table to steady myself. What was this judge getting at? Why were the judges talking about me? And what did he mean by "Miss" Brownstone? I always wore a suit and tie in court. Didn't I look just like every other man there? I always tried so hard to be professional, dignified, and respectful. And yet, obviously my tone of voice or comportment, or both, were considered offensive in some way, but how? Why? What had I done wrong?

I took a deep breath and replied, "Sir, most people call me 'Harvey,' but in court I'm called '*Mister* Brownstone,' as any other man would be. And with respect, Your Honour, if there's any ambiguity regarding my gender, I'm pleased to clarify that I'm a male and have been happy to be one all my life. Now, with regard to my adjournment request . . ."

The judge interrupted me, banged both his hands on the desk, leaned forward as if he were about to leap off the dais, and flew into a rage, yelling, "Listen you pathetic pipsqueak, you pitiful, degenerate wretch masquerading as a law student. How dare you show such insolence and disrespect to this court! I ought to cite you for contempt! Who do you think you are? You just sit right down there and stay put. I'll deal with this matter at the end of my docket."

What could I do? I sat there at the counsel table, trembling with both fear and rage, from ten-thirty in the morning until the judge finished the rest of his docket at five o'clock, after having taken an extra-long lunch break and numerous lengthy, unnecessary recesses for the sole purpose of prolonging my torture. I was beyond despondent. I was petrified.

Finally, at five, when there were no other cases to address and I was the last person in the courtroom besides the prosecutor and the court staff, Judge Dnieper glared at me, sucked his teeth for what seemed like forever, and said in his snarkiest voice, "I've given this matter considerable thought. I'm not prepared to deal with this case today. I'm ordering Mr. Adler to appear before me at ten o'clock tomorrow morning to explain not only the reasons for this adjournment request, but more importantly, his appalling choice of articling students. This court is adjourned." And with that he swept arrogantly out of the courtroom, like the Wicked Witch of the West on her broom.

I was numb and could hardly breathe. The Crown prosecutor packed up his briefcase, looked over at me, and said with a smirk, "Them's the breaks, kid. Don't let him get to you."

I couldn't believe what had just happened. How was I going to explain to my bosses that I wasn't even capable of doing the simplest of things, like getting a consent adjournment? Would I be fired? I rushed back to the office, my heart in my throat and fighting back tears, and explained to Leo and Bill exactly what had happened. They both burst into great peals of laughter. I was getting angrier by the second, watching them laugh at my expense.

Leo said, "Well Harvey, you've now been initiated into 'Dnieper hell.' Believe me, we all went through it. He does that to everyone, so don't feel bad. You're not alone."

I asked, "He does that to everyone? Why hasn't anyone reported him? He's a monster! Isn't there some kind of governing body that can have him disciplined or removed from office? We have to do something! What am I going to do if I have to appear in his court again? He should be fired, dammit!"

Once again Leo and Bill just looked at each other as if to say, *The kid just doesn't get it, does he?* Leo explained patiently, "Harvey, listen to me. The fastest and best way to ruin your career before it even starts is to report a judge to the judicial council. Do you want to be known as the one who brought down a judge's career? Every judge will have it out for you. Why do you think none of us have ever taken him on? Because we know better. You need to understand the politics of the justice system. So just forget it and move on. I think you need a drink. I'm buying." And off to the bar we went.

I took their advice and moved on, but I certainly didn't forget it. And a year later, I was before Judge Dnieper again, representing a gay man who'd been arrested at a bathhouse. I explained to my client there was no way he should plead guilty in front of this judge, but the client replied, "Look, I took a day off work to do this. I can't live with this stress any longer. I want it over with. Everyone else I know who was arrested got an absolute discharge, so what's the problem? How bad can this judge be? I'll take my chances. Let's go ahead."

No matter how hard I tried, I couldn't talk him out of it, and before I knew it he was pleading guilty before the notorious Judge Dnieper. My heart was pounding out of my chest.

The Crown attorney explained the facts. "Your Honour, this accused was arrested in the infamous bathhouse raids of which I'm sure Your Honour is aware. Defence counsel and I have agreed that the accused should receive an absolute discharge, given his previous good character and absence of a criminal record."

Judge Dnieper sat back in his chair, making that maddening sound with his teeth again. "Counsel," he sneered, "*what exactly* is a bathhouse? Doesn't your client have a bathtub at home?"

I could feel beads of sweat forming on my forehead and my fingernails were digging into the palms of my hands.

Choosing my words as diplomatically as I was able, I replied, "Your Honour, my understanding is that the premises in question consist of saunas, hot tubs, showers, locker rooms, and private cubicles where men congregate."

The judge's eyes grew wide, and he replied, "Congregate? *Congregate?* So is *that* what they call it now? That's quite a word for what goes on in those places."

I said in a pleading tone, "Please, Your Honour, I'm begging you to take into account that my client has already been through quite enough. Just being charged and having his name published in the newspaper have caused enormous stress to him and his family. He has asked me to assure this honourable court that he will *never again* go to such a place. He's throwing himself on the mercy of the court, and as his counsel, I'm respectfully requesting this honourable court to give effect to the agreement I reached with the learned prosecutor and grant him an absolute discharge."

He sucked his teeth once more and jeered, "Oh, he's promising not to go back to *that place*, but is he promising not to '*congregate*,' as you put it, ever again? That's what I want to know."

I clenched my teeth and turned to my client, giving him a look that said, "Keep your mouth shut and let me handle this," and said what I had to say to help him. With fingers crossed behind my back, I said to the judge, "Yes, Your Honour, the only place where my client plans to 'congregate' from now on is in church."

Judge Dnieper said, "Well, from what I hear, some churches would welcome him with open arms." There was an audible gasp in the courtroom. "But tell me, Counsel, why should I grant your client a discharge?"

To this day I have no idea how I came up with this answer. You know how sometimes your mouth operates before your brain kicks in? Well that's what happened in that moment. The words flew out of my mouth before I could stop them. "I'll tell you why Your Honour should grant him a discharge," I blurted, "because I believe this court should give my client the discharge he didn't get to have at the bathhouse on the night he was arrested." I stopped and suddenly realized what I had just said. I was beyond mortified. Even for me, this comment extended far beyond the bounds of good taste and proper decorum.

To my utter amazement, Judge Dnieper sat back, a look of shock on his face, and began to chuckle. "Well, Counsel," he replied, "that's possibly the best answer I've ever been given to that question." And with that, he turned to my client and pronounced in his most pompous voice, "Sir, you will be granted an absolute discharge. Have fun in church."

Afterwards, every lawyer in the room told me they'd never seen Judge Dnieper smile before. It was quite a moment and probably the worst close call I ever had as a lawyer. I'm relieved to say that was my last appearance before him.

Judge Dnieper passed away in 1993 and his funeral was jam-packed with every criminal lawyer in Toronto. We all attended the funeral just to make sure he was really dead.

After I'd worked as a duty counsel for two years, Bill Gorewich and his associate Steven Price offered me a position at their firm as junior counsel, and I immediately jumped at the chance. I loved all the lawyers at the firm and knew I'd get to work on even more complex cases than I'd been assigned at Legal Aid.

Over the next year, I continued to develop and refine my courtroom advocacy skills and was making a name for myself in the legal community. I'd been having great success in court. My unique blend of thorough preparation, common sense, passionate advocacy, and quick wit made me popular with judges. Juries liked me because I spoke plain English and delivered animated and sometimes entertaining submissions, unlike so many lawyers who, although highly competent, didn't understand the value of developing a sense of personal magnetism. Most of them were dull and boring, with sleep-inducing monotone voices.

I enjoyed practising criminal law. I even enjoyed answering one of the most common questions asked of criminal defence lawyers: "How can you defend someone you know is guilty?" What they're really asking is, *Where's your moral compass? How can you live with yourself if you know a client actually committed the crime, and yet you still got them set free?*

The answer starts with the fundamental principle known as "the presumption of innocence." An accused is presumed to be innocent unless and until the prosecution has proven their guilt. This means that in a criminal court trial, what actually *happened* in a case is not the question, because people may have different versions of what happened. Rather, it's what the prosecution can actually *prove* that matters. And since the proof of guilt must be beyond a reasonable doubt, the evidence of culpability must be so compelling that no other logical explanation exists, leaving the judge or jury with a high degree of certainty about the accused's guilt.

This means that a defence lawyer's most important task is to look at the prosecution's evidence and determine if it is credible and persuasive enough to convince a judge or jury of the client's guilt beyond a reasonable doubt. Although many people have great difficulty with what you're about to read next, the fact is that many guilty people are acquitted (found not guilty) not because they're innocent of the crime, but because the prosecution did not have sufficient evidence to prove guilt beyond a reasonable doubt. We can live with that because of this foundational principle of criminal justice: It's far better that one hundred guilty people go free than for one innocent person to be wrongfully convicted.

If a defence lawyer is satisfied that the prosecution does indeed have sufficient evidence to prove guilt beyond a reasonable doubt, a frank discussion will then occur between lawyer and client in which the pros and cons of going to trial will be weighed. If the client decides to plead guilty, the lawyer will attempt to negotiate the most favourable resolution possible with the Crown prosecutor.

I thought I'd clearly understood and embraced all those principles until a life-altering incident occurred in my third year as a criminal lawyer, causing me to reassess my values and suitability as a defence lawyer.

I'd just finished a lengthy trial defending a client, whom I'll call Bert, who'd been charged with sexual assault. The client was found not guilty and released from custody.

In the early hours of the next morning I received a call from my client, who was again in custody at the police station, having just been arrested for sexually assaulting someone else — a mere ten hours after being released. I couldn't believe it. Feeling nauseated, I realized that had I not gotten my client acquitted, he would still be in jail. If he was guilty of this latest charge, I was partly responsible for the terrible trauma inflicted upon his latest victim, because I had been the one who'd gotten him acquitted and released. After hanging up the phone I couldn't get back to sleep, and as the hours passed, I became more and more furious.

That morning, still enraged, I went to court to represent Bert at his bail hearing. Meeting with him in a cubicle next to the cells, I let him have it. "Bert," I yelled, "I just got you off yesterday! How the hell could you get yourself in exactly the same trouble the very night you got out of jail? Are you out of your mind? I can't believe it! I'm fed up with you. I don't even know if I want to be your lawyer anymore."

Bert sheepishly mumbled something incomprehensible, and the conversation was over. Unbeknownst to me, a senior criminal defence lawyer had been sitting in the cubicle next to mine, meeting with his client, and had overheard everything I'd said to Bert.

On my way to the courtroom, he stopped me. "Harvey, you're not cut out for criminal law," he declared. "You need to find something else to do."

Shocked at his comment, I replied, "What are you talking about? I've never lost a trial. I get great results for my clients. Why would you tell me that?"

He shook his head and responded, "I overheard what you said to your client. You're angry with him for getting arrested right after you got him off. You just don't get it. You're supposed to *want* your clients to get arrested. That's how you make a living, you idiot! But you gave him hell. I'm telling you, Harvey, if you can't understand the most basic reality of what defence lawyers do, you need to get out of this business." And off he went, leaving me standing there, speechless.

It was another one of those "aha" moments. I instinctively knew my colleague was right. It *did* bother me that my clients didn't learn from their behaviour. I *did* get upset when they kept committing offences after I'd promised the court, on their behalf, that they'd abide by probation orders, go to rehab, get counselling, look for employment, and stop breaking the law. I *did* feel badly when my clients kept victimizing people after I'd worked so hard to get great results for them in court. In that moment, I realized that being a criminal defence lawyer was really not a good fit for me.

What was I to do? The answer was obvious. If you love criminal law and you don't want to be a defence lawyer, be a prosecutor.

So I applied for a position as a Crown attorney. Two weeks later, I was interviewed by the senior Crown attorney for the Toronto region. Getting the interview was easy; all the Crown lawyers knew me and most of them liked me. Three senior members of the Crown's office acted as references for me, and even two judges served as references.

At the interview, after inviting me to be seated, the senior attorney got right to the point. "Harvey," he said, "I've heard great things about you. You really distinguished yourself as a duty counsel. And I understand you're even bilingual."

"Yes, sir," I replied. "My Mom is from France and has spoken to me in French my whole life, so I'm fluently bilingual."

Since the courts in Canada are required to provide services in both of Canada's official languages, and there was a need for prosecutors who spoke French, that was an important credential. I began to feel optimistic.

Then he dropped a bomb. "Harvey," he inquired, "you're gay, aren't you?"

My heart sank. I replied, "Yes, sir. But what does that have to do with my ability to do the job?"

"Well . . . nothing," he responded. "It's not a problem for me or my staff, but here's the thing. We work closely with the police, as you know. Those guys are very macho, rough around the edges, not very worldly or sophisticated, and quite frankly, I don't think they'd be comfortable working with someone like you."

I was dumbfounded and could feel myself almost starting to cry. Here I was, a successful, popular lawyer who'd proven himself over and over again, against all odds, and once more I was being hit with the "sorry, you're gay" nonsense.

I countered, "But, sir, I've dealt with the police every day since I started practising criminal law. I've never had a problem interacting with them. You can ask any of them."

He stood up, extended his hand to shake mine, and said, "I'm so sorry Harvey, I'd like to hire you. I really would, believe me. But you're just not a good fit for this office. But thanks for coming in." And that was the end of that.

It was 1984. There were still no legal protections for gay people. I had no recourse and had been kicked to the curb yet again. I went home feeling terribly dejected and had a good, long cry. I thought to myself, *I don't want to be a defence lawyer, and I can't get hired as a prosecutor. So, obviously, I have no future in criminal law. What am I going to do now?*

I licked my wounds for a while, and then, yet again, I had an epiphany, another watershed moment. What about taking the advice Rosie Abella had given me when I was her clerk? She'd said I had aptitude for family law. She even thought I had what it took to be a judge! Why not go into family law? That's exactly what I decided to do. And I never looked back.

That moment was another important life lesson. I learned to trust my instincts: that voice inside your head telling you what's right for you. If you can block out all the background noise — and by that I mean other people's expectations and your fear of being judged — the volume of that inner voice seems louder, and if you heed what it says, you will always do the right thing.

There's a very satisfying postscript to my heartbreaking interview with the senior Crown attorney. Flash forward eleven years to my swearing-in ceremony. The same man who'd interviewed and rejected me for a Crown attorney position was now sitting at the counsel table to bring official greetings from the Toronto Crown's Office. Our eyes met for a brief moment; I nodded regally at him, and his eyes immediately looked down.

At the reception following the ceremony, he came up to me with a hangdog look and, shaking my hand, said, "Congratulations, Your Honour, we're all very happy for you. You've worked so hard for this."

Before I could say "thank you," he went on, not letting go of my hand: "Your Honour, I want you to know I feel terrible about what happened when you applied for a job in our office. But as you know, it was a very different time back then. Thank God, attitudes have changed now. I hope you have no hard feelings."

I said, "On the contrary, sir, I'm grateful to you. If you'd hired me back then, I'd probably still be working for you today. But thanks to you, I switched to family law and had a meteoric career. And now I'm a judge. I can't thank you enough." He nodded slowly, as if in a slight stupor, and walked away.

And I meant it. It's often said that when a door closes, a window opens. That's certainly been true in my life. And once again, I was reminded that success is the best revenge.

CHAPTER 9

HURRICANE HARVEY

Once I decided to switch gears and pursue a career in family law, I faced two challenges: getting up to speed on the subject matter and finding a job. I was hoping there might be a way to do both at the same time.

A few weeks after my fateful interview at the Crown's office, I happened to meet an old Legal Aid colleague. He mentioned a job vacancy in the family law section at the Legal Aid Research Facility, a department that provided research services for lawyers in Ontario representing clients who'd been granted Legal Aid. I knew getting the job would be a long shot, as I'd never practised family law, but I remembered the old adage "nothing ventured, nothing gained," so I threw my hat in the ring.

I was interviewed by the director, Ken Chasse, a soft-spoken, kind man who seemed to take an instant liking to me. He was impressed by my previous work history with Legal Aid as a duty counsel. He then asked the question I'd predicted he would, and for which I'd prepared: "Why do you want to switch from criminal law to family law?"

I replied, "As a summer student, I was Judge Abella's clerk at the family court and loved it. The issues revolving around family breakdown and the best interests of children resonated with me in a way that criminal law never has. Practising criminal law gave me the opportunity to develop my courtroom advocacy skills, which I enjoyed. But to be candid, I didn't care much for the clientele, and even when I got good results for them, my job satisfaction left much to be desired."

I'd chosen those words carefully, knowing that any astute lawyer would immediately understand exactly what I was trying to convey about the pitfalls of being a criminal lawyer. And I got the job.

My next task, which I wasn't looking forward to, was to tell Bill and Steve I was leaving the firm. I knew they'd be disappointed, because they'd invested so much time and energy in helping me develop my lawyering skills, and I'd become a part of the family.

When I told them, they were stunned. Bill said, "But Harvey, you're so good at this. You have a great future in criminal law. Why are you walking away from it? Is this about money? Do you want a raise?"

"No, no," I explained, "it's just that I feel disappointed, betrayed, and even angry when my clients keep committing offences over and over again after I've worked so hard to get them on the path to rehabilitation."

Bill and Steve gave each other a knowing look that seemed to say, "Yup, he's definitely not cut out for this line of work." They each gave me a hug and wished me well. And so ended my career as a criminal defence lawyer.

I spent the next three years learning every aspect of the law regarding separation, divorce, marriage contracts, cohabitation agreements, division of matrimonial property, constructive trusts, the issues facing common-law (unmarried) couples, child custody and visitation, child and spousal support, child protection, and adoption. I truly enjoyed developing creative legal arguments and practical solutions to the many interesting fact situations, questions, and dilemmas presented by lawyers across Ontario. There was only one problem that kept gnawing at me: I missed the drama and excitement of the courtroom.

In 1987, the Ontario Ministry of the Attorney General, in response to the widespread problem of child poverty, created a department to enforce child and spousal support orders. At that time, over 90 percent of family court support orders were in default (non-payment), with millions of dollars in arrears owing. And the overwhelming majority of that debt was owed to single mothers, given that almost every child of divorce was in their mother's custody. Hence the term "deadbeat dad."

In 1989, I spotted an advertisement seeking a "research and litigation counsel" at the Support Enforcement Program, so I applied for the job. The legal director, Elisabeth Sachs, was a charming, no-nonsense woman who relied heavily on her razor-sharp intuition. At the interview, her first question was, "Why do you want to work here?"

I replied, "There are several reasons. Firstly, I've spent the last three years as a family law researcher and can assure you I'm highly knowledgeable and proficient in this area. Secondly, I spent a summer clerking at the Toronto family court, so I have first-hand knowledge of the judicial approach to support orders, and I understand the needs of the family court clientele. And thirdly, when I practised criminal law, I really wanted to be a prosecutor, but they wouldn't hire me because I'm gay. But this job is perfect, because I'd get to 'prosecute' delinquent support payors in a family law context. If you hire me, I'll get to be a prosecutor after all!"

I knew I'd taken a risk by mentioning my sexual orientation, but I trusted my instincts and sensed that Elisabeth liked me. And I was right. She offered me the job the next day.

The world of child support enforcement is a fascinating lesson in human nature. I discovered the myriad reasons that parents provide when they believe they shouldn't have to support their children. One father said to me, "I only slept with the mother once, and I didn't even enjoy it. Why should I have to pay?" Another father complained, "She tricked me. She said she was on the pill, so I didn't use a condom. Why should I have to pay?" And yet another man insisted he shouldn't have to pay child support because "when the condom broke, she fixed it with chewing gum and assured me it would keep her from getting pregnant. It's her fault. Why should I have to pay?"

In one extremely unusual case, a female college student asked a rather gullible male friend for a sperm sample "for a school science project." She then inseminated herself using a turkey baster, and nine months later a child was born. The man was stunned to find himself obliged by a family court order to pay child support. "I'm the victim here," he protested. "She tricked me. Why should I have to pay?"

The answer in every case (except for anonymous sperm donors at licensed sperm banks) is simple. It's a matter of DNA. If you're a child's biological parent, you must support the child, regardless of the circumstances creating the pregnancy. And if you think about it, it makes sense. If a man tricked a woman into having unprotected sex by lying, saying he'd had a vasectomy, would anyone expect her *not* to be obliged to support the child? Of course not. Every child has the fundamental right to be supported by both parents.

Probably the most common reason fathers gave for not paying child support was: "The mother's violating the visitation provisions of the court order. She's not letting me see the child, so why should I pay support? Why are you enforcing her right to child support, but you're not enforcing my right to visitation?"

Here's the big fallacy in that argument: Parents have no rights. Parents have *obligations*. It's the *children* who have the rights. If a custodial parent breaches a visitation order, it's the *child's* right to a healthy relationship with the other parent that's being violated. And if a child support order is being breached, it's the *child's* right to proper support (housing, food, clothes, and the necessaries of life) that's being violated. If one of the child's rights is being denied, it's entirely unacceptable and inexcusable to punish the child by violating *another* of the child's rights. Two wrongs don't make a right.

I was, of course, sympathetic to fathers who felt their court-ordered visitation schedules were being disobeyed by mothers without justification. Many fathers asked me to intervene on their behalf with the mothers, in the hopes of getting visitation reinstated. But every mother had an explanation for denying visitation, and every father had a counter-explanation.

As a lawyer whose sole function was to enforce child support, I wasn't authorized to resolve visitation problems. All I could do was reinforce to both parents that *every* provision in a family court order — custody, visitation, and child support — had to be strictly complied with unless and until the court changed or terminated it. And I spent countless hours explaining the procedures each parent could invoke to resolve disputes. But I had to make it clear that withholding child support was *not* a permissible way to enforce visitation.

I heard many other excuses for non-payment from delinquent fathers, such as, "I've got a new partner now and we've had another child. I can't afford to pay support anymore." I never ceased to be amazed at some fathers' capacity to emotionally disengage from their own children following separation. They had a rude awakening when our agency brought enforcement proceedings against them in court.

I loved everything about enforcing family support orders, even though the work was extremely challenging. Our staff tracked down delinquent payors' bank accounts, places of employment, and other income sources so that we could garnish funds to pay arrears. Some payors kept quitting their jobs and finding new employers every time we caught up with them to avoid wage attachment. Many self-employed payors engaged in a wide variety of schemes to conceal their true incomes. Some payors transferred all their assets into a family member's name. Some changed their names and absconded to other jurisdictions, thinking we'd be thrown off course (we weren't). The lengths to which some people went to avoid supporting their own children were mind-boggling.

And in court, I learned once again the importance of "knowing thy judge." I remember one case involving the enforcement of over fifty thousand dollars in arrears owed by a self-employed father who'd been evading his child support obligations for many years. The support recipient, who'd clearly made an effort to dress nicely, was seated in the courtroom. After making my final submissions, urging the court to incarcerate the payor for wilfully dodging his support obligations, the judge glared at the mother for a prolonged moment and huffed, "Tell her to sell her jewellery. Case dismissed." I later learned that the judge had endured a bitter divorce and deeply resented the support he'd been ordered to pay. I realized the old adage "know thy judge" applied not only in criminal court but in family court, too, and undoubtedly in every court.

In 1991, the position of director of the agency became vacant, and I applied for the job. It was an important senior management position, overseeing a large, province-wide organization with four hundred employees, eight regional offices, a call centre, and a head office — and I really wanted it. There were hundreds of thousands of support orders to enforce, hundreds of court proceedings ongoing at any given time, and millions of dollars being collected and disbursed every day. In the two years I'd been there, I'd enthusiastically learned every aspect of the operation, and was strongly encouraged by many of my colleagues to apply.

I was interviewed by Jack Johnson, the assistant deputy Attorney General, a gruff, disagreeable, cantankerous man in his sixties who appeared and acted much older. We didn't know each other, but his reputation as a rigid, stuffy, and intolerant manager was well known throughout the ministry. Minutes into our conversation, he said to me, "Look, Harvey, I've heard good things about you, but there's no way I'm promoting a homosexual into senior management."

I couldn't believe this was happening again, especially since the Ontario Human Rights Code had been amended in 1986 to add sexual orientation as a prohibited ground of discrimination. I said, "Mr. Johnson, are you aware that what you've just said is a violation of the Human Rights Code, and I could launch an official complaint against you?"

Without skipping a beat, he replied, "Oh really? Well, let me tell you something, young man. There's only you and me in this room and I'll deny what I said. Who do you think they're going to believe? You or me?"

In an uncharacteristic spasm of speechlessness and defeat, I could offer no rebuttal.

It turned out I didn't need to answer, because he kept talking. "Look, Harvey, it seems you're the best candidate for the job. You have a lot of support from the management team at the enforcement program. They obviously like you. How about this? We'll offer you an acting director position. For all intents and purposes, you'll be the director and get the same pay as a director, but it'll be an 'acting' appointment, so if things don't work out, we can send you back to being a regular staff lawyer."

I protested, "But Mr. Johnson, if I'm the best candidate, why won't you give me the job like you would with anyone else? My sexual orientation has never been an issue or caused the slightest difficulty in any job I've ever had. If you make me only an 'acting' director, what will everyone think? How will you explain it?"

He replied, "That's easy: You're young, only thirty-five. And you've been here only two years. This is a very big position for someone so young. My other directors are all at least ten years older than you. We'll say you got the job on a trial basis to see if you can handle it. And if it all works out, then in a few years, I can make you the full-fledged director."

I thought to myself, *Great. Now he's violating the Human Rights Code again, this time by discriminating on the basis of my age.* But for once, I kept my mouth shut and asked him if I could have time to consider his offer. He gave me twenty-four hours.

I felt such a mix of conflicting emotions: happy to be offered the job but angry and offended that, because I was gay, I would have to first "prove myself" as an "acting" director. I asked my two closest friends for advice. One said, "Do the right thing. Be principled. Tell that homophobe to either give you the full title or nothing. Call his bluff. Stick to your guns. If you're really the best candidate, he'll have to give you the job. He's just testing you." The other one said, "Take the job. Who cares if it's an 'acting' position. It's the same job and the same money. This is a huge promotion any way you look at it. It'll look great on your resumé. And besides, you'll prove yourself in no time, and he'll drop the 'acting' from the title." Each point of view seemed to be equally compelling. I was no further ahead.

After tossing and turning all night, and consulting that little voice in my head, I was struck by several compelling factors: Firstly, although the basis for giving me an "acting" appointment was deeply offensive, I had to admit the world had come a long way. I'd gone from being told six years earlier that a gay person couldn't be hired as a prosecutor *at all* to now being offered a senior management position in the government, albeit an "acting" position. I'd lived long enough to see that in the realm of human rights, progress comes in small steps.

Secondly, regardless of whether I took the job, I was still going to be working at the ministry and didn't want to make an enemy of Mr. Johnson, who was in a position to significantly impact my career. I was sure he knew at heart that he hadn't treated me fairly. If I took the high road with dignity and accepted his invitation to prove myself, I was confident I'd gain his respect. And hopefully one day he would remove the "acting" from the job title.

Thirdly, the promotion would increase my annual salary by eight thousand dollars, which was not an insignificant amount.

Lastly, and most importantly, I was damned if I was going to let someone less qualified than me get the job I *knew* I deserved and become my boss. The prospect of that happening was far too much to swallow.

When faced with a difficult decision, I've always trusted my instincts, and they told me to hold my nose and take the job. So I did.

Mr. Johnson and I ended up getting along well and he treated me with respect, although he never removed "acting" from my job title. Sometimes you have to be content to win the battle, and let the war take care of itself.

As acting director of the support enforcement program, I was instrumental in introducing major new enforcement tools, such as automatic wage deduction, whereby support payments were regularly deducted by employers from the support payor's wages. We also acquired the authority to suspend the driver's licences of defaulting payors to compel immediate payment of arrears. These mechanisms significantly enhanced our ability to effect compliance with parental support obligations.

One day, I received a piece of very important mail. The nondescript, handwritten envelope addressed to "The Director, Family Support Plan" had no return address. Inside the envelope was a single piece of paper with a photocopy of a cheque for fourteen million dollars, payable to the sender from the Ontario Lottery Corporation. Underneath the cheque, scrawled in handwriting, were the words "That bitch will never see one cent of this money."

I immediately went to our database and found the sender's file. He was a deadbeat dad who owed thirty-seven thousand dollars in child support arrears for his three children. He had indeed just won fourteen million dollars, which probably generated more than thirty-seven thousand dollars every few days in interest. And yet, his venomous anger and bitterness towards his ex-wife, the mother of his children, was so horribly toxic that he couldn't bring himself to pay what, for him, must have been a relatively meaningless sum to support his own children.

By the time we tracked down the money, the payor had secreted it in a bank account in Bermuda, a jurisdiction with which Ontario had no reciprocity. There was nothing we could do to get those funds. And to add insult to injury, by sending me that note with a photocopy of the lottery cheque, that man was thumbing his nose at my staff and me. I was beyond livid and hell-bent on doing something about it.

I marched upstairs to the office of Marion Boyd, the Attorney General, and demanded to speak with her. I didn't know her very well, but as director of an important program in her ministry, I'd briefed her several times, and she'd seemed receptive to my presentations. The receptionist inquired if I had an appointment. I replied testily, "No, but this matter's urgent." Her eyes grew wide. She called the minister's executive assistant, Victoria, and asked her to meet me in the foyer.

Victoria was a hard-working, gracious, and accessible woman with whom I'd frequently had dealings regarding important issues. I told her about the lengths to which one of our delinquent support payors had gone to avoid paying child support, even though he'd just won the lottery. I said, "Listen, Victoria, this can never happen again. How many other people who owe child support are winning large sums in the lottery and evading payment? The government controls lotteries in this province, so the government can fix this."

Victoria was stunned that someone with $14 million in their pocket would be so vindictive and heartless that they'd refuse to support their own children. She asked, "I think the minister would be sympathetic, but what exactly are you recommending?"

I replied, "In the United States, anyone who wins over a thousand dollars in the lottery doesn't get their money until their name has first been checked on the support enforcement agency's database. If the winner owes support arrears, the sum owing is deducted from the winnings. It's that simple. All we have to do is provide the Ontario Lottery Corporation with a computer link to our database, and if arrears are owed, they send the money to us for disbursal to the support recipient." I wanted to mention that, in the United States, the same procedure also applied at casinos for anyone winning over a thousand dollars, but I thought I'd better not press my luck. One step at a time.

Victoria said, "The minister is tied up in meetings all day, but let me talk with her about this and get back to you. Our ministry has nothing to do with lotteries, so she may not consider it appropriate to interfere in the operations of another ministry. I mean, after all, how big a problem is this? How often does a defaulting support payor win the lottery? Is this really worth getting all worked up over?"

I saw red. "Even *one* is too many," I replied emphatically. "We have over two hundred thousand support payors in default. I'll bet thousands of them have won over a thousand dollars over the years. Their children deserve to get the money they're owed before any winnings are paid. By imposing such a requirement, the government would be making an important statement about parental commitment and responsibility."

And then I went in for the kill. Flashing my most charming smile, I cunningly added, "Besides, how would it look if a certain brazen director of Canada's largest support enforcement agency called a press conference about this issue? Can you see the headlines? 'Deadbeat Dad Lottery Winner Skips Town, Leaving Children Penniless.' Think of the optics, Victoria. What will people think when they find out a simple computer search could have gotten the children their money — something that's routinely done in the United States? Why can't the Ontario government make child support a priority in paying out lottery winnings, just like the Americans do?"

Victoria shot me her best stern Sunday school teacher look. "Harvey," she said, "you wouldn't *dare* embarrass the government by doing such a thing . . . would you?"

I couldn't resist the bait, and I took it. "Victoria, hell hath no fury like a support enforcement director scorned, especially *this* old queen. Please tell the minister I want something done about this *now*!" And off I strode.

Four hours later I was summoned to the Attorney General's office. My heart was beating like crazy. Had I gone too far? Was this the end of my "acting" directorship?

Smiling, Marion Boyd shook my hand, asked me to sit down, and started giggling. "Harvey, Harvey, pretty soon I'm going to call you 'Hurricane Harvey.' Victoria told me what's got you all worked up. I've only got five minutes before my next meeting, so tell me quickly. What do I have to do to make sure you don't end up on the evening news?" I could tell by her chuckles that she hadn't taken my press conference threat seriously. Too bad, because a part of me had actually meant it!

Nevertheless, I breathed a sigh of relief, saying, "Madam Minister, I'm prepared to do all the work. If you can get me a meeting with the big shots at the lottery corporation, I'll do the rest. I know I can talk them into this. We're not asking a lot. All we have to do is give them a computer link to our database so they can do a search of the names and dates of birth of the winners and see if there's a match. If there is, they deduct the support arrears from the winnings and send us the money. No big deal, right?"

The minister thought a moment and responded, "Okay, I'll have my staff set up a meeting."

Two weeks later, several of my senior managers and I attended a meeting in a luxuriously furnished boardroom at the Ontario Lottery Corporation, hosted by a dozen or so stony-faced, officious executives. To describe the atmosphere as unwelcoming and glacial would be an understatement. It was like walking into a deep freeze.

I showed them the note I'd received from the lotto-winning deadbeat. Then I explained the database-search procedure I was suggesting should be utilized in the case of everyone winning over a thousand dollars. At that, one of the executives, clearly affronted by the audacity of my suggestion, and speaking with great authority, proclaimed, "What? Are you serious? This is totally unacceptable. People don't even pay taxes on lotto winnings in this country. *Nothing* should be deducted from winnings. That's what makes lottery money so special. If we start deducting child support, what's next? Property taxes? Income taxes? Unpaid traffic tickets? Overdue library fees? This is the thin edge of the wedge! People will stop buying lotto tickets! The answer is *no*."

I folded my hands on the table with a noticeable thud, straightened my back, stared directly at the man who'd just spoken, took a deep breath, and channelled Faye Dunaway's portrayal of Joan Crawford admonishing the Pepsi-Cola executives in *Mommie Dearest.* "Listen to me, ladies and gentlemen," I blared, "and you better listen carefully. Don't fuck with me. This ain't my first rodeo! First of all, how *dare* you compare child support to those other debts? Are you aware that not even *bankruptcy* can discharge child support arrears? The Americans have been deducting support arrears from lotto winnings for years. Do you hear them complaining about poor ticket sales? How would you like the media to find out you're willing to facilitate deadbeat parents because you're too smug and self-righteous to do a simple computer search before paying out funds?"

Then, in typical Harvey style, I delivered the pièce de résistance: "And besides, I'm sure you're well aware that in the United States, the *casinos* also check for support arrears before paying out winnings over a thousand dollars. You're damn lucky I'm not asking for that too. And come to think of it, I just *might.*"

Those poor jokers knew they'd met their match. They were stupefied. Every mouth in the room, including those of my own colleagues, was agape in disbelief. The meeting ended with assurances from their executive team that we'd hear from them soon. We did, and the answer was yes. Legislation was passed requiring support arrears to be deducted from all lottery winnings over a thousand dollars. I'm extremely proud to have had a role in making this happen and to finally allow support recipients to receive money they might not otherwise have received.

My staff and I believed passionately in our mandate to enforce child support. I made many other recommendations to the government to reinforce that mandate. For example, I believe no one should be allowed to get a marriage licence if they're in arrears of child support. If they want to live with someone, that's fine. But if they want the state to sanction their relationship through the institution of marriage, they should first have to prove they're in compliance with their obligations arising from their previous marriages. After all, if the government is prepared to suspend the driver's licenses of delinquent support payors, why not make marriage licences contingent upon being up to date with child support? Marriage licences are far more connected to the well-being of children than driver's licences.

And here's another suggestion. I believe you shouldn't be allowed to adopt anyone else's child if you're not supporting your own children. There are thousands of men who marry women with children and then adopt those kids. I'm one of those children, so I certainly understand the value and benefits of step-parent adoption. However, it strikes me as totally inappropriate and contrary to the best interests of a child if a court were to allow that child to be adopted by someone who isn't supporting the children who came first.

To date, my suggestions have fallen on deaf ears. I hope that one day, we'll see a government, somewhere, demonstrate the courage and fortitude to enact truly child-focused legislation that will finally bring home to parents the all-important necessity of properly supporting the children of family breakdown. This should be the number one priority in every parent's budget and on every parent's mind.

CHAPTER 10

DARING TO DREAM BIG: BECOMING A JUDGE

In 1994, five years after joining the support enforcement program, "Harvey the overachiever" became restless for another mountain to conquer. Running a government program was deeply rewarding when it came to overseeing the operational aspects of delivering a critically important public service. But I didn't enjoy the tedious bureaucratic aspects of the job, such as budgeting, human resource management, and the endless, superfluous administrative reports required by the executive branch of government. Anyone who's worked in a high-level government position knows the hours are gruelling, the pay is paltry, and the demands are endless.

I was also more than a little annoyed that Jack Johnson was in no hurry to remove the "acting" from my job title. Whenever I broached the subject, he'd say, "Harvey, you're doing well. If you rock the boat, you might get thrown off." I grew to hate that expression, along with the veiled threat it conveyed.

There was another factor at play in my growing restlessness. I missed the drama, excitement, and theatricality of the courtroom. For litigation lawyers, courtroom advocacy is addictive. Nothing compares to the adrenaline rush coming from a great cross-examination of a witness, or the heart-thumping anticipation moments before a verdict is delivered, or, most of all, the euphoria of winning a case.

Another longing had been planted in my heart by Rosie Abella when I was a summer student in her court. Why not apply to be a judge? After all, she'd said I had what it took, and that was even before I'd proven myself as a criminal lawyer, family law researcher, support enforcement lawyer, and director of a major government program.

Throughout my career, I'd appeared before dozens of judges ranging in competence from excellent to abysmal. I'd endured the entire gamut of judicial styles: from calm, respectful, compassionate, and patient; to poker-faced and stoic; to indecisive and anxious; and to manic, sadistic, and verbally abusive. I'd often said to myself after a particularly unpleasant court appearance, *I just* know *I could do a better job than that judge*. So, I started researching the judicial appointments process.

In Canada, unlike the United States, judges are appointed by the government, not elected. One must complete a comprehensive application form canvassing the applicant's education, employment history, major career accomplishments, record of community service, published works, and references both within and outside the legal profession. The candidate must also provide detailed responses to such questions as: "Why do you want to be a judge?" "How do you feel you would enhance access to justice?" "What do you believe are the greatest challenges facing the justice system?" and so on.

In Ontario, applications to be a provincial judge are submitted to the Judicial Appointments Advisory Committee, a group of thirteen members appointed by the Attorney General and comprising prominent judges, lawyers, and members of the public. The committee vets the applications, investigates the candidates' competence and suitability, and then interviews the top ten applicants, following which they forward a list of the top three names to the Attorney General, who must choose from that list. This process reflects a strongly held belief in Canada that judicial appointments should be based on merit, not politics.

I asked a few trusted friends and colleagues whether they thought I should apply. Everyone said the same thing: "Harvey, I'm sure you'd be a great judge, but no government in its right mind will ever appoint an openly gay judge. It would be political suicide. If you really wanted to be a judge, you should have thought about that a long time ago and stayed in the closet. But it's too late now. Everyone knows you're gay. Forget it."

Not one person in my professional circle offered even a scintilla of encouragement. One senior government lawyer put it this way: "For you to fill out an application form would be a waste of good paper. Do us all a favour and save a tree." After my swearing-in as a judge, I planted a tree in his honour, and I've done it every year since.

I refused to be discouraged by the negative advice because by then I was used to being told by naysayers that I wasn't the "right fit," and I'd built an entire career proving them wrong. Most importantly, Rosie's inspiring and uplifting words, uttered all those years ago, kept ringing in my ears. I decided to submit an application.

Lawyers seeking to become judges must not only be highly proficient and widely respected as legal professionals; they must also demonstrate a long-standing commitment to improving the quality of life in society through a strong and impressive record of community service. Filling out the application form, I outlined my history of community involvement.

My volunteer activities began in the early 1980s as a board member of the Toronto Lesbian and Gay Community Appeal, which raised funds for cultural programs serving the queer community. I was also on the board of the Toronto Out and Out Club, an organization that held a wide variety of recreational and social events of interest to gay men.

By 1984, AIDS was spreading like wildfire. Tens of thousands of gay men were succumbing to the HIV virus while the rest of the world, and especially governments, were wilfully oblivious to the devastation wrought on our community. I lost over a dozen good friends to that terrible disease, including several men whom I had dated; I had to watch them wither and die, ravaged by a relentlessly virulent infection resulting simply from having had unprotected sex. To this day I don't know how I miraculously avoided contracting the virus.

Around that time I became involved in Chutzpah, a social group for Jewish gays and lesbians in Toronto. At that time many of our members were estranged from their parents and families after having come out to them. Chutzpah provided an essential lifeline and support network for these marginalized and disenfranchised people. As the AIDS epidemic progressed, Chutzpah became even more crucial for our members who became desperately ill. I joined the board of directors, led by Howard Levine, who eventually became a Toronto city councillor.

It was heartbreaking to see so many young Jewish men dying with no family members to comfort them. Howard and I felt it was time to reach out to the mainstream Jewish community for assistance. Our members needed financial support, counselling, and myriad other services. And sadly, we also needed to finance and arrange funerals.

As I had grown up going to the Jewish Community Centre in Hamilton, my first thought was to call the Toronto Jewish Community Centre. I asked the receptionist, a woman who sounded older than my grandmother, if she could connect me with someone in charge of providing social services. "Social services for whom?" she asked.

I replied, "There are a number of young homosexual men in the Jewish community suffering from AIDS who've been rejected by their families. We need help providing them with end-of-life services."

There was a long pause, and finally she exclaimed loudly, "What? Homosexuals? AIDS? Oy! I've never heard of such a thing! There *are no* Jewish homosexuals!" And she hung up.

The situation now became urgent. One of our members had just died, necessitating that funeral arrangements be made immediately, as Jewish funerals should ideally be conducted the day after the death. We'd collected enough money to buy a burial plot and pay for the funeral. All we needed was a rabbi to conduct the funeral service. I called the Holy Blossom Temple, Canada's largest Reform synagogue, which was renowned for its progressive values. In fact, during the American civil rights movement in 1962, Holy Blossom made history by inviting Dr. Martin Luther King Jr. to address the congregation.

I told the Holy Blossom receptionist I needed to speak with a rabbi about arranging a Jewish funeral and was immediately put through to the senior rabbi, Dow Marmur. After I explained the situation, he asked, "Was the deceased a member of this congregation?" I told him the deceased wasn't a member of any congregation.

The rabbi responded, "Well, I'd have to speak to the board of directors about doing a funeral for a non-member, and their next meeting isn't until next week." I was floored.

"Rabbi," I pleaded, "this is an emergency. A young Jewish man died tragically and needs a Jewish burial right now. We're willing to pay for your services, but obviously we can't wait a week for your board of directors to approve it. Can't you just come and do it?"

Rabbi Marmur replied, "That's not how things work here. Lots of people die every day. We can't do funerals for everyone. Our obligation is to our members. And besides, where's this young man's family?"

I explained the man was gay, and that when he came out to his family, they'd cut him off. Without skipping a beat, the rabbi snapped into a measurably louder, more severe tone. "Well, what would you expect? Do you think parents throw a celebration when they hear such news? Do you have any idea what a heartbreak this is for parents?" I began to feel my blood pressure skyrocketing, my throat constricting, and my heart pounding.

"Rabbi," I said, trying desperately to maintain my composure, "I know *exactly* what parents go through, because I saw what *mine* went through. But Rabbi, do *you* have any idea what we gay people go through when we're thrown out and ostracized by our own parents for something we have absolutely no control over?"

He responded, "Well, thank God this doesn't happen very often in Jewish families. I've never heard of even one case in our congregation."

That did it. This man needed a reality check and I was about to give him one. "Rabbi, I *guarantee* you there are dozens of families at Holy Blossom dealing with this issue. And I can prove it."

"Oh really? Is that so? How?" he asked, the agitation in his voice approaching fever pitch.

"Why don't we advertise an event at the synagogue for members of the congregation who are parents and families of gays and lesbians?" I responded. "We can put together a panel of experts who are members of Holy Blossom — a psychologist, a doctor, a social worker, a lawyer, and yourself — to address issues like coming out, AIDS, human rights law, the Jewish perspective on homosexuality, and so forth. And we can invite questions from the audience."

He thought for a moment and replied, "Hmm, well I don't see any harm in that. I'm sure I can get our Social Action Committee to organize this. But don't expect a big turnout. I can't imagine a lot of interest in this topic."

Three weeks later, on a frigid winter weeknight, the event took place in a large, echoing auditorium at Holy Blossom. It was scheduled for seven o'clock in the evening. When Howard and I arrived at six thirty, only three rows of chairs had been set up. The janitor explained he'd been instructed by the rabbi not to put out a lot of chairs because he didn't want to draw attention to the poor attendance. By six forty-five, as more and more people flooded into the room, the janitor had to hurriedly assemble more rows of chairs and the auditorium was almost full. And by seven o'clock, there was standing room only. The rabbi was flabbergasted.

The event was one of the most memorable evenings of my life. One parent after another got up and tearfully poured their heart out, saying how embarrassed and alone they'd felt when their children came out, and how mortified they'd have been at the thought of ever telling anyone, let alone their rabbi.

To his credit, Rabbi Marmur gave a heartfelt, impromptu speech, apologizing for having been unaware that so many members of the congregation and their families were struggling with coming-out issues. He regretted that people had felt too uncomfortable to confide in him about what they'd been going through. And he pledged to be more supportive, sensitive, and accessible in the future.

That seminal evening at Holy Blossom Synagogue provided the impetus for the creation of a support group for parents and families of LGBTQ+ Jews, which has assisted hundreds of people in distress for many years.

As for Chutzpah's need to find a rabbi willing to conduct funerals on short notice for AIDS victims, we were indeed fortunate that Rabbi Arthur Bielfeld of Temple Emanu-El in Toronto enthusiastically came to our rescue every time we needed him, including the funeral for the fellow for whom we'd approached Rabbi Marmur. Rabbi Bielfeld and the board of directors hosted numerous events at the synagogue in support of Chutzpah, and we were always warmly welcomed there.

When Howard Levine was elected to Toronto city council in 1988, I became president of Chutzpah. We organized a major outreach effort to establish lines of communication and working relationships with every organization in the mainstream Jewish community, such as the United Jewish Appeal, Jewish Child and Family Services, B'nai Brith, the Canadian Jewish Congress — and yes, even the Jewish Community Centre. I wanted to make sure that never again would a gay Jewish person ask for help from a Jewish organization and be told, "There are no gay Jews."

In 1990, Councillor Levine invited me to join the Toronto Mayor's Committee on Community and Race Relations. The committee's mandate was to promote understanding, respect, tolerance, and acceptance of the vast multicultural and multiracial mosaic comprising the diverse Toronto population. I was honoured to work on the committee and, thanks to Howard's inspired leadership, became the chair of Toronto's first Lesbian and Gay Subcommittee. In that capacity, I coordinated a multi-faceted strategy to improve the badly fractured relationship between the gay community and the Toronto Police Service, a relationship plagued by unease and mistrust ever since the 1981 bathhouse raids. We were also instrumental in fostering a more positive, inclusive, and welcoming work environment for lesbian and gay police officers, who'd been terrified that their homosexuality would be discovered by their colleagues.

With this history of community service, combined with my track record of professional achievements, and the fact that I was bilingual (Mom had always insisted I speak with her in French), I was hopeful that the committee would look favourably on my application. But I first had to get through a critical stage in the process known as "discreet inquiries."

After reviewing the applications, the committee selects the candidates whose resumés warrant further investigation. After calling the references provided by the candidates, the committee members dig much deeper. They make numerous phone calls to prominent lawyers, judges, and community members familiar with the candidates' work, personalities, and reputations.

They want the "real scoop" about the candidates' competence, judgment, integrity, honesty, and interpersonal skills.

The committee takes this step for good reason. Let's face it: Anyone who's agreed to be a reference for a job applicant can be expected to say good things about the person. The idea behind the "discreet inquiries" is to gain credible insights from well-known people whom the candidate did *not* choose as references.

Most importantly, the committee wants to know whether a candidate will become egotistical, arrogant, self-absorbed, and narcissistic after becoming a judge — in other words, will the person develop an all-too-common affliction known as "judgitis"? Unfortunately, many highly competent, respected, and popular lawyers undergo a dramatic and appalling personality change almost immediately upon ascending to the Bench. They lose all sense of humility and transform themselves into insufferably vain, pompous, and egomaniacal tyrants. I've lost count of the number of very nice, kind, humble, gracious lawyers I've known who became unrecognizable after donning their judge's robes. It's a very real problem, and the committee does their best, through the process of "discreet inquiries," to eliminate candidates who in any way indicate a potential to develop "judgitis."

That being said, unfortunately the "discreet inquiries" process is fraught with difficulties. First, they're *anything* but discreet. The committee members are usually unaware of the state of a candidate's relationship with the person they've chosen to consult. The reality in any profession is that professional jealousy, rivalry, and antipathy can exist between colleagues. People's personal agendas may unfairly influence their assessment of a candidate about whom they've been consulted. I've seen it happen. Many times.

Let me give you an example. Assume the person being consulted has just lost a trial against the candidate and is angry, embarrassed, and resentful about it. If that person is lacking in integrity, morality, and a sense of decency, they could easily destroy a candidate's chances of a judicial appointment by trashing them.

Here's another example, which actually happened to me while I was a candidate. I received a call from a committee member asking me to comment on the suitability of *another* candidate! Since I was competing against that person for the same position, there was an obvious conflict of interest. So much for discretion! I respectfully declined to comment on the other applicant's suitability, and minced no words telling the committee member how inappropriate it was to be calling me about another applicant.

Another major problem with "discreet inquiries" is that, although such consultations are supposed to remain confidential, nothing could be further from the truth. In the weeks after I submitted my application, I was approached more than a few times by colleagues and acquaintances who would whisper acidly in my ear, "Harvey, I received a call from the committee, and I want you to know I gave you a good reference." Can you imagine how I felt? First of all, the fact that these people even *knew* I'd applied bothered me. It's not something I'd advertised.

Secondly, some of those people were in absolutely no position to comment reliably on my job performance. And lastly, I didn't appreciate the thinly veiled implication that, somehow, I owed them something for having spoken positively about me. And I was right. Following my appointment, several people came up to me half-jokingly and said something like, "Now Harvey, you'd better be good to me, because I was one of the people called by the committee, and I gave you a good reference."

Mercifully, I made it through the "discreet inquiries" stage, and to my great jubilation was invited for an interview. As that fateful day approached, my anxiety and apprehension compounded exponentially. What questions would I be asked? How does one prepare when one has no idea of the questions they'll ask? Ideally, I should have consulted a judge for advice on how to prepare, but I didn't know any, except Rosie Abella, who'd been appointed under a different process. Would my sexual orientation be mentioned? Would my comportment, tone of voice, and personality convey the desired degree of dignity, decorum, and solemnity to be considered suitable for the loftiness of the judiciary? My traumatic experiences at previous job interviews didn't bode well for this monumentally important interrogation.

The interview was the final step in the process. If I could manage to convince the committee that I was one of the top three candidates, they'd send my name to the Attorney General. The exciting thought of that happening gave me hope, because if the Attorney General, Marion Boyd, were to see my name on that list, I knew I had a distinct advantage. She knew me and had seen me in action with the support enforcement program, and I felt confident she might be inclined to appoint me to the Bench. But first I had to get through the interview and get my name on that list.

It was February 24, 1995. The crucial day had arrived. I wore a brand-new navy-blue suit with a pale-blue shirt and ruby-red tie, an outfit the salesman at Brooks Brothers had assured me was perfect for the occasion. The interview took place in a downtown Toronto hotel.

I was ushered into a large, nondescript meeting room that screamed of beige with grey industrial carpeting. At the front of the room stood a long table, draped with a white tablecloth, at which the thirteen committee members were seated. The table was littered with binders and papers in front of each member, and there were pitchers of water and glasses placed at regular intervals along the table.

The committee was relatively evenly divided between men and women. The members, all of whom were middle aged, and none of whom I'd ever met before, stared at me intimidatingly. I was struck by their monochromatic, neutral, bland business attire and wondered whether their personalities were as sterile and colourless as their wardrobes.

I was seated in the centre of the room in a lone hard, wooden chair facing that long table. I could feel myself trembling and wondered if the committee could see my legs shaking. My heart was thumping so intensely I was sure they could hear it pounding. I prayed I'd done enough to prepare for this ordeal, even though I knew there'd really been no way to prepare.

The chair was Mr. Justice Robert Walmsley, a grey-haired, soft-spoken gentleman in his late sixties with a warm smile, who began the interview by introducing himself and the other members. The committee members took turns asking questions. They asked why I wanted to be a judge. I told them I had a lifelong passion for utilizing the law not only to effect justice, but to make a positive difference in people's lives. They asked how my career as a lawyer had prepared me for the Bench. I spoke about having represented Legal Aid clients in criminal court and having worked diligently to enforce parental child support obligations. They asked whether, in my opinion, the law governing young offenders (youths under the age of eighteen who committed criminal offences) was too lax. I responded with my own question: "Are the jails doing such a great job of rehabilitating adults that we should be throwing teenagers in there too?"

Some questions seemed designed to throw me. For example, I was asked whether I believed a Black accused person could receive a fair trial with an all-white jury, a question that made no sense because I was applying to be a provincial judge and there were no juries in provincial court. The judges made all the decisions. After pointing out that fact, I said that in order for a jury to truly be comprised of the accused's peers, there should be a healthy mix of people reflecting the diversity of our community.

One member asked me to name the last three books I'd read. I wondered, *What are they getting at with* that *question?* I told them that when I wasn't reading legal briefs and other documentation relating to my work, I read celebrity biographies, as I hoped to learn as many life lessons as I could from highly accomplished people.

They asked whether I was in favour of having cameras in the courtroom. The question was timely, as the O.J. Simpson murder trial in Los Angeles was currently unfolding on television before millions of viewers. I replied, "I think there's already quite enough grandstanding and showmanship in our courtrooms. I believe court proceedings should focus exclusively on the best interests of the litigants, not on making celebrities out of their lawyers — or, for that matter, the judges," a comment that elicited knowing smirks from two of the judges seated at the table.

I was then asked which aspects of my life I felt had best prepared me to be a judge. I appreciated this question. It allowed me to reference the hardships I'd overcome, which gave me unique insights into the many challenges regularly faced by the people who appeared in court. "When I was nineteen," I said after having drawn a deep breath, "my parents threw me out because I'm gay. I spent the next five years on welfare and working part-time cleaning people's toilets to get myself through university. I'd be willing to bet that I'm the only candidate you'll ever see who knows what it feels like to be that poor, and to be on the outside looking in. Believe me, I understand our clientele. And I know my life experience has equipped me well for this position." So far, so good. I was actually beginning to relax and even enjoy the experience.

Suddenly, one of the lay members of the committee, a morose-looking woman, looked down at a document in front of her, then looked up at me and said sardonically, "It says here that you're fluently bilingual. With a name like 'Harvey Brownstone,' how is it that you speak French?"

I cheerfully replied, "The name 'Brownstone' comes from my dad. He's an anglophone from Winnipeg. But my mom is from France and she raised me speaking French."

With a half-smile, she flashed a look at the person beside her and nodded, as if to say, *Watch this, I've got him this time*. With raised eyebrows, she said sarcastically, "Oh really? Well go ahead then, say something in French."

I couldn't believe it. She was testing me to see if I was telling the truth. Did this moron actually think someone applying to be a judge would have the audacity to lie about speaking another language? I couldn't help myself. Donning the most enchanting smile I could muster, I replied, "Allez vous faire foutre, Madame!" Translation: "Go fuck yourself."

Her face lit up and she smiled from ear to ear, clearly ignorant of what I'd just told her. She exclaimed, "Oh, what a lovely accent!" Out of the corner of my eye, I detected another committee member, who'd obviously understood my reply, stifling a guffaw and winking at me. I knew I'd made my point. However, this unbearable woman wasn't done with me yet. She was like a dog with a bone.

"Tell me, Mr. Brownstone," she intoned officiously. "There are five hundred applicants for this position. What makes you think you're more qualified for the job than any of them?"

Seriously? I thought. I couldn't believe it. Wasn't it the committee's job to assess the applicants and decide who was most qualified? How was I to answer that question without having seen the other applications? I was fed up. Out came Hurricane Harvey, and before I could restrain myself, I snapped emphatically, "The difference between me and those four hundred and ninety-nine other people is that *I'm* going to get the job and they're *not*!"

There. I'd said it. Time stood still as my words seemed to echo endlessly in that cavernous room. Every jaw at that table dropped to the floor in shocked silence. I could feel my throat constrict, my stomach heave, and my head throb. All I could do was stare straight ahead, knowing without question that my judicial aspirations had come to an abrupt and wretched end.

The next thing I knew, the committee chair stood up and walked over to me, saying, "Well, I think that about wraps things up." He shook my hand and escorted me out of the room saying "Thanks so much for coming in. We'll be in touch."

I went home nauseated, dejected, and furious with myself for allowing my big mouth and lack of impulse control to decimate my hope of ever becoming a judge. Over the next two weeks I was broken-hearted, inconsolable, despondent, and full of self-rage. I relived that final moment at the interview a thousand times, imagining all the ways I could have answered that woman more appropriately. I thought of little else.

And then, exactly two weeks after that momentous interview, the Attorney General, Marion Boyd, called to tell me she was appointing me a judge. It was the phone call of my life and I almost fainted. I couldn't believe what I was hearing. She said she was thrilled when she saw my name on the list of the top three candidates, and that this was the easiest decision she'd ever made as Attorney General. Then she said, "And Harvey, I'm going to attend your swearing-in ceremony personally. Normally a senior Crown attorney speaks on my behalf at these events, but in your case, I wouldn't miss this for the world!" I was euphoric. Even now, as I write these words, I'm finding it hard to express the extent of my surprise, joy, elation, and gratitude.

Two weeks after my conversation with the Attorney General, I was sworn in as a judge. At the reception following the ceremony, the chair of the appointments committee, Mr. Justice Robert Walmsley, came up to congratulate me. I couldn't resist asking him the one question that had been burning in my mind ever since I found out I got the job. I said, "I can't believe the committee put my name forward to the Attorney General after what I said to that woman."

Smiling slyly, he moved closer towards me, put his hand on my shoulder, and whispered in my ear, "Harvey, what you didn't know is that we all hated her. She tortured every candidate we interviewed. Only you had the guts to put her in her place. We were really impressed by that. And just to bug her, we all voted to put your name on the list. She was outnumbered. There was nothing she could do about it."

Over the years, dozens of lawyers have asked me for advice about what to say at judicial interviews. I always smile to myself, thinking, *If they only knew what I did at my interview, they definitely wouldn't be asking me for advice.*

CHAPTER 11

LIFE ON THE BENCH

No matter how many times a lawyer has appeared in court, nothing can fully prepare him or her for being a judge. There's no school to attend or course one can take, although judges regularly attend continuing education programs to keep abreast of the law.

The only training a newly appointed judge gets prior to presiding in court is to "shadow" other judges for several weeks before being sworn in. That means sitting silently on the dais next to the judge, observing everything he or she says and does. The regional senior judge chose the judges I was to shadow. "I've selected a variety of judges who demonstrate a broad spectrum of judicial styles," he said. "Harvey, this is your chance to learn what to do and what *not* to do. It's the last time you'll ever get to see your colleagues in action, because once you're sworn in, you'll be flying solo in your own courtroom. So make the most of it."

I vividly remember the first time I sat on the dais next to a brand-new colleague. From that elevated vantage point at the front of the courtroom, the view was so different than it had been when I stood at the counsel table as a lawyer facing the judge. Now the lawyers were facing me, and the witness box was right beside me. I was struck by the immense honour and privilege that had been bestowed upon me, and was eager to soak up all the wisdom, expertise, and judging "tips" my colleagues could impart.

My first day of shadowing was in criminal court, observing one of the most notorious judges on the Bench, Justice Bill Ross, a wild-eyed, eccentric man in his late sixties with long, unruly, frizzy grey hair that bounced when he spoke and gesticulated. His extreme impatience, sarcastic and off-colour quips, and mercurial temper were legendary. I'd appeared before him numerous times as a lawyer and always found him amusing, in a menacing kind of way. Now, sitting directly beside him, in such close proximity to a man renowned for his impulsive and erratic behaviour, I was more than a little apprehensive about what I was about to witness and how his behaviour might reflect on me. Would the lawyers appearing before us assume he was training me to become just like himself? Would his actions tarnish my reputation before I even began presiding? Would I suffer from guilt by association?

Our first case involved a bank robber who pleaded guilty. The accused, a man in his mid-twenties, had a lengthy record of previous offences, though much less significant ones, and he had been in and out of jail since he was a teenager. After listening to the submissions of the prosecution and defence lawyers, Justice Ross simply pronounced, "Sir, I sentence you to seventeen years." That was it. No reasons given. During the morning recess I asked how he'd arrived at that sentence. "Simple," he answered. "I looked down at the calendar in front of me and saw that it was the seventeenth day of the month. So I gave him seventeen years." As the day wore on, it became abundantly clear that I'd been sent to Justice Ross's court to learn what *not* to do.

Several days later, I sat beside another judge, a kind-hearted, soft-spoken woman beloved by defence counsel and loathed by prosecutors. She conducted two criminal trials and found both accused not guilty, even though I thought the evidence of guilt in both cases was overwhelming. Over lunch, I asked her what it was about the evidence that raised a reasonable doubt as to the guilt of the two accused. She said, "Well, the way I see it, I wasn't there when the incidents happened, so I can't really be sure what happened. How am I supposed to know if someone's telling the truth or lying? So if an accused gets up and says he didn't commit the offence, that's enough to raise a reasonable doubt in my mind."

Hmm, I thought, *no wonder the defence lawyers love her!* From one extreme to the other, I was building my understanding of what to avoid.

And yet another judge, Ayres Couto, an irascible, crotchety old curmudgeon, well-known for never having a reasonable doubt, advised me, "Harvey, this job is easy. If the accused is guilty, send him to jail. If he's innocent, give him a fine." I swear, you can't make this stuff up.

The next day I sat beside a kindly, soft-spoken family court judge in his late fifties who was notorious for being indecisive. He greeted me first thing in the morning with, "Harvey, if I play my cards right, we'll be out of here by noon and I'll take you for a nice long lunch." The docket was filled with a lengthy list of hotly contested motions brought by hostile ex-partners fighting over custody, visitation, and child support. I wondered what "playing his cards right" meant. How in the world could my colleague complete such a lengthy list of cases before lunchtime?

I soon found out. In the first motion, we listened to the wife's lawyer's submissions, and then the husband's lawyer made his submissions. The judge sat there poker-faced, saying nothing. He then heaved a great sigh and said, "Counsel, it seems to me that if you *really try* to talk to your clients and work with each other more effectively, you'll be able to work this out. I want you all to go out in the hall and don't come back in here until you've reached a resolution." The same thing happened with the next three motions we heard. We then took the morning recess.

I was astonished and confused. Wasn't it obvious the parties were in court because they *couldn't* resolve their disputes? Why was the judge assuming the lawyers hadn't tried hard enough to negotiate a resolution *before* coming to court? He hadn't even asked them what efforts they'd made to reach a consensus. Wasn't it the judge's job to make a decision when the parties were at a stalemate? And besides, if he was going to urge them to try to negotiate an agreement, shouldn't he have given them some feedback on their positions to point them in the right direction?

During the recess, I peppered the judge with all those questions. He responded, "Harvey, here's the thing. These parents all have young children and will have to deal with each other for the next twenty years. They chose each other to have children with, so like it or not, they're stuck with each other and they have to make the best of it. They must find ways to work with each other as co-parents so they can raise their kids without constantly coming to court, expecting judges to do the parenting for them. The best thing judges can do for them is to keep pressuring them to communicate, cooperate, and compromise with each other."

Unsatisfied with his "pie in the sky," Pollyanna response, I pressed on. "Of course we should encourage parents in conflict to reach agreement, and in a perfect world, that would happen in every case. But we all know this isn't a perfect world. Some people are unreasonable, obstinate, and stubborn. Weren't courts created for the precise purpose of having a neutral third party, a judge, resolve disputes when people just can't do it themselves?"

He replied, "I get it. But parents aren't like other litigants who sue each other and never have to see each other again. Parents have to be there for their children until they grow up, and often far beyond that. Too many judges let parents off the hook by deciding everything for them in motion after motion. We're babysitting these parents, and in the long run we're not doing them any favours. And we're certainly not doing ourselves any favours either. Look at the family courts. They're imploding with far too many cases. We've become victims of our own success by making it far too easy for parents to abdicate their responsibilities."

Risking irking him even further, I still wouldn't give up. "In my experience, people don't choose to come to court lightly. Litigation is terribly expensive, time-consuming, unpredictable, and stressful. I think you should assume, when these people are standing there before you, that they and their lawyers have made every reasonable effort to settle the matter. They desperately need closure. They need you to make a decision so they can move on with their lives. And if you don't do it, I think *you're* the one who's abdicating his responsibilities."

Oops, now I'd gone too far. My vexed colleague shot me a look of righteous indignation, stood up, put his judicial robe back on, and in a decidedly stern tone of voice said, "Harvey, you seem to think judges are best qualified to decide these disputes, but you'll soon find out that we're not mind readers and we don't have magic wands or crystal balls. If I were to decide what should happen to these people's children, how do you know I'd be right? What if I'm wrong? I'd be blamed for whatever happened to those kids. But if the parents decide for themselves, then I can't be blamed. Your first responsibility as a judge is to protect yourself. We'll just have to agree to disagree. It's time to get back into court."

Back in the courtroom, one case after another was adjourned on consent to another day. The lawyers had clearly seen the writing on the wall: This judge was not going to make any decisions, so it'd be a waste of time to argue their cases. They'd convinced their clients to postpone their motions and perhaps try to get their cases transferred to another judge. And just like my colleague predicted, the docket was completed by lunchtime. Nothing substantive was achieved in his court that day.

Not surprisingly, my colleague remembered he had an important errand to run, so he couldn't have lunch with me. He wished me well, saying, "Thanks for the stimulating conversation. Can't wait to get your thoughts over lunch one day after you've been on the job for a few months." I'm still waiting to have that conversation and that lunch.

Luckily, I also shadowed some wonderful judges, including Justices Mary Jane Hatton, Joe James, David Main, Harvey Salem, and Sam Darragh, who exemplified the very best qualities we all want to see in judicial officers. They taught me so much about how to manage unruly lawyers, litigants, witnesses, and audience members; how to assess evidence; how to formulate and deliver decisions; and much more. And perhaps most importantly, they taught me to take my work seriously, but never to take myself too seriously. As you'll read in the forthcoming chapters, I put these lessons to good use.

The first thing I had to deal with when I began presiding as a judge was my youth. It was, and still remains, almost unheard of for a thirty-eight-year-old to be a judge. People entering the courtroom would look up at the dais to see who the judge was, take one look at me, and do a double take. One day an inebriated man staggered up to the front of the courtroom and shouted,

"Hey, wait a minute. *You're* the judge? You're *way* too young to be a judge. How old are you?"

I replied, "Well, sir, if you must know, I'm thirty-eight."

He guffawed, "Hell, I've got things in my *fridge* older than you!"

I responded, "And are *they* a little off, too, sir?"

One day, only several months after being appointed, I was conducting a trial in a fraud case. The defence lawyer was Jack Pinkofsky, an intolerably haughty, boastful, self-important, and smug gargoyle of a man in his late sixties, well-known for giving judges a hard time by making snide, sarcastic, contemptuous comments in response to judicial rulings. After I overruled one of his nonsensical and supercilious objections, he took a deep breath, exhaled as if beyond exasperated, and pompously proclaimed in a voice dripping with sarcasm, "Well, Your Honour, I've only been a lawyer thirty-five years. I couldn't *pretend* to have the depth and breadth of legal experience that *you* have."

Without skipping a beat, I replied, "That's all right, Mr. Pinkofsky. Maybe in another thirty-five years, you'll get there." The entire courtroom burst into applause, and Jack Pinkofsky never again gave me a moment of difficulty.

I spent my first few months on the Bench carefully developing my personal judicial style, and one key decision stemmed from a lesson I'd learned as a lawyer. Too many times, at the end of a trial, the judge would deliver an erudite, sophisticated, and complex decision loaded with legal analysis fit for a doctoral thesis, and then quickly exit the courtroom. My client would look at me blank-faced and ask, "What just happened?"

It disturbed me terribly that I had to be the one to explain the judge's decision to my client, especially if it was unfavourable to them. In my opinion, it's cowardly for judges to speak above the parties' heads and then make a quick escape to avoid having to deal with their reactions to the decisions. Early on I decided to always speak in plain language, and to disarticulate the law into manageable chunks, so that people appearing before me could clearly understand what I was saying. I wanted them to know not only what I'd decided, but also the *reasons* for my decisions. And if more explanation was needed, I wanted to be the one to provide it, not burden the lawyers with having to speak on my behalf.

Judges sometimes lose sight of the fact that many of the people appearing before them are unsophisticated and uneducated. They speak so far over people's heads that you need a legal dictionary to understand what they're saying. And their written judgments are incomprehensibly verbose, rambling, and convoluted. I used to jokingly tell some of my colleagues that they could turn a semicolon into a monologue! Although those judges are brilliant scholars, they're writing for law professors, legal publishers, and appellate courts, not for the litigants whose cases they're adjudicating. I was never a legal scholar, but I made sure to speak and write in a plain, simple, and relatable way, geared to the needs of the people whose cases I was deciding.

I'm reminded of a case in which a young man was in the witness box being asked to review a document. His lawyer got up and said, "Your Honour, that's impossible. My client is illiterate." Suddenly, his mother, who was sitting in the body of the courtroom, jumped up and yelled, "Your Honour, that's a dirty lie. I married my son's father three weeks before he was born!" You get the point.

Another important characteristic of my personal judicial style was that I wanted the litigants appearing before me to feel free to speak to me if they so desired, especially in family court. This was almost unheard of back in 1995 when I began presiding. In those days, judges spoke only to the lawyers in court, never to the litigants themselves. It was as if the clients weren't even there. It was considered disrespectful to a lawyer for a judge to circumvent them and speak directly to the client.

Lawyers care deeply about protecting their clients' best interests, and so they routinely tell them never to speak to the judge, and for good reason. The client may say something that could prejudice their case. I never compelled a parent in family court to speak to me if they had a lawyer. But if the parent wanted to — and most of them did — I was willing to hear them out and respond, although I always suggested they first run their comments by their lawyers. After all, these were high-stakes cases about *their* lives and *their* children. They shouldn't be made to feel invisible. I didn't want parents to leave my courtroom angry and frustrated, feeling they hadn't been allowed to fully explain their positions before I had to decide the issues at hand. And

I also didn't want them to be angry with their lawyers for shutting them up when they really wanted to tell me something.

I quickly learned there was another very important advantage to allowing parents in family court to speak directly to me. Without the sugar-coated filters applied by lawyers to portray their clients in the best possible light, I got to know these parents in a real way, and it became easy to understand the dynamics of their relationships and discover their true agendas. Letting parents speak frankly about what was really on their minds proved to be enormously helpful in cutting to the heart of the conflict and finding solutions.

For example, in one case the lawyers were engaged in a heated argument over custody. The mother wanted sole custody and the father wanted joint custody. At one point the father said, "Your Honour, everything my ex-wife's lawyer is telling you is a total lie. My ex-wife is a terrible mother and a total bitch. I'm done with her. I never want to speak to her or have anything more to do with her ever again! I hope she drops dead!"

"Oh really?" I said. "Well tell me, sir, how do you expect to have joint custody with someone you won't communicate with? What exactly do you think joint custody is?"

It was blatantly obvious that the father's lawyer hadn't adequately explained to him that joint custody requires both parents to communicate and cooperate with each other and make decisions together in a mature, civilized way. To put it bluntly, joint custody is for parents who don't *need* to go to family court to have a judge, a total stranger, make decisions for them about their own children. Had the father not been allowed to speak directly to me, I would never have known, from what his lawyer was saying, that he felt that way about the mother of his children. Scenarios like this occurred on a daily basis.

Well over 80 percent of parents don't have lawyers, so for family court judges, learning how to communicate directly with parents is a necessity. Extremely poor people will qualify for Legal Aid, and very rich people can afford to hire lawyers. But everyone in between is left to their own devices, which is very challenging and difficult for all concerned. The justice system was never designed or intended to be navigated without the benefit of legal counsel, and my heart breaks for those whose financial circumstances compel them to do just that.

Quite apart from those who'd like to be represented by a lawyer but can't afford one, there's a sizeable number of people who *can* afford a lawyer but don't believe they need one. Thanks to TV judges like Judge Judy, many people choose to represent themselves in family court. In countless cases, parents would say to me, "Why would I need a lawyer? It's my life. It's my story. Why would I pay someone to tell my story? Nobody had a lawyer on *Judge Judy*."

That used to infuriate me because, first of all, Judge Judy dealt with small claims court cases, not family court cases, which have a much greater impact on people's lives. Secondly, Judge Judy was first and foremost an entertainer whose style of adjudication was meant to amuse and sometimes shock the audience. Family court, while often shocking, is anything but entertaining (although I'm the first to admit there were some lighthearted moments in my courtroom). And thirdly, Judge Judy's cases actually took much longer than what was seen onscreen. The hearings were edited to show only the most compelling portions. In short, nothing about the television show reflected the reality of family court. It troubled and angered me that so many people actually believed that watching a TV show constituted sufficient preparation for their own court appearances.

Several weeks after my swearing-in, my mother called to announce that she and Dad were coming to come see "their son the judge" in action. A lump grew in my throat. For someone who's never been to a criminal or family court, the ambiance can be startling and off-putting. The clientele is frequently dishevelled, loud, vulgar, and highly emotional, and the subject matter — domestic violence, child abuse, substance abuse, mental illness, robberies, bar fights, home invasions, and the like — is not exactly what one would call genteel. This was no place for Mom. I just knew it.

I tried to dissuade them from coming, but Mom was having none of it. She was so proud of her son and wanted to witness all the pomp and circumstance that she imagined would be surrounding me. And she wanted everyone to know that she was the judge's mother.

They came to court on a day on which I was hearing criminal cases. My day began at nine o'clock in the morning, with a call from the senior court security officer saying, "Your Honour, there's a woman here at the front door refusing to go through the security check, claiming she's your mother. Is it true?" I could feel my face turning beet red and told the officer I'd be right there.

I ran apprehensively to the security gate at the front door of the courthouse to find a long line of people waiting with growing impatience to enter the building. At the front of the line, holding everyone up, was Mom, immaculately coiffed and in full makeup, glamorously dressed and bejewelled in a sequined gown, with a black gamma mink coat draped over her shoulders and posing as if she were on the red carpet at a Hollywood premiere. All she needed was a diamond tiara and she could easily have passed for royalty at Buckingham Palace. I was mortified.

"Harvey!" she yelled. "Thank God you're here! Tell these men who I am. How dare they expect me to open my purse? Didn't you tell them your *mother* was coming?"

The security officer took one look at my embarrassed face and immediately understood that this crazed woman was indeed telling the truth. He waved my parents through the security gate, and Mom sashayed right by him, stopping momentarily to give him the once-over — accompanied by a loud and indignant "harrumph" — as she swept into the courthouse lobby with great pageantry.

I hurried my parents to my chambers, hoping no one would notice us. No such luck. The senior security officer had already called the court manager to let her know Justice Brownstone's parents were visiting. Oh, how I wish he hadn't done that.

The court manager, Donna, was an efficient, no-nonsense, humourlessly bureaucratic woman in her fifties with jet-black hair pulled back into a tight bun and round spectacles that were much too big for her face. Moments after my parents and I entered my chambers, there was a knock at my door. I opened it to find the manager accompanied by the administrative judge, Derek Hogg, a lecherous but good-natured, red-faced alcoholic known for his uncouth, crass, tasteless utterances. He drank so much that he loved to say, "The last time I gave a urine sample it had an olive in it." Derek was barely coherent at the best of times, and almost comatose after lunchtime.

Thankfully, it was still morning, so he was able to walk without assistance and with only a moderate stagger.

Before I could open my mouth, Donna said, "Justice Brownstone, we're all so delighted to have your parents here." I introduced my parents perfunctorily to our visitors, praying silently that Mom would graciously say "Hello, nice to meet you" and let them be on their way. Not bloody likely.

Mom took one look at Donna and blurted, "Oh my dear, you're the manager? Is *this* how you dress for court, working with judges like *my son*? This will never do!"

Donna, clearly taken aback, looked down as if to remind herself of what she was wearing, and before she could utter a single word, Mom declared, "This is your lucky day, my dear. I'm sure my son's told you I have an exclusive French fashion boutique [I hadn't]. I can dress you from head to foot, and of course you'll get a discount." She then pulled a business card out of her purse and handed it to Donna, who was nonplussed beyond recognition.

Before Donna could open her mouth to respond, Derek grabbed my mother's hand, shook it enthusiastically, and chimed in with "Well now, *here's* a lady with real class. Harvey, your mother is what I call a *real* queen." The pun went right over Mom's head. He then blurted, "We could sure use a few more dames like you in this joint, that's for sure. And I love the French accent. I spent time in France during the war. Ooh la la, those French girls, I'll never forget 'em. Hey, by any chance, did you happen to know Brigitte Bardot?"

Mom looked at Derek as if she'd just come face to face with decayed roadkill. Brusquely disengaging her hand from his and wiping it on her dress, she scathingly replied, "Yes, we French people have class. And I raised my son to be classy too. I'm sure you can see that. It was very nice to meet you but I'm here to see *my son* and I have a lot to tell him." And with that she turned to me, hissing in French, "Get these bourricots [boors] out of here. They smell. They're making me sick."

Derek and Donna left my office completely stupefied. Heaven only knows what they must have thought of their encounter with my mother. I'll never know because we never spoke about that visit.

At ten o'clock, I asked my clerk to take my parents to the courtroom so they could be seated in the audience. I was in the middle of a sexual assault trial and the complainant was testifying. Throughout her testimony, an audible series of gasps emanated from where my mother was sitting. Each time the witness described something dreadful the accused had done to her, a look of horror would cross my mother's face and she'd whisper to my dad, who'd then whisper back to her. I could tell he was explaining terms like "fellatio" and "cunnilingus" to her. Her level of agitation was increasing by the moment, and I feared the powder keg was about to explode.

Suddenly, in the midst of the witness's testimony, my mother turned to my dad and asked in a voice much too loud, "Sam, qu'est-ce que c'est le 'digital penetration'?" Dad whispered something into Mom's ear, triggering a look of horror. "*What?*" she shrieked. "I can't believe it. Is *this* what I raised my son for, so he could sit here and listen to this garbage? Mon fils, mon fils, is *this* why you wanted to be a judge? No wonder you don't want to have sex with women. Look what you're listening to! I'm sick, just sick over it. Come on, Sam, we're leaving. I'm not listening to one more second of this trash." And with that, she grabbed my poor, dazed father's hand and, dragging him along in her wake, stormed out of the courtroom in a flurry of French expletives and a tornado of dust.

I wanted the floor to open up and swallow me whole so I could fall through it and die. Now everyone in the courtroom knew this glamorously attired but crazed and disruptive woman was the judge's mother. Without waiting for instructions from me, the clerk stood up and yelled, "*All rise.* This court is now in recess." God bless my clerk.

She then rushed out of the courtroom to fetch my parents and bring them back to my chambers. Mom was enraged and in tears. "Harvey, I just can't believe it," she cried. "You wanted to be a judge to listen to all these horrible things? How could you want to be in such a hideous place? Did you see the look of the people here? Walking down the hallway, I was sure we'd be attacked. I had no idea being a judge was so awful. I'm just sick over it. This is *not* what I wanted for *my son.*"

I replied, "Mom, what did you *think* it'd be like? Did you think I'd be dealing with the crème de la crème? This is a criminal court! We deal with criminals!"

Disheartened, my parents went home. That was their one and only time watching "their son the judge" in court. Thank heavens for small mercies.

I'm often asked whether the subject of my sexual orientation ever came up at work. I'm happy to say that, for the most part, my judicial colleagues were accepting and supportive of me and treated me very well. But there was one unforgettable incident that I must share with you.

Justice Derek Hogg regularly filled the fridge in the judge's lunchroom with beer, and he and several of my other colleagues gleefully imbibed all day long, much to the chagrin of some of my other colleagues and myself.

Derek loved women. Frequently. He talked about his lust for women all the time, and in the most graphic detail. It was Derek's idea to bring a television to the judges' lunchroom so we could all view reruns of *Baywatch*. He and some of my other workmates loved ogling the beautiful, sexy actresses posing suggestively on the beach wearing revealing swimsuits. My colleagues would spend their lunch hour spiritedly debating such earth-shattering subjects as whether the actresses on *Baywatch* applied ice cubes to their nipples before filming in order to make them appear hard on camera. No female judge lasted at that courthouse very long, and I couldn't blame them.

Times were very different back then. The judiciary was largely populated by old white men, "hail fellow well met" types who came from an era that tolerated and even encouraged sexism, misogyny, racism, and homophobia. I was appointed at the tail end of that era. Thankfully, things changed dramatically for the better within a few years of my appointment.

One day, after watching an episode of *Baywatch* — which he called *Babewatch* — Derek said, "Harvey, I just don't get it. Look at those babes on the screen. How can you possibly not be aroused by those bodies? What does a man have that could possibly compare to those luscious babes?"

Oy. Seriously? What could I say? And why bother? He was three sheets to the wind. I just chuckled and replied, "Derek, if you ever *really* want to find out what you're missing, just let me know. It can be arranged." Derek's face went blank, there was a stunned silence, and that was the end of lunch.

The next day, Derek and a few of our more boisterous colleagues came up to me and said, "Harvey, get ready. We're taking you out for lunch. And don't try wriggling out of it. You're coming with us." I wondered what in the world they had in mind.

Lunchtime came and the four of us piled into a fellow judge's gleaming black BMW and headed to a now-defunct strip bar located not far from the court called the Landing Strip. I couldn't believe it. "Guys," I said, "are you kidding me? We're going into a strip club? I have no interest in seeing a bunch of naked women. And I'll bet the food sucks."

Laughing, Derek said, "Harvey, it'll do you good. And who cares about the food? We're here to satisfy a *much* different appetite. Leave it to me. I have it all arranged." And he certainly did. We entered a dimly lit, dingy, red-velvet-wallpapered room that reeked of smoke, stale beer, and vomit. Beneath flashing lights there were small round nightclub tables, occupied by lecherous drunks, placed strategically around the numerous floor-to-ceiling poles on which scantily clad female strippers were gyrating and cavorting to the thumping music.

My colleagues led the way as I stepped gingerly across the repulsively sticky carpet to our table located just beneath the stage. Derek ensured that I was seated directly in front of the stage. A top-heavy, svelte waitress, with curvaceous hips and lipstick that extended from one ear to the other, came up to our table to take our order. "Hi, Red!" she exclaimed, greeting Derek excitedly. "Hi, guys," she said to my other colleagues. And then, nodding in my direction, she asked, "Who's the cutie?"

Derek said, "Oh, this is Harvey, our latest rookie. We're breaking him in." I smiled faintly, mumbling, "Hello."

Everyone ordered a beer except me. I had a club soda. The guys ordered wings. Taking my life in my hands, I ordered a club sandwich and fries.

When the waitress left our table, I turned to Derek, asking, "Who's 'Red'?" He replied sheepishly, "Oh, she loves to call me that because she gets my blood pressure up and my face goes red." Enough said.

Suddenly, a spotlight glared on the stage and a male voice blared over the sound system announcing their star attraction, unsurprisingly named

"Ineeda Man." A buxom redhead wearing nothing but a G-string — that left little to the imagination — bounced onto the stage and began wrapping herself around the pole like a giant boa constrictor.

Before I knew it, she'd slithered off the stage and onto my lap, her thighs enveloping mine, leaving me hopelessly trapped. Paralyzed, I glanced pleadingly over to my colleagues, who were laughing uproariously at my predicament. "Come on, Harvey," Derek jeered, "show her what you got!"

The dancer's gyrations in my lap continued until she realized she wasn't getting a "rise" out of me. She quickly disengaged herself and pranced back to the stage to complete her performance, which included some rather ingenious uses for Oreo cookies and Ping-Pong balls, prompting some desultory applause and catcalls from the crowd. All I could think was, *I can't wait to get home and take a shower.*

We quickly ate our lunch and headed back to the court, not a moment too soon as far as I was concerned. On our way back, Derek joked, "Well, Harvey, if *that* experience didn't do it for you, nothing will. I give up." And so ended their pathetic, yet amusing, attempt at conversion therapy.

In my twenty-six years as a judge, my homosexuality came up only three times in the courtroom. The first occurred several weeks after I began presiding. Some lawyers had been saying the only reason I'd been appointed was because the government wanted to appear progressive by putting a "token" gay on the Bench. I was surprised that anyone could believe such a thing, as I'd repeatedly been told before applying for the job that no government in their right mind would ever appoint an openly gay judge. And now that I had that position, those same people said, "Well, he only got the job because he's gay." You just can't win.

One day, several weeks after being appointed, I was presiding over a hotly contested motion being argued vociferously by two fiery lawyers. There were other lawyers at the counsel table whispering among themselves, waiting for their cases to be called. Suddenly, a lull occurred in the proceedings, during which I clearly heard one female lawyer, whom I'll call

Ms. Fleming, say to the colleague next to her, "I sleep with men, too, and they didn't appoint me."

She immediately realized I'd heard what she'd said. A horrified, ashen look crossed her face, and she began visibly trembling and appeared ready to collapse. I actually felt sorry for her. I simply said, in my most campy voice, "Well, Ms. Fleming, perhaps you need to improve your technique. I'd be happy to give you some tips after court."

The second time occurred in youth court. A fifteen-year-old boy was pleading guilty to having badly beaten up a classmate at school using brass knuckles. He'd broken the nose of his victim, another fifteen-year-old boy. His lawyer delivered the usual perfunctory sentencing submissions such as, "My client is very remorseful. This act was out of character, an isolated event, and will never happen again."

I wasn't satisfied. There was something missing in the recitation of the facts. This attack appeared to have occurred out of the blue with no precipitating event. I wanted to know what had provoked the accused to assault his classmate so viciously. I asked his lawyer, "Counsel, I don't understand. What got into your client to do such a thing? Why did he beat up this young man?"

Before the lawyer could respond, the offender blurted out, "Because he's a faggot," in a tone conveying the confidence of someone who felt completely justified in doing what he'd done. Contrary to what his lawyer had said, this boy was anything but remorseful.

I saw red. My blood boiled. This was a moment of truth for me. I had to say something that this kid would never forget. I snapped, "Oh yeah? He's a faggot? Well let me tell you something. *So am I.*" I could hear an audible gasp throughout the courtroom, as if the walls were caving in. Pointing to my judicial robe, I blared, "You take a good look at *this*, young man, because *this* is what faggots grow up to be now." And I sent him to youth custody for nine months.

There are no words to adequately describe that boy's reaction to what I'd said. Never in a million years had he thought the judge sentencing him would be gay. He'd gotten the lesson of a lifetime that day. But much more significantly, so had the fifteen-year-old victim who was seated in the first row next to his parents. Both the victim's and his parents' eyes filled with tears as they looked at me in disbelief.

I then said to the tearful victim, "Young man, I just did that for you, for me, and for everyone who's ever been bullied." I then invited him to come up to the dais and stand beside me. Slowly and hesitatingly, he did so. I smiled at him and shook his hand, saying, "If you're ever in a courtroom again, I know you'll be sitting right here." That was quite a moment. It still gives me goosebumps.

The third and final time my homosexuality was mentioned in court occurred during a custody case. The mother, who had custody of the parties' two young boys, aged five and seven, vehemently opposed the father's request for weekend visitation with his sons. The marriage had ended when the father had come out. The father, a commercial pilot, had always been an active and loving parent. The mother could point to nothing disqualifying him from having the same visitation with his children as would any other father. She argued, "Your Honour, he's gay. I have no idea who his friends are or what he's doing at night. I can't take the chance of having my sons exposed to his lifestyle, in such a dangerous environment."

This couple had already appeared before me numerous times. I felt she had a good sense of who I was and trusted me. I replied, "Ma'am, if I wanted your children to spend a weekend with me in my home, would you be okay with that?"

She immediately responded, "Well of course I would. You're a judge. I'm not worried about you, sir."

I continued, "Well, ma'am, I'm gay."

She was stunned. I had made my point, and she consented to a generous visitation arrangement.

Writing this chapter has reminded me that, during my twenty-six years on the Bench, I had the great privilege of meeting and getting to know thousands of people who appeared in my courtroom. I'm humbled and grateful to have had the opportunity to, in some small way, impact the lives of those people. And, there's no doubt, they certainly impacted mine.

CHAPTER 12

THE BITTER REALITIES OF FAMILY COURT

I'm often asked about the difference between presiding in criminal court and presiding in family court. Family court is much more emotionally draining than criminal court for three reasons: Firstly, although criminal court deals with many human tragedies — homicides, sexual assaults, and other violent offences — the ambiance is generally civilized and orderly because the trials occur many months after the events took place, due to court backlogs. Victims and witnesses have had time to recover, or at least adjust, to what they've been through. But in family court, there's a sense of immediacy and urgency, as the events flowing from the relationship breakdown are progressing even as the court case is ongoing, making the parties' emotions and anxiety levels extremely raw.

Secondly, in criminal court 95 percent of accused persons plead guilty, meaning there's no trial, and the judge's only function is to sentence the offender. Victims don't have to testify and relive the traumas they've been through. They simply provide a written statement to assist with sentencing, and most of the time they don't even attend court.

And, finally, even if there is a trial in criminal court, the judge's job of adjudication is relatively simple. If the judge is convinced beyond a reasonable doubt that the accused is guilty, the accused will be convicted. If the judge believes the accused is innocent, the accused will be acquitted (found not guilty). And if the judge can't make up his or her mind, then obviously they have a reasonable doubt, so the accused will be acquitted. But in family court, a judge doesn't have the luxury of making a case go away by having a reasonable doubt. Unless the parties reach a consent, the court must make a decision to resolve the dispute, no matter how complicated or unpleasant the issues and results are.

There's a common saying that describes the major difference between criminal court and family court: In criminal court, we see bad people at their best behaviour. They're well behaved and respectful because they want to make a good impression on the judge in the hopes of not being sent to jail. But, in family court, we see good people at their worst behaviour. They're so enmeshed in the turmoil they're going through in the breakup of their relationship that they often can't control their behaviour in court. Ask any court security officer which court they would rather work in, and I guarantee you they'll choose criminal court any day.

The hardest thing about being a family court judge is that decisions must frequently be made based on incomplete information. Judges don't have private investigators to assist them. They're dependent on the evidence produced by the parties, and that evidence is often woefully inadequate, mostly comprised of "he said / she said," with little or no proof to support each party's allegations against the other. Family court judges often have to rely on their own intuitive abilities to read between the lines and draw reasonable inferences from the parties' behaviour. I'm reminded of British comedian Rowan Atkinson's famous comment: "I feel like a blind man in a dark room looking for a black cat that isn't there."

In child protection cases involving allegations of neglect and/or abuse of children by their parents, judges are required to make critically important decisions assessing parenting capacity and risk of harm to children. The stakes are high for parents because the court may terminate their parental rights and place their children for adoption. But the stakes are even higher for the children. A judge's wrong decision could mean the loss of a child's relationship with his or her parents, and in the worst-case scenario, grievous harm or even death.

The gravity of my responsibility in child protection cases was made abundantly clear to me on my very first day presiding in family court. I was having lunch with the other judges when one of them inquired, "Harvey, did you know the judge whose position you filled when he retired?" I replied that I didn't know him personally but I certainly knew of him.

My colleague went on to ask, "Do you know why he retired?" I didn't. "He left the Bench," my colleague continued, " because he ordered the child protection authorities to return a baby to the parents, and two weeks later they killed the child. It absolutely destroyed him. He was never the same after that and retired a little while later."

I was dumbfounded and terrified. A wave of fear surged through me from head to toe. What was I getting into? Was I cut out for this job? Did I have the necessary judgment to make good decisions? What would I do if I became too paralyzed by the fear of making a mistake and couldn't come to a decision? And worst of all, what would I do if I made a bad decision, resulting in someone being injured or killed?

Every judge is acutely aware of the awesome risks and responsibilities inherent in every decision they make. It's a fundamental component of the job with which one must learn to live. Like every judge, I learned to make the best decisions I could, based on the evidence before me, and hope that I'd been correct, then move on. As far as I'm aware, in my twenty-six years on the Bench, I never made a decision that resulted in a tragedy, and I am exceedingly grateful for that.

When I think back to my years presiding in family court, the word that immediately springs to mind is "heartbreaking." The toxicity and hostility with which warring ex-spouses attacked each other was mind-boggling, and it never ceased to amaze me. I used to listen to the appalling things ex-partners would say about each other and wonder to myself, *Were these people actually in love with each other at one time?* They say love and hate are opposite sides of the same coin. In family court I saw only the one side. What happened to make them hate each other so much?

The answer to that question, in 90 percent of the cases upon which I presided, was infidelity. I know because, out of curiosity, I kept statistics in my courtroom for many years. In my experience, the remaining 10 percent of breakups resulted from myriad other issues including interfering in-laws, financial problems, mental illness, substance abuse, and domestic violence including physical, emotional, and verbal abuse.

Infidelity is an epidemic in modern relationships, thanks to the facility with which the internet enables people to connect with others looking to find partners, or perhaps to stray into the world of casual "hookup" sex. Later, I'll share my perspectives on internet dating and the impact it's had on modern relationships and especially marriage breakdown. But for the purposes of this discussion, infidelity is relevant because, for the deceived partner, it's the ultimate betrayal of the relationship and frequently triggers extreme reactions.

The vast majority of people have had at least one relationship that didn't work out. Statistics in this area are hard to find and probably unreliable, because they generally refer only to marriages, not to common-law relationships (unmarried couples who live together). However, it's generally believed that about 90 percent of people who break up are able to resolve their issues amicably, or with the help of lawyers who negotiate separation agreements for them without court intervention.

It's the remaining 10 percent of couples who, unable to resolve their disputes, end up in family court and engage in what we refer to as "high-conflict litigation." And what are they fighting over? The major issues are division of property, child custody and visitation, spousal support, and child support.

I never cared much about cases involving only money or property, because those litigants almost always had lawyers to whom they were paying at least five hundred dollars per hour. Ideally, matrimonial property litigation should be strictly a business matter, with each party making decisions using a cost-benefit analysis. One has to weigh how much money is at stake versus how much it's costing to pursue the litigation. I used to say to couples, "There's one big pile of money here, and our task is to make it into two piles. But the longer this court case goes on, we're making four piles: one for each of you, and one for each of your lawyers. You need to remember that with every step you take in this case."

Simply put, the major challenge for high-conflict couples is this: Their decisions and actions are fuelled by emotion rather than logic. Their feelings of betrayal, anger, and pain in reaction to their ex-partner's conduct (usually infidelity) totally override their judgment and common sense. I've seen parents spend thousands of dollars on legal fees for arguing a full day in court over pillowcases, lawn furniture, or other inexpensive items that could easily have been replaced at minimal cost. Some couples spend hundreds of thousands of dollars litigating over family pets. I even saw a couple fighting over Air Miles and spending so many days in court that they both lost their jobs for taking too much time off work!

When I asked these litigation-obsessed couples how they could justify making such mountains out of molehills, the answer was always the same: "It's the principle of the thing." These were people who'd lost all sense of proportion, and quite frankly, if they wanted to spend their money paying lawyers to fight such petty battles, I didn't get fussed over it.

What *did* trouble me greatly were the high-conflict custody cases impacting the well-being of children. I've seen parents fight over everything: how to split the child's time during weekends and holidays, which school a child should attend, what Hallowe'en costume the child should wear, who should pay for school trips, which TV shows the child should be allowed to watch, what medical treatment a child should get, whether a child could get a tattoo, and even how long the child's hair should be. I've even had cases where a mother brought the father to court after a weekend visitation because she'd sent the child to his home on Friday wearing a T-shirt, and the shirt came back on Sunday with a stain on it. Some parents will stop at nothing, and no subject is too trivial to justify a court motion.

One of the most incredible cases I had was a custody and visitation dispute between two young, extremely immature parents. Normally, parents argue over which one the children are going to live with, and how often the other parent will have them. In this case, neither parent wanted the children on weekends because they were both dating new partners and wanted to go out and have fun with them on weekends.

I'd never seen that before, so I thought I'd give them a good scare and said, as sternly as possible, "If neither of you wants your children on the weekends, I'll have to consider placing them in foster care."

The mother's eyes widened, and without skipping a beat, she looked me in the eye and asked, "Is that free? Or would we have to pay?" Sad but true.

When parents allow their mutual hatred to govern their parenting decisions, using their children as weapons, pawns, and spies, that's of grave concern. Children caught in the middle of such conflicts are extremely vulnerable because when they witness their parents arguing and fighting, it's a form of child abuse.

One of the worst cases I ever had involved two extremely immature parents whose twelve-year-old son was the subject of a hostile and prolonged custody battle. Each parent had embroiled him in the dispute by attempting to recruit him as an ally, placing him in a terrible conflict of loyalties because he loved both parents equally.

At one of their court appearances, the parents, neither of whom had a lawyer, showed up with the boy. This was a terrible thing to do. Children should be shielded from parental conflict, not play a role in it. They should be in school, not in a courtroom witnessing their parents arguing with each other in front of a judge. But here were these parents standing before me with their young son, all while making terrible allegations against each other and insisting I speak privately with the child.

Each parent emphatically told me, with great confidence, that the child wanted to live with him or her. Both parents were likely telling me the truth, in the sense that they were repeating what the child had told each of them separately. Children want to be loved and don't want to disappoint either parent, so they'll tell each one what he or she wants to hear. What else would you expect from a child who's caught up in such an impossible situation?

I explained that the appropriate way for the court to ascertain the child's wishes and preferences was to appoint a lawyer for him. Children's lawyers work with a team of social workers who can take the time to ensure a child's expressed wishes are genuinely felt, and aren't the product of undue pressure from the parents or anyone else. Requiring the child to meet with the judge is fraught with risks, not only because this places enormous pressure on the child, but because most judges, including me, receive no training in how best to conduct such interviews.

The parents were agreeable to a lawyer being appointed for their son but still insisted I meet with him immediately. They wanted a temporary decision to be made about the child's living arrangements, pending a report from the child's lawyer, which would take a few months.

Because the parents' allegations against each other were equally severe, and no reliable evidence existed to assess their credibility other than what the child might tell me, and because there was an urgent need to make an immediate custody decision, I reluctantly agreed to meet in my chambers with the twelve-year-old boy, whom I'll call Kevin.

Before my clerk brought Kevin into my chambers, I took off my judicial robe and changed into my street clothes — a sweatshirt and jeans — so I'd look like an ordinary person. We sat on my sofa, facing each other. He was fidgeting with his hands nervously, eyeing the big jar of jellybeans on the coffee table. I took off the lid and told him to help himself. He took a handful, carefully removing the black ones. I said, "Oh Kevin, you're just like me. I don't like the flavour of black jellybeans either!"

That prompted a smile. Then his eyes lit up as he said, "Why don't you take out the black jellybeans before you put them in the jar?"

Smart kid. I replied, "That's a great idea, Kevin. Thank you. I'll do that next time." We sat quietly while he ate his candies, and I munched on a few to keep him company. I had no idea what to say or do, and with each passing moment, I regretted more and more my decision to meet with him.

So I decided to let Kevin lead the way. He was looking at a *Wizard of Oz* movie poster on the wall behind my desk, so I told him how much I loved that movie when I was a kid, because sometimes I was sad and the song "Over the Rainbow" gave me hope about one day finding a happier place to live. Bingo. That was the magic key to getting Kevin to relax and open up. Thank you, Judy Garland.

Kevin talked about his favourite subjects at school, his little dog Toby, his favourite TV shows, the music he liked listening to, and playing soccer. Eventually he asked, "What's it like being a judge? Do you get to meet lots of kids like me?"

I replied, "No, Kevin. Very few kids ever come to court. It's their parents' job to work out their differences, and you shouldn't have to be involved in all that. Your job is just to enjoy being a kid and have a loving relationship with both your parents."

Kevin thought a moment, then asked tearfully, "What's wrong with my mom and dad? I have friends at school whose parents broke up, and they don't go through all this fighting. I don't even understand why I'm here."

My heart was breaking. Searching for the right words to say, I responded, "Well, Kevin, I think your parents brought you here because they love you very much and they want me to make the best decision I can that will make you happy."

Kevin replied, "Well here's what will make me happy. Can you make my parents get back together?"

A lump grew in my throat as I said with a sigh, "Kevin, I wish I could make that happen for all the parents I see, but I can't. I'm just a judge, not a magician."

Kevin paused briefly and then asked, "Well then, can you make my parents stop fighting?"

I sighed again, thinking, *This innocent, naïve kid sure has a knack for pointing out, with great precision, all the things a judge can't do*. Rarely have I ever felt so powerless and inept.

"Kevin," I replied, feeling my voice cracking with emotion, "I wish I could. But they're having a difficult time right now working out a few problems. But believe me, this won't go on forever, and things will settle down, hopefully soon."

Kevin's eyes lit up again and, moving right next to me on the sofa until he couldn't move any closer, he looked up at me and asked plaintively, "Well, then, I have an idea. Can I live with you until my parents work everything out? I'm sure they wouldn't mind. You're a judge. They'll have to say yes. And can I bring my dog? We'd be no trouble, I promise."

Tears streaming down my face, I took that little boy's hand in both of mine and said, "Oh, Kevin, that's the nicest thing any kid has ever said to me. And if I had a son, I'd want him to be just like you. And I'm sure I'd love your dog too. But you already have two great parents who love you so much. They'd miss you terribly. Besides, I'm not much of a soccer fan."

Kevin took his hand out of mine, slumped down in defeat, and with the saddest, most painful voice I'd ever heard, cried, "Well then, I wish I were dead. It's the only way my parents will ever stop fighting." Tears were flowing down his cheeks.

I was numb. Stupefied. Paralyzed. Those words sent a knife through my heart. I took some tissues from a box on the side table and gave them to him, keeping a few for myself. I knew I had to say something meaningful and healing to that poor child, whose anguish was clearly tearing him apart. I wiped my eyes, and putting my hands firmly on both of his shoulders, I said, "Kevin, you've got to listen to me. I need you to understand something very important. Your parents are *not* fighting about you. I know it feels like they are, but you've *got* to believe me. This has *nothing* to do with you. They're upset because they feel hurt by each other. And sometimes, parents who feel that way get confused about how to handle their pain. But I promise you, Kevin. Even if you weren't here anymore, your parents would still keep on fighting. And if you really think about it for a minute, I know you'll see I'm right."

Kevin sat silently for a moment and whispered, "Yeah, I guess so."

We both wiped our eyes and I stood up. "It was really nice meeting you, Kevin. Thanks for coming to see me. You're a great kid. I promise I'll do the best I can to help your family. Now let's see about getting you back to school." It was lunchtime. He could still make it back to school for afternoon classes.

When we returned to the courtroom, I told the parents I'd had a very impactful visit with their son, but that I would not deal with their case until they got him back to school. We recessed over the lunch period and they took Kevin back to school, then returned to court.

When we resumed I did my best to convey, in the most heartfelt and poignant way possible, how profoundly traumatizing their behaviour was for their son. I asked them whether they thought Kevin was at fault for their breakup. "Of course not," they each told me.

"Well then why are you both making him feel like your failed marriage *is* his fault?" I asked. Neither parent could answer me. I told them that if they didn't find a way to insulate and protect Kevin from their conflict, I would consider turning the case over to child protective services, which might result in their son being placed in a foster home. I wasn't above scaring parents who needed a jolt of reality. And it worked. I spent the afternoon mediating a mutually satisfactory parenting plan that maximized each parent's time with Kevin.

A week later, I received a letter from Kevin saying things were getting better, and that he'd decided he wanted to be a lawyer when he grew up. You can imagine my surprise and delight when, twelve years later, I received an invitation to Kevin's graduation from law school. Attending that ceremony was one of the highlights of my career.

I never again met with a child in my chambers. It was too emotionally draining, and I felt woefully unqualified to help children in such distress. But I did develop another helpful technique when confronted by parents who each insisted their children wanted to live with them and wanted to prove it by having me talk to the children: I would always ask each parent to tell me which child he or she loved the most (if they had more than one). I never met a parent able to answer that question, even when I persisted and urged them to give me an answer. Then I would say, "You're adults, yet you're not able to tell me which of your children you love the most. But you expect your children, who are just kids, to decide which parent *they* love the most. Do you think you're being fair to your children by making them choose between you?" Sometimes my words got through to parents. Sometimes they didn't.

Although I regularly poured my heart out to parents in an effort to help them successfully reinvent themselves from ex-partners to co-parents, I learned early on that people in an emotional state don't listen with their ears. They listen with their triggers.

Here's an example. I often told parents that the only way to successfully co-parent their children after a bitter separation was to love their children more than they hated each other. One time the father stood up in a rage and screamed, "How *dare* you tell me I don't love my children?" That wasn't at all what I'd said, but that's what he'd heard.

What else have I learned from high-conflict parents? I learned that family law cases are not about the facts of the case; they're about the personalities of the parties. Different people handle the same situation differently. For example, in couple A, the wife finds out that her husband has been having an affair. Heartbroken, she immediately ends the relationship. She and her husband are able to work out a mutually agreeable parenting plan for the children, because the wife understands that although her husband was a bad partner, he wasn't a bad father. She also understands that turning every minor disagreement with her ex-husband into World War Three is detrimental to her children. She knows that when it comes to such minor matters, making peace is more important than being right. The children are not exposed to parental conflict, and everyone gets on with their lives.

In couple B, the wife who discovers her husband's infidelity is just as heartbroken as the wife in couple A, but her personality doesn't allow her to separate her husband's qualities as a parent from his qualities as a spouse. She's determined to punish her husband in every way she can. She refuses to let him see their children and does her best to turn them against him, engaging in behaviour known as "parental alienation." She becomes fixated and obsessed by her feelings of anger, pain, and betrayal and can't move on from the relationship in a healthy way. Her sole motivation is vengeance, not the best interests of her children.

Any ex-partner experiencing the feelings of the wife in couple B (and to be sure, men and women experience such feelings with equal frequency) will find family court a most frustrating and unsatisfying experience. Judges aren't in the vengeance business, and they're not interested in dissecting relationships and conducting post-mortems to determine which ex-partner is the "victim." Their only interest is in making decisions in the best interests of the children.

High-conflict parents who keep finding reasons to haul each other back to court for one motion after another may be physically separated, but they haven't disengaged emotionally. I remember one case where the parents spent a half-day in court arguing vehemently over which summer camp their children should attend and whether it should be in July or August. Each parent had a lawyer, and by the end of the motion, they'd cumulatively spent more money on legal fees to resolve that one issue than the cost of university tuition for both children for two years.

I used to say to such parents, "You know something? You two are actually still dating, except instead of going out to dinner and a movie, you're coming here to see me!"

Why did I say that? Because anyone who truly wants nothing more to do with an ex-partner would never keep engaging with them through protracted court proceedings over the most trivial issues. Thanks to family court, some high-conflict parents interact with each other more after separation than when they lived together!

I firmly believe the major problem with family court is that we treat child custody and visitation as a legal issue, when in reality it's a public-health issue. Every mental health professional agrees that children caught up in parental conflicts are at great risk of emotional harm. And yet, the justice system expects lawyers and judges, whose only training is in the law, to resolve these issues. Law school cannot possibly prepare lawyers and judges for the many challenges of assisting emotionally disturbed parents to overcome the wounds of a traumatic breakup.

High-conflict parents need intensive counselling from trained psychologists, therapists, and social workers just as much as they need legal advice and representation — if not more. The court system is highly adversarial. Everyone, including lawyers and judges, thinks in terms of "winners" and "losers." But, taking a line from the movie *War of the Roses*, there is no winning in family court — only degrees of losing. And the biggest losers are the children. It's no wonder that parents embroiled in family court proceedings end up hating each other more at the end of a case than they did when it started. If family courts are ever to achieve the oft-stated goal of enabling parents to learn how to communicate and cooperate with each other for the sake of their children, a much more therapeutic and less antagonistic model is needed.

Over the years I've been asked several times whether it was difficult to pass judgment on other people's parenting when I wasn't a parent myself. And once, it even came up in court. After I forbade a mother from physically disciplining her adolescent daughter for violating her curfew, the mother hissed, "Why should I listen to anything *you* say? Where do you get off telling me how to parent my children? How many kids do *you* have?"

I replied, "Ma'am, I consider every child whose life I affect in this courtroom, including yours, to be my child." And that's truly how I felt. It's certainly undeniable that, had I been a parent, I would have benefited from the many insights that come from raising a child. But you don't have to be a parent yourself to know what constitutes good and bad parental conduct. We were all children once and were parented by someone. Our own life experiences as children frequently inform our perspective on parenting.

I've also been asked whether being gay, and never having been in an opposite-sex relationship, made it difficult to understand the dynamic in male-female relationships. The answer is no. I was raised by parents in a heterosexual relationship. The vast majority of my friends and acquaintances are in heterosexual relationships. I've had plenty of opportunity to observe and absorb that dynamic. But most importantly, in my experience, the issues that couples face in romantic relationships are exactly the same regardless of the parties' genders. Love is love, and when love comes to an end, the fallout doesn't change because of the partners' sexual orientation.

Another question I'm often asked is how I coped with all the unhappiness, tragedy, and toxicity permeating family court. Like other professionals, especially doctors and nurses, who deal with unpleasant situations and great sadness in their work, I developed what I liked to call "emotional Teflon." I dealt with each case to the best of my ability and with all my heart, but when the case was over, I let it go. Like Teflon, nothing stuck to me. I never took my work home, and learned to develop short-term memory loss, which is a very useful job skill when dealing with high-volume fact situations.

I don't want to convey the impression that my time in family court was always sad. Many funny things happened. For example, one day a woman stood before me wearing a T-shirt with huge letters reading JUICY PUSSY.

In a rather stern voice, I asked, "Ma'am, do you think that shirt you're wearing is appropriate attire for a courtroom?"

She looked down at the shirt, then back up at me, before pointing to it and saying, "Oh, *this*? Well, they told me to dress up, so I did!"

Looking suitably indignant, I said, "Well, ma'am, I'm not going to sit here and look at that. Go to the women's washroom and turn that shirt inside out, and then you can come back here."

A lawyer sitting at the counsel table turned to the colleague beside him and whispered much too loudly, "Boy, did *she* get the wrong judge!" Touché.

Another time, during a trial, I was about to hear testimony from a child witness, a lovely, precocious nine-year-old girl. Prior to allowing her to testify, I was required to conduct a brief inquiry to determine whether she understood the solemnity of the occasion and the importance of telling the truth. After asking a few perfunctory questions to determine if she understood the difference between the truth and a lie, I asked her, "Now do you know what would happen if you promised to tell me the truth, and you were to lie?"

Without skipping a beat, she smiled from ear to ear and responded, "Oh yes, my mommy's lawyer said we'll win!" That was most definitely a "Depends™" moment for the lawyer, who ended up being removed from the case.

One of my most satisfying moments in family court happened in a child support enforcement proceeding. Having so passionately enforced child support obligations as a lawyer, you can imagine how gratifying it was to do so as a judge. I got to see, first-hand, the results of the enforcement legislation I'd worked so hard to convince the government to enact. And my efforts to get delinquent support payors' lottery winnings seized were handsomely rewarded in one of the most unusual cases I ever had.

I'd been a judge just over a year and was presiding in family court on a highly unusual motion brought by a support payor, whom I'll call Bill. I couldn't believe what I was hearing. Bill owed twelve thousand dollars in child support arrears. He'd won twenty-two thousand in the lottery and, determined to avoid the seizure of those funds by the lottery corporation, gave the ticket to his friend Jack to cash in. What he didn't know was that

Jack himself owed twenty-five thousand in child support arrears! All of Bill's winnings were seized and paid out to Jack's children!

Bill wanted me to order Jack to pay him the twenty-two thousand back. If I wasn't prepared to do that, he wanted the court to apply a credit to his arrears in the same amount, even though his children hadn't received one cent. Did I do it? Not a chance. And Bill ended up in jail for failing to pay child support. Now that's what you call karma.

In 2009, after presiding in family court for fourteen years, I authored a book titled *Tug of War: A Judge's Verdict on Separation, Custody Battles, and the Bitter Realities of Family Court*. I wrote it out of frustration, because I could no longer keep silent about the carnage occurring in family courts because of high-conflict litigation. I wanted to give separated parents the information they needed to decide whether family court was the best way to resolve their parental disputes. I wanted them to know about the alternatives to litigation, such as mediation, arbitration, collaborative law, and hiring a parenting coach.

Tug of War was a landmark book. Never before had a sitting judge spoken out publicly to inform the general public about what really went on in court. The prevailing view within the judiciary, then and now, is that judges should speak only through their court decisions. Judges are highly discouraged from making public statements through the media, in speaking engagements, or in publications for fear of compromising their independence and neutrality by addressing issues over which they may have to adjudicate. But I believed, and still strongly believe, that judges should not just be adjudicators — they should also be public educators, because while they can't offer legal advice, they have a lot of information and insights about the justice system that they can and should share.

Tug of War was a crie de coeur, a passionate plea to parents entangled in custody battles to choose non-adversarial ways to develop post-separation parenting plans. I was eager to publish the book because I knew it could help people, but I worried about the consequences to my career of doing so. I knew there were lawyers and judges who disagreed with the book's major theme, that family court is often bad for families and should be an avenue of last resort. There were many old-timers, traditionalists in the family justice system, who truly believed the system was perfect.

I told my chief justice, Annemarie Bonkalo, that I'd written a book and sent her the manuscript. I heard nothing. I didn't even know if she'd read it. After a few weeks, I called her to ask whether she thought I should publish it. After an ominously lengthy pause, she said, "Harvey, I can't tell you what to do. I'm sure it's a good book because I know you're a good judge. But surely you understand the risks of putting yourself out there in such a public way, and you have to be prepared to deal with whatever happens." I got the message. I was on my own and shouldn't expect any support from the court. If I got into trouble, I'd be hung out to dry. I wasn't surprised. No one in the judiciary sticks their neck out for a colleague. They're too busy covering their own butts.

I turned to my dear friend and mentor, Justice Rosalie Abella, who by then was presiding on the Supreme Court of Canada. She read the manuscript in two days and called excitedly. "Harvey, go ahead and publish it," she exclaimed. "It's an important book that tells people exactly what they need to know if they're contemplating family court proceedings. Don't be afraid. You've got my support." Rosie gave me the courage to submit the book to a publisher.

Tug of War was extremely well received by the media and legal profession. Within a week of its release, the book became a national bestseller, which was most gratifying because all my royalties went to the Children's Wish Foundation, which grants wishes to children suffering from fatal illnesses. Thinking back to my conversation with Kevin, the twelve-year-old boy who'd met with me in chambers, I figured that if I couldn't grant children's wishes in court (to make their parents get back together or at least stop fighting), the least I could do was donate my book royalties to a wonderful organization that fulfills their wishes in a very different way.

I spent the next eighteen months criss-crossing North America, appearing on TV and radio interview programs, giving newspaper interviews, making keynote addresses at legal conferences, and speaking at law schools — all of which was done on weekday evenings, weekends, and during vacations. I never missed a day of presiding in court.

Six months after *Tug of War* was released, I was approached by Nancy Kinney, a TV producer in British Columbia, who'd seen one of my television interviews. She said, "Justice Brownstone, you've got a personality made for TV. How would you like to host a talk show where you could bring world-renowned experts to educate and enlighten the public about the justice system?" I was hooked. And that's how *Family Matters with Justice Harvey Brownstone*, the first and only television show in the world hosted by an actual sitting judge, was created.

The trepidation and apprehension I felt about publishing a book paled in comparison to my anxiety about hosting a television show. None of my colleagues thought it was a good idea, but I went ahead anyway, because I knew the public was hungry for reliable and helpful information about many aspects of the justice system. The producer agreed to give me final approval over the content of the show, so I felt confident there'd be no problematic material in the finished product.

Family Matters was filmed in the CHEK television studios in Victoria, B.C. Hosting my own TV show was daunting and yet exciting. Having watched so many talk shows growing up, and having always dreamed of being an interviewer, I was almost giddy at the idea of having my own show, a wardrobe, director, and crew, and being part of the world of show business.

The first season of the show, which aired in 2010, consisted of an online YouTube series. There were eight episodes dealing with such timely subjects as mediation, child support, collaborative law, elder abuse, the role of children's lawyers, child protection, and prenuptial agreements. This was long before the advent of online web series and podcasts. We were way ahead of our time and were astounded at the phenomenal reaction to the subjects we discussed. We received thousands of letters from viewers suggesting further topics for future shows.

The next year, *Family Matters* began broadcasting as a prime-time national television show on the CHCH-TV network, with fifteen episodes addressing a variety of topics including parental alienation, domestic violence, grandparents' rights, pets and divorce, and men's rights. I was thrilled that the show had evolved to the point where we could impact an even greater viewership and hopefully influence, educate, and enlighten parents in need of information about the justice system.

In 2013, *Family Matters* returned for another season with sixteen episodes in which we discussed even more compelling subjects including gambling addiction, infidelity, online dating, same-sex parenting, bullying, child abduction, spousal support, and anger management. I was even able to convince a number of wonderfully progressive judicial colleagues to appear on the show, including Justices Victoria Starr, Stanley Sherr, and Robert Spence. They contributed to the show's legitimacy, credibility, and gravitas.

Although critically acclaimed, the show wasn't renewed for another season. The network executives were dissatisfied with my restrained and rather bland personality as a TV host. They compared me to pablum — no flavour, no texture — and insisted, "We want more Harvey and less Justice Brownstone." I knew exactly what they were getting at. As a sitting judge, I'd had to be extremely careful not to express any opinions about ongoing cases, or about issues over which I might be required to adjudicate. While I truly wanted to show the audience my real personality, sense of humour, and opinions, I knew full well that one wrong move would result in an onslaught of harsh criticism from my colleagues, some of whom were only too ready to embark on such an exercise, and I couldn't take that risk.

Although the show was on television for only two years, I'm immensely proud of this groundbreaking achievement, and all these years later I still receive great feedback from viewers watching the show on YouTube.

Unsurprisingly, and as I've already hinted, not all my colleagues were supportive of my venture into the world of television. Sadly, the tall poppy syndrome is alive and well in the judiciary.

The show's positive reception didn't stop some of my judicial brothers and sisters from suggesting it was unseemly and off-putting for a sitting judge to host his own TV show. One day, at a judicial conference, I was riding a jam-packed elevator with a number of colleagues when one snidely asked, his voice dripping with sarcasm, "Hey, Mr. TV Star, pray tell, what's the *next* episode of your show going to be about?"

Without skipping a beat, I replied, "Professional jealousy." There was stunned silence. That was the longest elevator ride of my life.

At Burlington Beach, 1960. The earliest photo of me and my parents. We became a happy family unit from the moment Sam and Odette began dating.

My parents, Sam and Odette, were married on December 29, 1960.

Within a month of arriving in Canada, and with only the most rudimentary English skills, Mom opened Odette de Paris, a French ladies' wear boutique at 473 King Street East in Hamilton, Ontario, which quickly became a sensation.

Dad and me, 1961. He was the best dad in the world.

Me with my parents at my bar mitzvah, May 24, 1969. Dad was the Director of the Hamilton Jewish Community Centre, so the entire Jewish community was there.

My Queen's University law school graduation photo, May 1980. After having worked diligently for five years to get top grades and maintain my scholarship, and after myriad financial struggles as a welfare recipient and working countless part-time jobs, I was filled with optimism for a bright future. Can you see the hope in my eyes?

The day I was called to the Bar of Ontario and became a practicing lawyer, March 1983. Little did I know that I would have a meteoric career, first in criminal law, then in family law, culminating in my appointment to the judiciary a mere twelve years later.

After a five-year estrangement following coming out to my parents, they surprised me by showing up at my law school graduation. It was a tearful and joyful reunion.

Mom and Dad with me at my swearing-in ceremony as a judge of the Ontario Court of Justice, April 4, 1995.

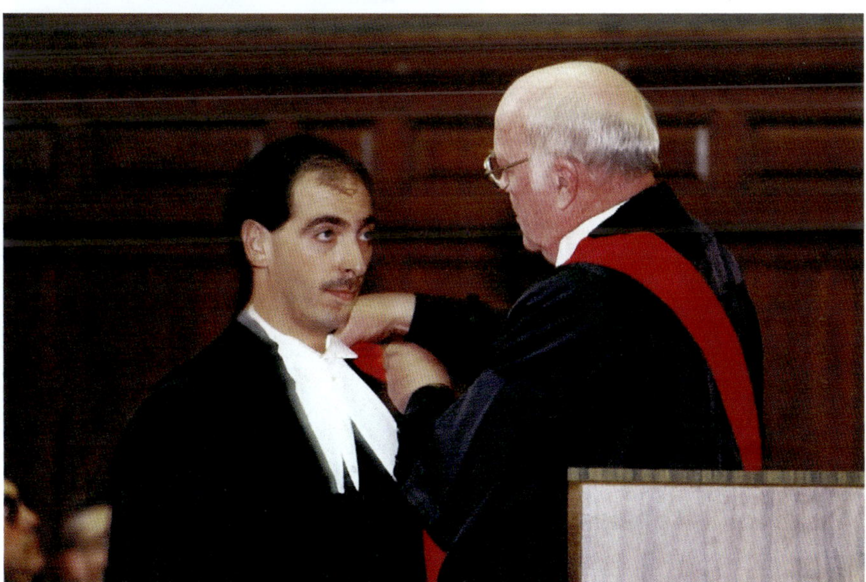

Chief Judge Ted Andrews affixing the red sash to my robe at my swearing-in ceremony. I got to know Ted when I was in law school, and he was a cherished mentor and friend throughout my life. The look of love and pride in his eyes while "sashing" me will remain entrenched in my heart forever.

My inaugural address at my swearing-in ceremony. When I tearfully told my parents how much it meant to me to have finally gained their love and acceptance, there wasn't a dry eye in the house.

My first day as a presiding judge, April 5, 1995. Within the first hour, an intoxicated accused person staggered to the front of the courtroom, saying I looked far too young to be a judge. When I told him I was thirty-eight years old, he said, "What? I've got things in my fridge that are older than you!" I replied, "And are they a little off too, sir?"

With the happy couples after officiating at their historic weddings. LEFT: American LGBT rights activist Edith Windsor and her partner of forty-four years, Thea Spyer, 2007. RIGHT: Canadian Olympic champion figure skater Brian Orser and Rajesh Tiwari, 2008. Little did I know that the Windsor/Spyer wedding would lead to the landmark 2013 U.S. Supreme Court decision overturning the restrictive definition of marriage in the Defence of Marriage Act, paving the way for the legalization of same-sex marriage in the United States.

Tug of War (2009), the first book ever written by a sitting judge intended for the general public. I wanted to demystify the justice system and urge separated parents to find alternatives to family court litigation, which is extremely toxic and highly damaging to the best interests of children. The book instantly became a national bestseller, and all my royalties went to the Children's Wish Foundation.

On the set of my TV show *Family Matters* interviewing Debbie Moskovitch, author of *The Smart Divorce*, in 2011. This was the first national television show in the world hosted by a real sitting judge. With a focus on enhancing access to justice, the show provided a platform for the public to gain valuable insights from lawyers, judges, psychologists, and child development experts who would not normally appear on television.

Me with my elementary schoolteacher and guardian angel, Barbara Jarrett. She was the only teacher I ever had who went out of her way to protect me from the relentless bullies. When I told her I wanted to be a lawyer when I grew up, she said, "No, Harvey, you should aim higher. Be a judge. Judges always have the final say." She told that story to a captivated audience in her speech following my swearing-in ceremony as a judge.

With my role model and mentor, Supreme Court Justice Rosalie Abella, 2013. When I was a law school summer student in 1979, I was Rosie's clerk at the Toronto Family Court. She taught me how to apply the law as a problem-solver and healer, not just a legal technician and scholar. I spent twenty-six years on the Bench doing my best to channel Rosie, asking myself, "What would Rosie do?" before making every decision.

Osgoode Law School Dean Lorne Sossin presenting me with the Pro Bono Students Canada Supporter Award, May 13, 2016. This award was granted in recognition of my spearheading a national program to have law school students work at family courts to assist indigent parents in completing the paperwork to launch their court cases.

In 2016, Supreme Court Justice Thomas Cromwell presented me with a Distinguished Alumni Award from Queen's University Faculty of Law, by reason of my groundbreaking efforts to enhance access to justice through my book, television show, and advocacy for same-sex marriage. Eight years later, in 2024, I was once again presented with a Distinguished Alumni Award, this time in recognition of the global success of *Harvey Brownstone Interviews.* I was delighted and honoured that Justice Cromwell was there to congratulate me. To date, I'm the only alumnus of Queen's Law School to receive two Distinguished Alumni Awards.

Me with some of my most popular guests on *Harvey Brownstone Interviews*: the legendary Marie Osmond, pop music icon Tony Orlando, pop diva Taylor Dayne, singer-songwriter Melissa Manchester, Canadian superstar Burton Cummings, and stand-up comic Zarna Garg. Getting to interview these artists, whom I've loved and admired for so long, has been a great honour. But getting to know them as a friend has been a dream come true.

My parents in their eighties. Although our journey together was at times turbulent, tempestuous, and exasperating, they made me a survivor and an overachiever. They taught me the power of forgiveness and that love conquers all.

On the set of *Harvey Brownstone Interviews*. I've been a talk show junkie my whole life and always dreamed of hosting my own interview program once I retired from the Bench. What started out simply as a post-retirement hobby quickly evolved into a full-time career because my unique "examination-in-chief" interviewing style brought recognition and acclaim to the program. The show started out on YouTube and audio podcast platforms, then progressed to cable television in the U.K., and is likely headed to a major North American network or streaming platform in the near future. So, as they say, stay tuned!

CHAPTER 13

HOMO IMPROVEMENT: THE LONG ROAD TO MARRIAGE EQUALITY

When I was growing up, the notion that two people of the same sex might one day get married was not only unheard of, it was unthinkable. Until I was almost thirty years old, homosexuals were a despised minority with almost no legal protections. I'm extremely fortunate to have lived through a monumental and relatively rapid evolution of legal and social reforms culminating in the legalization of same-sex marriage. And I'm even more fortunate that, during my judicial career, I had a front-row seat to some of the most historically significant developments in what many human rights lawyers refer to as "the last civil rights movement."

Homosexuals in Canada have travelled a long and difficult road to equality. During the 1950s and 1960s, the Royal Canadian Mounted Police monitored the activities of individuals suspected of being gay. Homosexuals were banned from working in government, law enforcement, and the military. Homosexuality was a criminal offence punishable by life imprisonment. The last Canadian sent to jail simply for being gay was Everett Klippert, an auto mechanic from the Northwest Territories. In 1965, he was given an indefinite life sentence as a "dangerous sex offender" even though all his sexual activities had been with consenting adults. The Supreme Court of Canada upheld his sentence in 1967, describing his incarceration as "preventive detention."

Homosexuality in Canada was decriminalized in 1969. Prime Minister Pierre Trudeau famously said, "There's no place for the state in the bedrooms of the nation." Despite the passage of these amendments, Everett Klippert wasn't released from prison until 1971.

The Stonewall riots of June 1969 in New York City are widely considered to have launched the gay liberation movement in North America. Throughout the next thirty years, public attitudes regarding homosexuality slowly improved, reflecting increasing levels of tolerance and acceptance. And beginning in the late 1970s, a series of legislative reforms and landmark court decisions occurred that gradually improved the lives of gay people.

In 1977, Quebec became the first province in Canada to include "sexual orientation" in its human rights code, making it illegal to discriminate against gays in housing, public services, and employment. And in 1978, the Canada Immigration Act finally eliminated the long-standing ban prohibiting homosexuals from entering the country.

In 1992, the Ontario Court of Appeal ruled that Captain Joshua Birch had suffered illegal discrimination when he was discharged from the Canadian Armed Forces for disclosing that he was gay. This led to a decision lifting the ban on homosexuals in the military, allowing them to serve openly and live on-base with their partners.

In 1993, in the case of *Canada v. Mossop*, the Supreme Court of Canada ruled that the denial of bereavement leave to a gay partner was not discriminatory. But two years later, in *Egan v. Canada*, the court ruled that sexual orientation is a prohibited ground of discrimination under the Canadian Charter of Rights and Freedoms. Finally, homosexuals in Canada were constitutionally protected from discrimination. That was the state of the law when I was appointed to the Bench in April 1995.

Several months after my appointment, my dear friend and colleague Justice James Nevins, with whom I presided at the same courthouse for many years, delivered a landmark ruling in the Re K. adoption case, permitting same-sex couples to adopt children. When I congratulated Jim on his brilliant and insightful application of constitutional equality principles to same-sex couples, he replied, "Well, Harvey, getting to know and becoming friends with a gay colleague like you helped me to understand the real-life implications of the legal issue I had to decide."

That comment made me realize, in a very profound way, that having diversity on the Bench itself was truly important for judges to have a better understanding of the issues they faced. I understood that, for many of my colleagues, I was the face and voice of the gay community. And I took that responsibility seriously.

Numerous judicial colleagues told me that, prior to my appointment, they hadn't known any openly gay people (which amazed me), and that their comfort level increased after getting to know me and my partner, with whom I'd begun living prior to becoming a judge. I always made a point of bringing my partner to every judges' conference and to all social events with my colleagues so that they'd see for themselves that same-sex couples were no different than any other couple. And, as time passed, I was called upon by numerous colleagues to help them and their spouses adjust and respond appropriately when their children came out. I was happy to be known by my colleagues as "the gay judge," giving personal advice, speaking on panels, and organizing a judicial education program on same-sex rights, because I considered it my privilege and responsibility to serve as a positive ambassador for the gay community.

In 1999, the Supreme Court of Canada rendered another landmark decision, *M. v. H.*, ruling that same-sex couples are entitled to the same treatment under the law as opposite-sex couples. As a result, we began seeing same-sex couples coming to family court to apply for spousal support upon separation, in the same way that heterosexual couples litigated.

Mind you, there are some glaring differences between straight couples and gay couples in family court. When two gay men separate, neither of them wants the furniture, because gay people view separation as a fabulous opportunity to redecorate. And some lesbian couples argue vigorously over clothing — especially those prized lumberjack shirts and workboots — whereas it's unheard of for straight couples to fight over each other's clothes.

Of *course* I'm just kidding. The truth is, the parties' genders make absolutely no difference in family court.

Same-sex marriage became legal in Ontario on June 10, 2003, making the province only the third jurisdiction in the world, after the Netherlands and Belgium, to legalize same-sex marriage. Over the next year, through a series of court decisions, same-sex marriage became legal across Canada, culminating in a landmark ruling (in *Reference re Same-Sex Marriage*) by the Supreme Court of Canada on December 9, 2004. In contrast, same-sex marriage didn't become legal nationwide in the United States until June 26, 2015, as a result of the Supreme Court ruling in *Obergefell v. Hodges*.

Interestingly, not everyone in the lesbian and gay community agreed that we should be advocating for the right to get married. Many people argued, "Divorce rates are skyrocketing. The institution of marriage is an abysmal failure. Why would gay people want to be part of a failed institution? Why are we aiming so low?"

My answer was simple. Being truly equal means having the right to make the same decisions and mistakes as everyone else. No one was being forced to get married. Marriage isn't for everyone. But now everyone had the choice, and I felt that was important.

The legalization of same-sex marriage changed my life dramatically. Because Ontario doesn't have a residency requirement, gay couples from everywhere in the world now had the opportunity to come to Ontario to be married. Of course, the question of whether such marriages were legally recognized in their home jurisdictions depended on the law where they lived. But even if they knew their marriages wouldn't be valid at home, that didn't stop them from travelling to Toronto just to experience the sheer joy and elation of getting married.

A few days after same-sex marriage became a reality in Ontario, I was asked by several members of the Toronto gay community if I'd be willing to officiate at weddings. I immediately answered, "Sure, just give people my work email address and I'll make arrangements for them to come to the courthouse and get married in my chambers." I figured it would be fun to conduct the occasional wedding, which would certainly be a pleasant diversion from the daily misery of family court proceedings, in which declarations of love are non-existent.

At that time, very few churches, other than the Metropolitan Community Church and the Unitarian Church, were willing to conduct same-sex weddings. And besides, a lot of couples wanted a civil ceremony, not a religious one. The only other option for a civil ceremony was to go to city hall, which charged a fee. Judges aren't permitted to charge a fee for carrying out a judicial duty, so couples could save money by getting married at the courthouse.

These were the early days of the internet, and I was incredibly naïve about the impact of giving out my email address, and even more naïve about the volume of demands for wedding officiants from same-sex couples around the world. Suddenly, my email address was on every website that advised gay and lesbian couples about how to get married in Toronto. In two weeks I received eight thousand emails, causing the courthouse server to crash!

Before same-sex marriage became legal, I'd attended many weddings of straight friends and family members. Although they were happy events, I couldn't help feeling a tinge of sadness, dejection, and envy, because, like every gay person, I was on the outside looking in.

And on the few occasions I was obliged to attend family weddings with my mother, it was a nightmare. She'd wear oversized dark sunglasses, and as the ceremony proceeded she'd start moaning with increased volume, "My son! My son! Why? Oh, God, why?" Eventually she'd be sobbing uncontrollably and everyone would turn and look at us in astonishment, but Mom was oblivious to their stares. Then, after the ceremony, Mom would turn to me and whisper, "Thank God no one heard me. People have no idea what I go through at their damn weddings!" To be sure, weddings were not enjoyable events for me.

Imagine how surreal it felt, as a judge, to officiate at weddings for straight friends. I had the power and authority to bestow the status of marriage upon them, but being gay, I wasn't entitled to that same status myself. But all that changed in June 2003.

It's hard to describe the flood of emotions flowing through me the first time I officiated at a wedding for a gay couple, two lawyers who'd appeared in my court many times. As tears streamed down my face, I thought of all the gay and lesbian couples who'd come before me who hadn't lived long enough to see this day arrive. I felt immensely grateful to be living in

Canada, a progressive country that embraced diversity and inclusivity. And most of all, I was extremely grateful to be a judge during such a monumentally important time in our community's history, and to be in a position to make the institution of marriage a reality in their lives.

Until same-sex marriage became widely available in the United States, thousands of couples flocked to Toronto to get married. My life revolved around my commitment to being available to conduct wedding ceremonies for as many couples as needed me. In addition to presiding in court full-time, I conducted five wedding ceremonies per day in my chambers: one before court started, one during morning recess, one during lunch hour, one during afternoon recess, and one after court ended. I don't know exactly how many marriages I officiated at, but they numbered well over a thousand.

My colleagues were astonished by the sheer number of couples pouring into the courthouse every day to get married. And on rare occasions when I was held up in court or unwell, a few of them filled in for me so that no couple would ever be turned away. Although I never heard a word from my chief justice or anyone in senior management, my fellow judges at the courthouse were very supportive and appreciative of the service I was providing to the gay community.

I got to share countless unforgettable moments with numerous interesting and highly accomplished people. These included one of Canada's national heroes — Brian Orser, the figure skater who was 1987 world champion and a two-time Olympic silver medallist — who married his husband Rajesh in my chambers in 2009. That same year, popular radio host and Canadian jazz singer Adi Braun married her wife Linda in their beautiful garden. And in 2016, former Queen's University law school dean and current president and vice-chancellor of the University of Alberta, Bill Flanagan, married his husband Senthuran in a memorable outdoor ceremony at the University of Toronto.

Most of the couples I married were from the United States. Some individuals were very well known, including renowned filmmaker and activist Brendan Fay, City University of New York Professor Emeritus Kenneth

Sherrill, New York Family Court Judge Paula J. Hepner, prominent podcaster John Selig, and internationally acclaimed conductor Gary Thor Wedow. I kept in touch and became friends with many of the couples I married, which was such a lovely by-product of my wedding experiences.

I was particularly touched by the dozens of courageous couples who made their way to Toronto from such places as Afghanistan, Turkey, Iran, Russia, Singapore, and other countries where homosexuality was illegal and punishable by lengthy terms of imprisonment or, in some cases, death. Tears still come to my eyes when I think of how many couples told me they could hardly believe they were being married by a judge, which for many people was a symbol of the "establishment" that had persecuted our people for so many years. I felt like an ambassador, proudly showing them how progressive, compassionate, and inclusive we were here in Canada.

Most of the couples arrived at the courthouse by themselves, with no friends or family to share their joy or act as witnesses. When I asked why they hadn't brought any loved ones to help celebrate, many said they were estranged from their families, who didn't approve of their lifestyles. That always broke my heart and brought back painful memories. My secretary, court clerk, and other court staff gladly stepped in to serve as witnesses and help create a festive ambience. Still, it deeply saddened me that these couples were alone for one of the most important and joyful days in their lives, with no one else who loved them in the room.

Every wedding ceremony was unique. Most couples had given a lot of thought to making their weddings reflective of their unique personalities. Some wanted me to read a specific poem ("The Art of Marriage" by Wilferd E. Peterson was very popular). Some wanted a certain song played ("I Knew I Loved You" by Savage Garden was a favourite). Some couples came in drag, paying tribute to their favourite celebrities (I lost count of how many Cher, Bette Midler, Diana Ross, and Barbra Streisand impersonators I met). Many couples brought their dogs with them as ring bearers. And one couple wanted to be married in the nude — but that's where I drew the line. I sent them to the nearest nudist colony.

In 2005, the Global Television Network approached me with an unusual request. They were launching a reality show called *My Fabulous Gay Wedding*, starring comedian Scott Thompson, who'd achieved fame in the popular television series *The Kids in the Hall*. Every episode of the show would feature a gay couple preparing for their big day with the help of a team of wedding planners, and the episode would culminate in a wedding officiated by — you guessed it — me!

I met with the show's producers and was intrigued by their desire to show the public that gay couples were no different than straight couples. I was interested in participating in a project that would foster public acceptance of same-sex marriage, so I agreed to officiate at one wedding before deciding whether I wanted to sign on for the entire series. And because judges couldn't accept payment for performing an official function, the network made a donation to the Children's Wish Foundation in the amount they'd have paid me. So it was a win-win.

A few days later, one of the producers brought the engaged couple to meet me in my chambers, along with a camera crew. The purpose of the meeting was for the couple to provide input on how they'd like me to make the wedding ceremony special and unique for them.

One of the partners, Todd, was a quiet, timid, nerdy-looking man in his late twenties with a "deer-in-the-headlights" look that seemed to say, "How did I ever get into this?" His partner, Lucien, was an outrageously flamboyant, foul-mouthed, self-absorbed queen wearing a lime-green silk pantsuit and sporting a Louis Vuitton clutch bag. He flitted about the room, pouting and posing for the cameras, showing absolutely no interest in his partner or the topic of conversation. I thought I was meeting one of the stars of *Priscilla, Queen of the Desert*. And I knew I was in trouble.

I tried asking the couple about their relationship, hoping to get a few tidbits to personalize the wedding ceremony. I asked if they'd like any poems or readings added to the ceremony. I asked if they'd like to exchange personal vows. Lucien was having none of it. He was too busy asking the producer who was designing his wedding outfit whether they could get Paris Hilton to attend the event, whether the network would pay for Botox treatments prior to "airtime" (which is how he repeatedly referred to the wedding day), and whether the network would finance their honeymoon in Key West. He then grilled the cameraman about whether he'd be filmed from his left or right side during the all-important kiss at the end of the ceremony (he preferred his left). Neither poor Todd nor I got a word in edgewise.

After fifteen minutes of listening to Lucien babble on, I stood up, cleared my throat loudly to get Lucien's attention, and said in my most judicial voice, "Gentlemen, we're out of time. I have to get back into court. You don't seem to care about the wedding ceremony itself, so I'll just do my best."

With that, Lucien stood up, took Todd by the hand, and said, "Come on, honey. We've got to get to the gym. I have to lose ten pounds before airtime, and it's only two weeks away."

I was hoping to have a word with the producer before they left, but Lucien grabbed her by the arm and whisked her out the door, whispering in a not-so-subtle voice, "Darling, is there any way we could get a hunky actor to do the ceremony? That judge has no star quality or sex appeal. He'll ruin my big moment." I had to suppress my urge to run after him and snap his neck like a twig!

Later that day, I called the producer to let her know I was having second thoughts about participating in this project. I didn't feel Todd and Lucien reflected well on the gay community because they were reinforcing age-old stereotypes. She said, "Don't worry, it's all in the editing. We'll take out anything that would make the show look bad. It'll be fine." I still felt uneasy but agreed to proceed.

Not surprisingly, the wedding was a circus. The crowd was composed of drag queens, rent boys, and various other denizens of Toronto's gay village, including numerous Village People impersonators and what looked to be the entire cast of *The Rocky Horror Picture Show*.

Todd and Lucien brought their two perfectly coiffed toy poodles, who were supposed to prance down the aisle with a ring box tied to each of their backs. As they reached the halfway mark, one of the creatures squatted and urinated on the red carpet. Lucien shrieked, "Fifi, you're embarrassing me terribly! Todd, I told you to take her out before bringing her in here. She's ruining my big moment!" Could this have been an omen of what was to come?

After the furor died down, I began the ceremony but didn't get far. I had just asked the couple to exchange their vows when Lucien began heaving and sobbing uncontrollably, gasping, "Oh Todd, you're the love of my life! You've made me so happy! I can't wait to spend the rest of my life with you!" After this performance, he wiped his eyes with great panache and turned to one of the cameramen, asking, "Did you get all that? Do you need me to do it again?"

That was the point at which I decided to simply pronounce them legally married and get this farce over with. Luckily, that fiasco of a wedding was never broadcast. Instead, the producers got me to perform a wedding for a lovely couple, Michael and Charles, which reflected much better on all concerned. That was my one and only experience with reality television, and I learned a good lesson: If you're going to get involved with reality television, make sure the show's reality matches your reality.

One of the highlights of my life was officiating at the 2007 wedding of Edith Windsor and Thea Spyer, a prominent New York couple who'd been together for forty-two years. My involvement in this marriage began with a phone call in April of that year from New York activist Brendan Fay, at whose marriage I had officiated in 2003. He told me about Edith, affectionately called "Edie" by everyone who knew her. She was the first female executive at IBM. Her partner, Thea, was one of the most successful and respected psychotherapists in New York. Edie and Thea had decided to come to Toronto to get married, and Brendan wanted to know if I would officiate. Before I could say yes, he interjected, "But Harvey, there's a catch."

Brendan explained that the situation was urgent. Thea, a quadriplegic in the final stages of multiple sclerosis, had just been informed by her doctor that she had less than three months to live. It was her dying wish to marry Edie, who was the love of her life. And as same-sex marriage wasn't yet legal in New York, they felt their best option was to get married in Toronto.

Because of Thea's condition, she was ineligible for travel insurance. And because her personal care needs were so demanding, the prospect of spending any time in Canada was out of the question. As it was, they'd have to travel with a private nurse and a team of support workers. Therefore, the plan was to fly to Toronto, have the marriage take place in a hotel room at the Toronto airport, and immediately fly back to New York.

Brendan asked, "Harvey, I know this is highly unusual, but would you be prepared to meet us at the Toronto airport and marry them there?" There was no hesitation in my mind. Of course I said yes.

On May 22, 2007, I packed my judicial robe into a suit bag and drove to the airport. I arrived at the hotel early and asked to speak to the manager, an extremely helpful and accommodating young woman. When I told her what was about to take place at the hotel, her eyes lit up and she exclaimed, "Oh my heavens! These people are going through so much just to get married. We just can't let it happen in an ordinary hotel room. Let me give you one of our meeting rooms so everyone will be more comfortable. And we'll decorate the room with the floral arrangements from the lobby. We'll also provide complimentary champagne for the couple and their guests. Let's make this really special for them." Thanks to the enthusiastically supportive hotel staff, the bland, sterile room quickly became a colourful, warm, flower-bedecked space for this momentous event.

Several minutes later, the couple and their entourage entered the room. Edie, a petite blonde woman in her late seventies, with a radiant, charismatic smile and dressed in a white silk pantsuit sporting a white rose corsage, approached me and shook my hand. "You must be Harvey," she said warmly. "I'm Edie Windsor. And this is my partner, Thea." Next to her in a large wheelchair sat Thea, a stoic-looking woman with short and greying brown hair, wearing a tuxedo-style black pantsuit with a red rose corsage pinned to the lapel. "Nice to meet you," she said. "Thank you for doing this."

I replied, "It's my great pleasure."

I was then introduced to their team of about twelve friends and caregivers, and was deeply moved by the obvious effort this couple and their team had made to undertake this voyage.

I then noticed two individuals, one carrying a large video camera on her shoulder, clearly filming the event, and the other carrying a large boom microphone. Edie, noticing my look of curiosity, smiled and explained, "Harvey, I hope you don't mind, but they're making a documentary about us, and they want to film our wedding. So, get ready, you're going to be a movie star!" I wish I'd known. I would have called for makeup.

This was by far the most poignant and emotional wedding ceremony I've ever performed. For most couples, a wedding signifies the beginning of a life together. But for Edie and Thea, their wedding denoted the culmination of a long and happy life already lived. The words "till death do us part," uttered by this devoted elderly couple who'd been through so much together, took on a whole new meaning and brought a flood of tears to everyone. It was an unforgettable moment, captured forever in the critically acclaimed 2009 documentary *Edie & Thea: A Very Long Engagement*.

Following the ceremony and the champagne toast, Edie and Thea spoke about their struggles living a closeted life, their activism following the Stonewall riots, and the jubilation they felt to have finally overcome the last hurdle, marriage. Thea touched my heart deeply when she said, "We are particularly gratified to have been married by Canada's first openly gay judge." Edie reiterated this sentiment in her memoir, *A Wild and Precious Life*.

I would have loved to have spent more time with them, but their return flight was imminent, and so we tearfully hugged, said our farewells, and promised to keep in touch. And that's exactly what we did. I travelled to New York twice to spend time with Edie and Thea prior to Thea's death in February 2009. She'd miraculously outlived her doctors' predictions by a full eighteen months.

In June 2009, I had the great honour of accompanying Edie to the world premiere of the documentary at the historic Castro Theatre in San Francisco. I will never forget the thunderous standing ovation Edie received at the conclusion of the movie. The filmmakers, Susan Muska and Gréta Ólafsdóttir, gave me another honour in connection with the movie. They interviewed me about my experience officiating at the wedding and included the interview as a special feature on the DVD.

This wedding, far from being a simple event in the life of a couple, unexpectedly took on monumental proportions and changed the course of history. Following Thea's death, Edie was hit with an estate tax bill of over three hundred and fifty thousand dollars. Had they been a heterosexual married couple, Edie would have been exempt from this tax. But because the Defense of Marriage Act (DOMA) restricted the definition of marriage to being only between a man and a woman, Edie was required to pay the tax. She sued the federal government, the case ultimately reaching the Supreme Court, which in June 2013 struck down the restrictive definition of marriage in DOMA as being unconstitutional. This landmark ruling opened the door to marriage equality throughout America.

In June 2014, Toronto hosted the WorldPride celebrations. I was asked by the organizers if it might be possible to convince Edie, then eighty-five years old and in poor health, to return to Toronto to receive an award. Her reply to my request was, "Harvey, for you, anything." At a pre-event press conference, I proudly referred to Edie as "the Rosa Parks of the gay rights movement." We then gave a joint presentation at the WorldPride International Human Rights Conference. Speaking at the gala event honouring Edie, my heart bursting with pride, I reminded everyone of the important role Canada had played in the evolution of same-sex marriage rights in the United States. And once again, I expressed my immense gratitude to have had the honour and privilege of participating in the furtherance of those rights.

I saw Edie in New York one last time after that, only three months before she passed away in September 2017 at the age of eighty-eight. I'm tremendously grateful to have had Edie and Thea in my life, and they will live in my heart forever.

As far as I know, I was the only judge in Canada who made himself publicly available to perform same-sex marriages on an ongoing basis. As time passed, I became known internationally as the face and voice of same-sex marriage in Canada. *People* magazine featured one of my weddings in their August 18, 2003, issue. In 2008, Canada's premier queer publication, *Xtra Magazine*, named me Best Behind the Scenes Champion. That same year, the New York state senate honoured me by issuing a proclamation in recognition of having officiated at hundreds of same-sex weddings for citizens of New York. In 2010, I received the Colleague in the Spotlight award from the Canadian Bar Association Judges' Forum. In 2016, I received the Justice Thomas

Cromwell Distinguished Public Service Award from my alma mater, the Queen's University faculty of law. And in June 2023, I participated in the launch of Pride Month at the historic Stonewall Inn in New York City, birthplace of the gay liberation movement in 1969.

My involvement in advocating for and facilitating same-sex marriages has been one of the greatest joys and blessings in my life. To have seen so many couples attain their dreams of equality and dignity through the legal recognition of their relationships, giving them the societal respect they deserve, has given me the most satisfaction a judge can ever hope to have.

CHAPTER 14

MISTRIAL: MY EXPERIENCE IN CRIMINAL COURT

Despite all those exciting, dramatic trials you see on popular television shows like *Law and Order*, *Suits*, *The Good Wife*, and *Better Call Saul*, the reality of criminal court is very different. Unlike those brilliant TV scripts, which always resolve each case within the one-hour time slot, the evidence in a real court isn't always clear, the lawyers aren't always well-prepared or articulate, the witnesses don't always have perfect recall, and not every verdict produces a satisfying result. But one thing is always true: For the accused person, the experience of being charged with a serious criminal offence is terrifying. The consequences of being found guilty can result in a broad scope of punishments: probation, the imposition of a fine, house arrest, or at worst being sent to jail.

In my twenty-six years on the Bench, I presided over many thought-provoking trials, dealing with every imaginable offence — from shoplifting, spousal and child abuse, drunk driving, assaults, robbery, and white-collar crimes to sexual assaults and homicides. My task was always the same: to decide whether the prosecution had satisfied me, beyond a reasonable doubt, of the accused's guilt. If that stringent burden of proof wasn't met, I had to render a verdict of not guilty.

One of the most common questions judges are asked is, "How can you tell if someone is lying or telling the truth when they testify in court?" Sadly, there's no completely reliable way to assess someone's credibility. Some people are very good liars, and others who are actually telling the truth may, out of nervousness, create the impression they're lying. A person's demeanour while testifying isn't a very reliable indicator. Judges examine a person's testimony for internal consistency, meaning their story remains uniform throughout, as well as its consistency with the rest of the evidence presented. In the end, it's really just an exercise in common sense and logic.

Although the police may sometimes use lie detector tests, the results aren't admissible in court as the technology isn't considered sufficiently reliable. I remember one case where an accused said to me, "Judge, I'm telling the truth and I can prove it. Why don't you give me a lie detector test?"

I wearily replied, "Sir, *I* am the lie detector."

Sometimes the accused is guilty and everyone knows it because the evidence of guilt is overwhelming. They may have been "caught red-handed," found in possession of illegal drugs or the property they were accused of stealing, or DNA evidence may point conclusively to guilt, or perhaps the accused confessed to committing the crime. And yet, the accused is found not guilty. "How can this possibly happen?" you ask.

If the police violated the accused's constitutional rights in obtaining the evidence, such as by conducting an improper search, obtaining a confession under duress, not allowing the accused to call a lawyer, or not providing a reason for the arrest, the court may have no option but to exclude the evidence, necessitating an acquittal.

I'm frequently asked what it felt like to find someone not guilty when I knew he or she was guilty. I explained in chapter 8 how it felt, as a lawyer, to represent someone who I knew was guilty, and my feelings didn't change as a judge. I understood that the only way to protect citizens from police overstepping their authority was to exclude illegally obtained evidence.

Not every violation by the police will result in an exclusion of the evidence. Only glaring and heinous instances of police misconduct will result in evidence being thrown out. If the court decides allowing the evidence would bring the administration of justice into disrepute, it must be excluded. So the judge is engaged in a balancing act between the rights of the accused to a fair trial and the right of society to protection.

The first time I encountered this issue was a case against a young Black man charged with possession of illegal firearms. He had been driving a new BMW and was filling it up at a gas station in an upper-class neighbourhood. The arresting officer noticed the BMW and the Black driver and decided to approach him. After asking the driver for his name and driver's licence, the officer ordered him to open the trunk, in which he found numerous prohibited firearms. The officer arrested the man and then conducted a licence plate search that found the vehicle was stolen.

At the trial, the officer testified he approached the accused and decided to search the BMW because "the driver didn't look like he belonged in such an expensive car, especially in that high-class neighbourhood. I was acting on a hunch. I've been a police officer over twenty years, and I've learned to trust my hunches." In cross-examination conducted by a highly skilled defence lawyer, the officer ended up admitting that had the driver been white, his suspicions wouldn't have been aroused.

Had the officer run the licence plate search *before* approaching the man, he'd have discovered the car was stolen, which would have given him reasonable grounds to search it. But because he acted on a hunch, obviously grounded in racism, he violated the accused's constitutional right not to be subjected to an unreasonable search. The court couldn't condone such behaviour. I was compelled to exclude the evidence of the guns and find the accused not guilty. That case taught me that policing is perhaps the only profession in which relying on one's experience and following one's hunches can be a bad thing. But that's the reality of criminal law. The only consolation to this case was that at least the guns were seized.

Did I see a lot of police misconduct during my time as a judge? No. Every profession, including the judiciary, has its share of "bad apples," but overall, the police officers I encountered were highly professional, dedicated, and ethical. The police have an extremely difficult job, dealing with some of the most horrific and traumatizing situations imaginable. They endure tremendous abuse from people whose behaviour is affected by substance abuse, mental illness, or just plain rudeness. And their job is dangerous. They put their lives on the line every day for the sole purpose of protecting the public. Over the years, I've developed great respect for the police.

The most frustrating cases I dealt with in criminal court, by far, were those in which men were charged with assaulting their female partners. Domestic violence is an epidemic, and while it's certainly true that women can be just as violent as men, the sad reality is that the vast majority of perpetrators coming before the court are men.

Like many large cities, Toronto has a multicultural population with many new immigrants from countries where women and children have no rights. Over the years, many men in my courtroom who had been charged with domestic violence would look at me in stunned disbelief when I told them they were not allowed to lay a hand on their wives or children. I remember one angry man who, upon being convicted for beating his wife with a wooden spatula, shouted, "What? You? You're telling me I can't hit my wife? She's mine. My family *paid* for her! In my country, I can do whatever I want with my wife."

"Sir, I thought *this* was your country now," I replied. "And in *this* country, you *cannot* hit your wife, your children, or anyone else."

He repeated, "But my family *paid* for her!"

I huffed, "So what do you want from me, a refund?"

Many newcomers to North America, particularly refugees from developing countries, experience severe culture shock trying to adjust to our way of life. In my opinion, immigration authorities do far too little to provide these newest members of society with basic information about our system of values. Too many times it's left up to the judges, after a serious criminal offence has been committed, to provide a course in "Canada 101." And, by then, it's too late.

The justice system does a terrible job of protecting women victimized by domestic violence, and everyone knows it, especially the women. If a woman reports her partner's abusive conduct to the police, or dares to testify against him at trial, she's at great risk of suffering further violence when he retaliates upon getting out of jail — sadly, a frequent occurrence. Sure, courts impose restraining orders against the perpetrators, but those orders commonly aren't worth the paper they're written on. Restraining orders are among the most violated of court orders. The police woefully lack the resources necessary to protect every woman living in fear of her partner. We've all seen far too many cases where women, after being granted restraining orders, were murdered by their ex-partners, despite having begged the police for protection.

Soon after I became a judge, one of my colleagues released a man accused of wife-beating on bail pending his trial, despite the prosecutor's urgings to keep the man in custody. The next day, the man murdered his wife. It was shocking that a woman was dead because of a judge's wrong decision. I asked my colleague how he could live with himself after such a horrible result from his decision. He glibly replied, "Harvey, in every domestic assault case, the victim will tell you she's afraid for her life and beg you not to release the guy. In one out of a thousand cases, she'll be right. But does that mean we keep the other nine hundred and ninety-nine guys in jail until their trials? Is that the kind of society you want to live in, where merely being accused of something is enough to keep a person in jail until their trial?"

His response, although callous, made a valid point with which I couldn't completely disagree. If the presumption of innocence is to have any meaning, we can't keep everyone accused of a crime in jail until their trials. And judges, being only human, do make mistakes. But when some mistakes happen, the consequences can be catastrophic.

The question of how to protect victims of domestic violence is a troubling and multi-faceted one. Of course, there are women's shelters available for victims of domestic violence. But for women with jobs, living at a shelter won't protect them from being stalked by their abusers. For women with children, they still have to get them to and from school, and they have to deal with family court applications brought by their partners claiming custody or visitation. And shelters are only temporary residences. Eventually, the women have to find permanent homes. The challenges of separation for abused women are daunting.

Many abused women are financially dependent on their partners. If a woman testifies truthfully against her abuser and tells what he did to her, the judge will likely send her partner to jail and he'll lose his job. For many women in this situation, the prospect of rendering the family's sole breadwinner unemployed, and the family penniless, is simply out of the question.

Another obvious reason abused women don't cooperate with criminal prosecutions against their abusers is that they still love them. They're trapped in a prison of co-dependency fuelled by low self-esteem. Relationships are complicated, and while none of us has the right to pass judgment on other people's romantic choices, there's immense frustration for judges watching victimized women clearly lying to protect their abusers. I've listened to hundreds of women claim their bruises were caused by walking into doors — or, even worse, say the abuser was really acting in self-defence. It's heartbreaking, frustrating, and unfortunately totally understandable. And it makes judges feel completely powerless to make a difference in these women's lives.

Prosecutors do their best to proceed with domestic violence cases, even if the victims are uncooperative, by relying on other available evidence such as videos or the testimony of other witnesses. But the reality is that without the willing participation of victims, there's very little the criminal justice system can do about the scourge of domestic violence plaguing society.

I remember one case where the victim, having been subpoenaed, failed to attend court to testify at the trial. The prosecutor asked me to issue a warrant for her arrest. Now the victim was about to be re-victimized by the justice system! I couldn't bring myself to do it, but that's a perfect example of just how topsy-turvy the system can be when it comes to domestic violence.

However, the situation in family court is dramatically different. If a child witnesses his or her parents arguing and fighting, this is a form of child abuse. Parents who don't insulate their children from domestic violence run the risk of losing them. The stark reality for abused women is grim. If a husband is abusive, the only person children can rely on to protect them from that abuse is their mother. If she fails to do so, the child protection authorities are likely to step in and apprehend the children, even though their mother's failure to protect them understandably stems from her fear of retaliation by the abuser.

I remember many cases where I had to tell mothers, point blank, to either "dump the dude" or lose their children. The most horrific case I ever had involved an abused mother of a twelve-year-old girl whose stepfather, the woman's husband, had been making pornographic movies with the child for four years. It turned out that not only was the mother aware of what was going on, she was the camera operator. The child ended up in foster care, and both parents were charged criminally. At the trial, the mother argued that her participation in the child abuse resulted from extreme duress imposed by her husband, who regularly beat her and threatened to kill her if she ever reported the abuse to the police. I convicted her. During the four years the abuse was ongoing, she'd had countless opportunities to contact the police and hadn't. Parents are expected to put their children's best interests ahead of their own.

In yet another heart-wrenching case, a father of a four-year-old boy, angry that his son had wet the bed, put the boy's hand through a meat grinder. The child lost two fingers. When they couldn't stop the boy's bleeding, the father reluctantly allowed the mother to take the child to the hospital. Initially, the mother made up an improbable story explaining the injury, but the doctors, sensing they weren't hearing the truth, finally convinced the mother to tell them what the father had done.

When the police and child protection authorities investigated, it turned out that the father had been abusing both the mother and the boy for years. The mother was too terrified to take any steps to protect her son. After the father went to jail, the mother worked diligently with the child protection authorities to overcome her parenting deficits, and she was eventually reunited with her child.

I've learned over the years that domestic violence is learned behaviour. Boys who grow up watching their fathers beating up their mothers are at great risk of doing the same to their partners when they become adults. I remember one case involving a thirteen-year-old boy charged with putting a knife to his teacher's throat and threatening to kill her when she gave him a D on a test. The boy's mother said to me, "My son's been watching his father do that to me for years." Bullies learn how to be bullies by watching other bullies. It's that simple.

The case I just mentioned involved a young person charged with committing a crime. When youths under the age of eighteen commit criminal offences, the judge's task is to not only suitably punish the offender, but, perhaps more importantly, help steer the youth onto the right track to living a positive, constructive, and crime-free life. This is far easier said than done. Many of these youths have had terrible childhoods replete with parental neglect and abuse, poverty, domestic violence, and substance abuse. Many were born with fetal alcohol syndrome or other developmental delays and cognitive deficits. While they require a wide array of mental health and social services to overcome these challenges, governments, sadly, don't allocate anywhere near the resources necessary to make a positive difference in these children's lives.

Knowing that so many people who come before the court, especially young people, are damaged and therefore unpredictable, judges have to be careful about what they say and do. I learned that lesson early in my judicial career in a case involving a sixteen-year-old boy who pleaded guilty to breaking into a woman's house while she was at work. He ransacked the place and stole many of her prized possessions.

During the sentencing, the victim chose to attend court and read aloud her victim impact statement. She tearfully spoke about the jewellery left to her by her mother, which the youth had stolen and sold to buy drugs. Her presentation was truly heartbreaking.

When she finished speaking, I turned to the boy and asked if he had anything to say to the woman whose life he had so terribly upended. I assumed he'd want to apologize to her. But he simply said, "Nope."

I couldn't believe it. I said, "Young man, you've just heard how devastated this woman is to have lost some of her most cherished possessions, which you stole to buy drugs. Don't you think the *least* you could do is apologize to her?"

He rolled his eyes and exhaled deeply to express his annoyance. Shrugging his shoulders, he blurted sarcastically, "Big deal, she's insured."

I saw red. I said, "Young man, step into custody. You're going to spend the next few hours downstairs in the cells. I want you to do some thinking about your behaviour, and I expect to see an entirely different attitude when you come back here. I'll deal with this case after lunch." The court officers then handcuffed the boy and escorted him out of the courtroom.

Feeling smugly self-satisfied, I bragged to my fellow judges in the lunchroom about what had transpired. I was so proud to show them what a great judge I was. Upon hearing my story, my colleagues' faces turned white, as if they'd seen a ghost. One of them said in a gravely funereal voice, "Harvey, I did exactly the same thing a few years ago, and the kid hanged himself in the cell." I thought I was going to faint.

"What?" I exclaimed. "How could such a thing happen?"

My colleagues explained that when a person was sent to a cell during a recess, the officers didn't bother removing belts, shoelaces, and the like because the person would be returning to the courtroom in a little while. And the youth cell was not in the officers' direct line of vision, so they didn't see what the young person was doing.

I couldn't believe it. What had I done? What if this young person, about whom I knew nothing, were to panic and do something horrible to himself? Suffice it to say I ate nothing during that lunch hour, and was counting the minutes until I could get back into the courtroom and have the boy returned to me. When I saw his face enter the courtroom, I was so relieved that I wanted to hug him. That being said, I'm sorry to report that my effort to scare him didn't work. When I asked him if spending a few hours in custody had changed his attitude, all he could bring himself to say was, "The cheese sandwich I got for lunch was stale." So much for the impact of spending lunch hour in a cell.

Nevertheless, that case taught me to be careful and think twice when dealing with people whose life experiences may have rendered them susceptible to behaving impulsively and drastically.

There's a common misconception that the justice system is much too lenient on young people. Judges are often criticized for not "throwing the book" at young adults who commit crimes. Why don't judges impose lengthy jail sentences on them? Well, if the offender has committed an extremely serious violent offence, they *will* be sent to jail for a long time. But for less serious offences, judges try very hard to keep young people out of jail.

Why is that so? Consider the case of a nineteen-year-old boy who's gotten in with the wrong crowd and stolen a car. He's sent to jail for three months. Who do you think he's going to meet and befriend in jail? Who will his role models be? What will they teach him? I guarantee he will not come out of jail rehabilitated. On the contrary, he'll have learned how to break into homes, where to find drugs and guns, and which gang to join upon his release to advance his criminal career. I've seen it happen.

I can say beyond the shadow of a doubt that judges are not doing society any favours by immersing impressionable young people into a milieu that very strongly militates against rehabilitation. That's why judges first try community-based sentences such as probation, community service, and house arrest. Jail should be a last resort for vulnerable young people who are prone to being turned into hardened criminals.

In recent years we've seen a number of high-profile sexual assault cases in which the victims have come forward to accuse someone many years, even decades, after the offences allegedly occurred. Commonly referred to as "historical" sexual assault cases, these are among the most challenging and difficult ever encountered in criminal court.

The first and most obvious question that arises is, why would a complainant (alleged victim) wait so long to report such a serious crime? Psychologists have taught us there are many valid reasons why this may happen, having to do with the emotional makeup of the victim, the circumstances surrounding the offence, and the relationship between the parties. Whatever the reasons may be, the sad reality is that the longer a complainant waits, the harder it will be to prove that the incident occurred.

Sexual assault cases are almost always "he said / she said" cases because there are rarely any witnesses to such incidents. People's memories fade with the passage of time. And there's almost never any DNA or other forensic evidence in historical sexual assault cases because such evidence must be collected as soon after the incident occurred as possible. And so, courts are left with the extremely challenging task of deciding these important cases by assessing the credibility of the complainant and the accused, should they choose to testify.

Almost all the historical sexual assault trials I conducted involved adult women alleging that a male relative, often a stepfather, grandfather, or uncle, abused them as young children. These are terribly tragic situations for everyone. Complainants must relive the traumatic events when they testify, and they're subjected to vigorous cross-examinations by defence counsel. The accused perpetrators, who are usually quite elderly by the time the complaint is made, are made to feel they have the impossible task of proving that something *didn't* happen, even though the legal burden of proof is always on the prosecution to prove that it *did*. And inevitably in such cases, every extended family member ends up choosing sides. Family relationships are destroyed forever, no matter the verdict.

Sometimes, these cases are determined by a single piece of evidence that might otherwise have been considered irrelevant. In one of my cases, a forty-two-year-old complainant testified that her uncle sexually abused her when she was between five and ten years old. She repeatedly asserted that these assaults always occurred in her uncle's basement while they were sitting on a red leather sofa. She was quite adamant about that.

The defence was able to prove, without question, that the uncle didn't have a red leather sofa in his basement until the complainant was in her twenties. That one simple fact was enough to raise a nagging doubt in my mind, and I acquitted the accused. Was I correct? We'll never know.

In another case, a nine-year-old girl testified that her mother's ex-boyfriend molested her. By the end of her examination-in-chief, I was totally convinced this girl was telling the truth, and had the trial ended right there and then, I would have convicted the accused without hesitation. But when defence counsel cross-examined the girl, it became apparent she'd been coached by her mother to fabricate this complaint. The mother was angry with the accused for breaking up with her, so she enlisted her daughter in a vindictive scheme in an attempt to destroy his life. The mother ended up admitting her wrongdoing in her own weepy testimony. That case reinforced the importance of keeping an open mind until the very end of the case.

I don't want to give the impression that most historical sexual assault cases result in a finding of not guilty. In my experience, the opposite is true. In the vast majority of such cases that I have tried, I found the complainants' evidence to be credible and reliable, and their reasons for not having come forward much sooner were totally understandable.

Some jurisdictions have enacted limitation periods for sexual assaults. I have mixed feelings about that, because I appreciate the arguments for and against the concept. All I can say is that, for judges, life would be much easier if victims came forward right away after being so terribly abused.

Most people think of trials when they think of criminal court. Actually, approximately 90 percent of criminal cases are resolved by the accused pleading guilty due to plea negotiations between the prosecution and defence counsel. As a result, criminal court judges spend significantly more time sentencing offenders than conducting trials.

There are three objectives in sentencing people who commit criminal acts: Firstly, the offender's conduct must be punished in a way that reflects the gravity of his or her conduct. Secondly, the sentence must be harsh enough to deter the offender from repeating the offence or committing any other crimes, which is known as "specific deterrence." And thirdly, the sentence must send a message to the community to deter others from committing offences, called "general deterrence."

The major challenge for judges in sentencing offenders lies in trying to achieve the second objective, specific deterrence, commonly referred to as rehabilitation. In order to fashion a sentence that will deter the offender from repeating the criminal behaviour, one needs to understand what caused the person to commit the offence in the first place.

The criminal court clientele is overwhelmingly populated by people living with a multitude of severely challenging socio-economic issues, including poverty, mental health problems (mostly undiagnosed and therefore untreated), social isolation, addictions, domestic violence, developmental delays caused by fetal alcohol syndrome, illiteracy, learning disabilities, and a whole host of special needs. You only have to attend any criminal court anywhere, and watch the proceedings for even an hour, to see this is true.

The best way to rehabilitate those who engage in antisocial and self-destructive behaviour is to address the underlying reasons for that behaviour. When drug addicts told me they had a "drug problem," I'd always quote a famous line used by drug rehab counsellors: "Drugs are *not* your problem. Drugs are the *solution* you found to the *real* problem. Until you remove that solution, you won't see clearly what the real problem is." Drug addicts need intensive residential rehabilitative treatment, not jail.

There's an old saying that resonated with me as a judge — "There are no bad people, just lost children." No one is born a criminal. Bad behaviour results from trauma and pain. Another familiar saying comes to mind: "Hurt people, hurt people." In my experience, most criminals desperately need focused, comprehensive, professional help to overcome their challenges, and that requires major resources, especially mental health services, drug rehabilitation, and subsidized housing.

You can play a game well and lose sight of the fact that the game itself is broken. The criminal justice system is broken. Governments are spending a fortune warehousing people in jails, which ultimately achieves nothing. You can't throw a socially maladjusted, damaged person into a community filled with a bunch of other socially maladjusted, damaged people and expect the person to come out rehabilitated. On the contrary, the opposite will be true: The person will leave jail even more immersed in the criminal subculture. Everyone in the justice system knows this to be true. It's a recurring topic of conversation at every judicial conference and in every judges' lunchroom in which I've ever been. It's the elephant in the room that, for some reason, judges won't speak out about publicly. But they should.

The cost of arresting, prosecuting, and incarcerating drug addicts who commit offences to feed their addictions is huge. Similarly, there are enormous costs in processing undiagnosed mentally ill people who commit offences not because they're criminals, but because they're ill. Think of how much money governments must spend on police, prosecutors, judges, court staff, Legal Aid, staffing and operating jails, probation, and parole officers.

If that money were spent diverting mentally ill people and drug addicts out of the criminal justice system and into the intensive rehabilitation and mental health services they require, we'd see a massive reduction in crime, the courts would have the time they desperately need to deal with real criminals, and, most of all, the people who so urgently need help would receive it.

Some jurisdictions in North America have introduced drug treatment courts and mental health courts, but they're generally poorly resourced and very limited in scope. Most of them won't admit offenders who've committed serious crimes into their programs for fear of conveying the message that addicts can get away with criminal acts. It's a complicated policy issue, but one thing is indisputable: Our current way of dealing with mentally ill people and drug addicts *isn't working*.

Most criminal court judges will tell you the job is immensely frustrating because the resources required to effect true rehabilitation are woefully inadequate. Waiting lists for mental health services and addiction rehabilitation programs are inordinately long in every major city. The criminal court clientele has no voice or power. Politicians don't care about sentencing reform because these issues are never brought to the public forefront. They'll talk about "law and order," imposing mandatory minimum sentences, and public safety, but they demonstrate no interest in rethinking the way in which we deal with mental illness and substance abuse.

It's always troubled me that judges, who are in the best position to speak out about these issues, have remained silent, by and large. The conspiracy of silence within the judicial culture stifles any possibility of progress. While judges cannot speak publicly about individual cases, or legal issues over which the court may have to adjudicate, I strongly believe they should advocate loudly about matters affecting access to justice, the administration of the courts, and much-needed law reform. One of the great things about being retired is that I can now speak my mind with impunity.

CHAPTER 15

FLAWS OF ATTRACTION: DATING TIPS FROM AN EX-JUDGE

When I began presiding as a judge in 1995, very few people had computers, and the internet, though invented in 1983, was virtually unheard of. People hoping to meet romantic partners had to do it the old-fashioned way by going out to places like nightclubs, bars, churches, social clubs, gyms, or maybe even their workplaces. Sometimes friends and relatives acted as matchmakers, and in those cases, you received advance information about the person that was usually reliable.

When the only way to meet other people was to do it in person, we used all our senses and instincts to "size people up." We would engage in conversation and assess the person's attractiveness and suitability in terms of physical appearance, voice, personality, conversational and interpersonal skills, body language, and a host of other intuitive skills. The "chemistry" we sensed in the physical presence of the other person played a large part in helping us decide if that person was who we were looking for.

Most importantly, because it wasn't as easy to meet someone in the old days as it is now, couples made more of an effort to stay together. They worked at their relationships and tried hard to resolve their differences. The word "commitment" meant something. Yes, relationships broke up, but in most cases people gave it a really good try before deciding to pull the plug. The Neil Sedaka song "Breaking Up Is Hard to Do" reflected the way most people felt about terminating relationships.

Everything changed in the late nineties, when computers became a staple in every household and the internet created a global network, giving rise to social media and internet dating websites. And in the 2010s, the rise of smartphones led to the popularity of online dating apps. The impact on modern relationships has been nothing short of colossal.

It's difficult to find reliable statistics about the percentage of couples who meet online because most surveys capture only married couples, not the couples who choose to live together without getting married. However, it's indisputable that a significant number of people find romantic partners through the internet, whether it be for a long-term relationship or a "hookup." And I can say for certain that the vast majority of couples I dealt with in family court met each other online, because, out of curiosity, I always asked them how they met.

When I first started presiding in family court, most separated couples I met had been together at least five years. They had a history together, which created a status quo prior to separation. The court could make use of that status quo in developing post-separation parenting plans for their children that attempted to maintain, as much as possible, the parenting patterns prior to separation.

Starting in the 2000s, when internet dating sites became popular, family court judges began seeing an influx of couples who had very little history together. Their relationships were of short duration, usually under a few years. We began to see more and more couples who had been in a casual relationship and subsequently broken up even before their children were born. Some of them had never even lived together. Developing parenting plans for these couples presented new challenges for family court judges because there were no pre-separation patterns of parenting on which to base the plans. We were starting from scratch.

I believe the reason so many couples break up after having been together only a short time is because online dating has made it so easy to find someone else. If you've had an argument or disagreement with your partner, a few clicks on the computer will bring you an inbox full of potential new dates. There are always more fish in the sea. Why settle for someone who doesn't check off every box on your wish list? The temptation to see if there's someone out there who's better for you than your current partner can be irresistible. And for some people, it can become addictive.

I can remember dozens of cases where at least one member of the couple had been in court three times before, with different ex-partners. Online dating has made serial monogamy an easy lifestyle. I even had a few cases where the couples actually met in the family court waiting room! Imagine coming to court to litigate against an ex-partner only to meet someone else who's there for the same reason, and the two of you strike up a new relationship. I used to jokingly brag that our court was better than an online dating site because people could meet potential partners in person, and then watch their behaviour in court to get an idea of what will happen when they break up!

Another significant by-product of online dating sites is the convenience they provide to people wishing to stray outside their relationships. It's never been easier than it is now to cheat on one's partner. There are even specific websites designed to facilitate casual hookups for people who are married or in supposedly committed relationships. It's one thing to have an open relationship in which the parties have agreed they're free to have sexual encounters with other people. But it's quite another matter when one partner believes he or she is in a monogamous relationship while the other partner is surreptitiously screwing around with other people.

I mentioned in chapter 12 that, in my experience as a family court judge, the principal reason for family breakdown is infidelity. And consider this: In family court, we saw only the couples where a partner's infidelity was discovered. In other words, we saw only the people who got caught. Imagine how many people there are cheating on their partners who haven't yet been caught. I truly believe infidelity has become an epidemic in our society, thanks to online dating sites.

One of the most telling cases I ever had involved a young couple in their late twenties who'd met online. They'd been together only eighteen months and had agreed to be monogamous. Unbeknownst to each other, they both began searching online for casual sexual partners. Naturally, to protect themselves from getting caught, they used pseudonyms as screen names. One day each of them made a date to meet up with someone at Starbucks, and — you guessed it — they'd made a date with each other! They'd been communicating on the dating site for over two months, badmouthing their partners, only to discover they'd been talking to each other *about* each other. You can imagine how bitter and angry they were and the impact this had on the custody dispute over their infant child.

If you're wondering how the majority of cheating partners are discovered, I kept statistics on that too. In 75 percent of the cases I saw in my courtroom, the infidelity was uncovered from the cheating partner's cellphone, on which the "innocent" party would find a text message, photograph, social media post, or unknown phone number. In 10 percent of the cases, the cheating partner's computer revealed the incriminating evidence, often from an email. In 5 percent, a credit card bill or other receipt disclosed a suspicious expenditure. And in the remaining 10 percent, the infidelity was discovered either by someone telling the "innocent" party, or by that person figuring it out on their own due to the cheater's changed behaviour (an increased interest in grooming and hygiene often raises suspicions), reduced interest in sex, or being caught in a lie about their whereabouts.

In the vast majority of short-term relationships I encountered in court, especially those that began online, it was immediately apparent that these people barely knew each other at all. Other than a strong physical attraction, which produced babies they then fought over incessantly, these people knew almost nothing about each other's family backgrounds, education, careers, finances, likes and dislikes, recreational interests, or relationship histories.

None of this would have mattered had they not had children. But when a couple produces a child, they're tied to each other for at least twenty years, whether they like it or not, and whether or not they ever loved or even liked each other. My heart breaks for all the children out there caught in the middle of these often-dysfunctional relationships.

I'm not suggesting online dating is necessarily a bad thing. In fact, I've had great success with it, although there were some memorable moments. One fellow asked me on our first date whether I had any pets. I told him I had a cat. Bristling with annoyance, he blurted, "Well, you'll just have to get rid of it. I'm allergic to cats."

When I replied that I loved my cat and would never get rid of it, he angrily hissed, "Are you telling me your cat is more important than *me*?" There was no second date.

Speaking of cats, one guy in my online inbox asked me for a photo. I sent a nice headshot. He wrote back asking for a photo that "aimed farther down." I wasn't about to send anyone a photo of my nether regions and told him so in no uncertain terms. He wrote back saying, "No, you don't understand. I want to see your feet." I sent him a photo of my cat's paw. And that was that. Another one bit the dust.

Yet another gentleman I met online googled me on his cellphone as soon as I gave him my name as we were sitting down to have a coffee. Within seconds, he squealed with excitement, "Oh, you're a judge! You'll be perfect. I'll bet you live in a beautiful home in an expensive neighbourhood. I was born to be supported by a man like you. And by the way, I think we should adopt a child, as we're both getting on in years and we'll need someone to take care of us in our old age." I left before the coffee was delivered.

Another guy I met seemed to be a promising prospect. He was good-looking and had an interesting career as a school board executive. I was attracted to his intelligence and sense of humour. We went out on two dates and I felt we were enjoying each other's company. And then he "ghosted" me. He didn't respond to my phone calls or text messages. I had no idea what I'd said or done to turn him off. I soon learned from others with more experience than me that "ghosting" is a common occurrence in the world of online dating.

Contestant number five turned out to be Mr. Right. My partner and I have been together almost a decade, and without the advent of online dating, we would never have met any other way. So I'm grateful these websites exist. And let's face it: Online dating is here to stay. But it must be used intelligently and with caution. What I've learned from my courtroom experiences is that con artists are everywhere.

One of the most common dating tricks I saw as a judge was immigration fraud. Many people have had their hearts broken by falling in love with a foreign fraudster whose only interest in marrying them was to become a legal resident of their country. I've seen this happen more times than I care to remember, and each time, it's devastating.

Here's the typical scenario: A successful, financially well-off career woman in her mid-thirties, who's never had much success with relationships, is feeling lonely. Let's call her Juliet. She knows her biological clock is ticking and feels now is the right time to find a partner and have a baby. She goes online and connects with Romeo, a handsome man from another country.

Over the next few weeks they exchange dozens of emails, and very soon Romeo professes a strong infatuation with Juliet. He tells her he's smitten, and that she's the most beautiful woman he's ever seen. Very soon thereafter, he's professing great love for her, saying she's the soulmate he's been looking for and he wants to spend the rest of his life with her. Juliet, who's never received such intensely romantic attention, is swept off her feet by his effusive declarations, which are often accompanied by very sexy photos. Romeo is one hot dude and he loves showing her exactly what he's got. She's in lust. But she's convinced herself it's love.

I never thought I'd ever hear someone tell me they'd fallen in love with someone they'd never met, but in court, I heard people tell me that many times. It may be hard to understand, but there are a lot of lonely, vulnerable people who, despite being professionally successful and appearing confident, have low self-esteem when it comes to romantic relationships. They're craving romance, love, and affection, and they're ripe for the picking by swindlers.

Back to our scenario. The couple arrange to meet in person. Juliet might travel to visit Romeo where he lives, but often he'll persuade her to invite him to visit her at her home. He wants to check out his potential new digs. And besides, if Juliet were to see where and how Romeo lives, she'd probably realize he's a loser and ditch him.

Romeo and Juliet spend a few weeks together at Juliet's home. It's pure magic, a dream come true. Romeo gives Juliet the best sex she's ever had and treats her like a queen. He only has eyes for her. She can't believe her good fortune in meeting such a perfect man who wants to build his whole world around her. She sees her unborn children in his eyes. Yup, no doubt about it. She's in love.

During Romeo's sojourn into Juliet's world, she excitedly introduces him to her family and friends. Most if not all of them are skeptical. They say things to her like "How much do you know about this guy?" and "There's something about him I just don't trust" and "You're getting way ahead of yourself. Slow down!" She disregards everyone's admonitions and advice, because she knows better. She knows what's in her heart, and her heart would never lie to her. Besides, those other people are probably jealous.

Romeo and Juliet start planning a life together. Because she's the one with the successful career, it's obvious that he will be the one to relocate, not her. And besides, he doesn't really have much of a career (fraudsters never do), so he's happy to leave his country, which of course is what he was planning all along. They may or may not have a few more visits before getting married. Why do they get married so quickly? Because they can't bear being apart, and most importantly, she's going to sponsor him as a new immigrant.

You can guess what happens next. As soon as Romeo gets permanent residency, it's "Farewell Juliet, parting is such sweet sorrow." He's out of her life, except for one little problem. Because they're legally married, Romeo's entitled to a division of matrimonial property (which will include half of Juliet's house), and he'll claim spousal support because, after all, she made him leave his whole world behind to be with her, and now he has no way of supporting himself. The relationship may or may not have produced a child, but if it did, Juliet will find herself unable to collect child support from Romeo because he's a deadbeat.

Did I see cases of immigration fraud where the scam artist was a woman who defrauded a man? Yes, of course I did, but nowhere near as often as I saw men being the scammers. Nevertheless, regardless of the genders of the parties, the tragic results were the same, and my heart broke for the poor victims.

That's why I strongly recommend that, when searching for potential partners online, narrow your search geographically to include only your country or, better yet, only a reasonable commuting radius from where you live. Long-distance relationships are fraught with problems.

However, con artists can be homegrown too. Regardless of where the person you've hooked up with lives, there's always the potential that he or she might be a trickster. Anyone can go online and create a profile replete with falsehoods. It's so easy to create a backstory comprised of sheer fantasy regarding one's age, family history, education, marital status, and financial circumstances. And technology enables the creation of fallacious or distorted photos. How do you really know the person you're dealing with?

The biggest enemy of online daters is protection of privacy legislation. It's almost impossible to obtain reliable and accurate information about other people. Even private investigators find it difficult to pierce the veil of privacy surrounding total strangers.

Over the years I had numerous cases involving people who'd been duped by grifters they'd met online. In one case, a couple opened a joint bank account after getting married, into which their salaries were automatically deposited. One day, the wife discovered to her horror that the account had been garnished by the child support enforcement agency to pay child support arrears of thirty-two thousand dollars owed by the husband to his former wife. The wife was aware her husband had been married before and had two children, but he had neglected to tell her he was in default of his child support obligations. And there was no way for her to discover this independently.

I dealt with even more shocking cases where a person had no idea whatsoever that his or her partner had been married before, or worse, was still married. And there were many other cases where people discovered too late that their spouses had: changed their names; had criminal records prohibiting them from driving or from travelling to other countries; had gone bankrupt; had evaded taxes, fines, or other debts; or had children they were unaware of from previous relationships. I saw people duped into believing the person they'd met online had a particular job, only to discover that the person was engaged in illegal activity such as drug trafficking. When you don't know anything about someone other than what they choose to tell you, common sense dictates you should proceed with caution.

Here's what I recommend before getting involved with someone you meet online, and by "getting involved" I mean deciding to live with them, marry them, comingle your finances with them, or *especially* have a child with them. Each party should sign a consent authorizing the other to obtain any information in government databases, such as criminal records. Each party should provide full disclosure of all bank account and investment records. Insist on meeting the person's family so you can ask them questions and gauge their responses. And make sure you see for yourself where they're working. I know this may sound like overkill and detracts from the romance, but take it from someone who's seen it all: It's better to be safe than sorry.

Before deciding to cohabit with or marry someone, it's definitely worth consulting with a family law lawyer to discuss the desirability of entering into a prenuptial agreement. Given the reality that almost half of all relationships break up (and if we include couples who cohabited without getting married, the breakup numbers are much higher), prenuptial agreements are definitely worth considering.

The moral of the story is that if someone seems too good to be true, they probably *are*. When meeting people with whom you've connected online, it's always advisable to keep your eyes wide open and maintain a healthy sense of skepticism until you have solid proof that the person is who they say they are.

CHAPTER 16

KNOWING WHEN TO LEAVE: RETIRING FROM THE JUDICIARY

The position of chief justice of the Ontario Court of Justice is filled every eight years by way of appointment by the Attorney General. In 2015 it was time to replace Chief Justice Annemarie Bonkalo, who was about to complete her eight-year term. I was approached by numerous colleagues from across the province who encouraged me to put my name forward. They felt I would be an excellent candidate because of my pre-judicial administrative experience as a director in the government, together with my twenty-year history of having presided in both criminal and family courts (which none of our prior chiefs had done), my public profile attained through my book and television show, my progressive ideas about enhancing access to justice, and my being bilingual.

The only other candidate was Associate Chief Justice Lise Maisonneuve, who had the obvious advantage of being next in line to the chief. She'd also served as a regional senior justice, so she was steeped in the world of senior judicial management. She was part of the chief justice's inner circle and was widely considered to be the heir apparent.

But many of my colleagues, who'd been longing for much-needed modernization of the court system, viewed her as part of the problem, not the solution. They felt she was part of the old guard and therefore represented a continuation of the archaic and outmoded way of doing business, whereas I was brimming with fresh ideas to bring the delivery of justice services into the modern age. For example, I wanted to open the courts during evenings and weekends, much in the way that banks have, to enhance access to justice. I envisioned a streamlining and integration of criminal and family court cases for families involved in both courts due to domestic violence criminal charges and family proceedings resulting from marriage breakdown. Those parallel cases should be dealt with at the same time and by the same judge. Similarly, I wanted family court cases involving spouses living in different jurisdictions across the country, or even in different countries, to be heard by video conferencing instead of the ridiculously unwieldy paper-based process being used. I felt strongly that administrative barriers between jurisdictions should be eliminated. I advocated for expediting trials involving child witnesses to reduce delays and minimize the stress on children of having to remember traumatic events for inordinate periods of time. I foresaw technological and administrative efficiencies, such as introducing a paperless system and online scheduling of court appearances, to make the administration of justice less cumbersome, time-consuming, and expensive. There was far too much wasted time in the courts, which exacerbated delays and increased the cost of every aspect of the system. And I wanted to create a community-based steering committee comprised of laypeople — actual users of the court — to provide much-needed input into the delivery of justice services.

I spent countless hours considering the pros and cons of the move before finally deciding to put my name forward. Over the next few weeks, I received over two hundred letters of support from colleagues recommending my appointment. Word began spreading that my candidacy was being well received by the government, which at that time was led by Canada's first openly gay premier, Kathleen Wynne. I was receiving regular messages from numerous political insiders that the government was impressed with my qualifications and that, under Premier Wynne's leadership, the government was ready to make history by appointing the first openly gay chief justice not only in Canada, but in the world.

And then, on February 24, 2015, the unthinkable happened. *The National Post* featured an article written by Christie Blatchford, a prominent journalist, reporting she had been contacted by "an anonymous tipster" who said there was "unease on the Bench" about the very real possibility of my being appointed chief justice, given that the premier and I were both gay. The tipster went on to suggest that I didn't have "the necessary gravitas" required for the position. Ms. Blatchford suggested that, because of my reputation as "an approachable innovator," I might be seen as a threat to some on "the oft-stuffy Bench." She slammed the tipster and his cohorts for engaging in what she labelled a "smear campaign."

I was devastated. Never before had the process for appointing a provincial chief justice been politicized — and to think it was done by a cowardly colleague deliberately attempting to weaponize the media! Moreover, the expressed concern that an openly gay premier might appoint an openly gay chief justice, combined with the reference to a lack of "gravitas," a long-used trope well understood to mean "not straight," reeked of blatant homophobia. After all the progress the gay community had made, the thought that there were still judges expressing such abhorrent prejudices was beyond demoralizing.

What made the matter particularly egregious was that, despite receiving demands from outraged colleagues to launch an investigation into the source of the article, and urging her to, at the very least, send an email to the entire court denouncing the despicable conduct of the colleague in question, and despite a heated telephone conversation with her in which I clearly expressed my outrage, Chief Justice Bonkalo chose to do nothing. The obvious and inescapable implication from her glaring idleness was that she, too, shared the opinion that I was unsuitable for the position.

Did I know the identity of the culprit who contacted Christie Blatchford? Of course I did. Ms. Blatchford was so disgusted that a judge would behave in such a despicable manner that she told me. The "anonymous tipster" was a member of the court's senior management and a well-known homophobe. Did I report my colleague to the judicial council for engaging in blatantly inappropriate conduct totally unbecoming to the judiciary? No.

I've always understood that when a judicial career crashes, the entire Bench is diminished. My desire for retribution was nowhere near as important as the need to preserve the dignity of the court's public image. Enough damage to the judiciary's reputation had already been done by Ms. Blatchford's article. Besides, I'm a strong believer that karma has a way of taking care of people who hurt you.

Despite Ms. Blatchford's well-intentioned support, her article engendered such backlash that my fate was sealed. No politician, especially a gay one, was going to run the risk of being accused of appointing someone to such a prominent position merely because they both "played on the same team." Lise Maisonneuve got the job, and none of the major innovations I was contemplating materialized. For the first time since becoming a judge in 1995, I began to feel disillusionment with the institution I had worked so hard to support.

In retrospect, I'd dodged a bullet. One year after the new chief was appointed, the court was thrown into turmoil by the Supreme Court of Canada's landmark decision in *R v. Jordan*, which mandated that all criminal cases had to be decided within eighteen months of a charge being laid. Suddenly, hundreds of thousands of cases that had been languishing in the court system for well over eighteen months were at risk of being thrown out. A total re-engineering of the court's case management system had to be devised and implemented.

Then, the chief had to contend with a comprehensive and intrusive audit by the Ontario public auditor, whose 2019 report slammed the court for being deplorably inefficient. The report was an embarrassment that no chief justice could ever overcome.

And then, in 2020, an unimaginable tribulation occurred. The courts had to be shut down due to a global pandemic. The chief justice's life had become a living nightmare. At that point, I thanked my lucky stars that she had gotten the job and not me.

The last time I spent any time in a courtroom was March 13, 2020. That afternoon, everything was shut down everywhere due to the pandemic, and everyone was forced to work from home. I was sixty-three years old and presiding exclusively in criminal court. For the first few months, judges presided over their dockets by telephone, adjourning cases week to week in the hopes that the pandemic would be brought under control and in-person court appearances would resume. No such luck!

Although Zoom was launched in 2013, it wasn't approved for use in the courts until the fall of 2020. Thanks to the invention of online video conferencing, and our adoption of it, we could actually see the lawyers, accused, and witnesses on our computer screens and were able to hear guilty pleas and conduct minor trials. But the work of judging was changed dramatically by this method of communicating. Dealing with people remotely on a computer screen gave rise to a number of significant challenges, the most serious of which, for me, was at the human level. My inability to observe people's body language and look them right in the eyes when speaking with them made the interactions considerably less impactful than being physically present with them. It was extremely difficult to establish an emotional connection with the people who appeared before me, and the ability to do that had always been my trademark and my forte as a judge.

And there were other problems. Remote proceedings were cumbersome. Accommodations had to be made whenever a lawyer needed to confer privately with their client so that no one else could hear their conversation. In addition, the prisons had immense difficulties accommodating the inmates' needs to appear in court remotely. They had to construct dozens of private booths with video conferencing capacities for all the prisoners appearing in different courts at the same time, and there were significant delays throughout the day as we waited for prisoners to be brought from their cells to the video booths.

As judges weren't physically present at the courthouse, the court staff had to complete paperwork on our behalf, and since we couldn't verify the accuracy of the documents, serious errors were sometimes made. In one case, I sentenced an offender to a fine and gave him thirty days to pay it. My clerk misheard me and issued a warrant committing the man to jail for thirty days. These kinds of errors weren't infrequent.

And, as anyone who uses the internet knows only too well, there were endless technical glitches due to poor internet connectivity, audio problems, video freezes, and the like. Many accused persons didn't have computers and had to log on using cellphones, with varying degrees of success based on their locations. Frustratingly, it often seemed like the entire focus of the proceedings was on trying to make the technology work, rather than on addressing the substantive issues before the court.

As you might expect, many calamities occurred when dealing with accused on their cellphones. In one case, a man used his cell phone to plead guilty to impaired driving while driving his car. In the middle of the proceedings, he was pulled over by a police officer and charged with using a cellphone while operating a motor vehicle. We resumed the guilty plea after the officer gave him a ticket and left. But another problem suddenly arose. The conviction for impaired driving resulted in an immediate suspension of the offender's driver's licence — while he was actually driving! So unless he instantly stopped driving, he'd be guilty of committing a further offence.

In another case, a woman using her cellphone pleaded guilty to shoplifting while she was at a grocery store. Before we could finish the case, she was arrested by store security for stealing yet again. So much for criminal prosecutions having a deterrent effect.

I had one trial conducted on Zoom during which the prosecution's main witness suspiciously kept correcting herself and changing her story. She finally confessed that someone off-camera was coaching her, telling her what to say. After that, I was extremely reluctant to conduct trials on Zoom because there was simply no way to ensure the integrity of the process.

As the pandemic wore on, my frustration level compounded exponentially. It was lonely sitting in front of a computer screen all day long. We had no contact with our colleagues, who were busy in their homes doing the same thing I was. I missed the physical interaction with them and with the court staff, lawyers, and members of the public. And most of all, presiding in court over Zoom made the job profoundly unsatisfying. I knew in my heart it was time to prepare an exit plan. As Snaggletooth used to say in the cartoons, "Exit, stage left!"

In Canada, judges are permitted to keep working until their seventy-fifth birthday, and most do. They love the intellectual stimulation, interpersonal contact, and the satisfaction that comes from dispensing justice, not to mention the salary, social status, and prestige that comes with the position. And for many judges, their entire identities are completely enmeshed in their judicial roles — they *are* what they do. They can't imagine their lives having any purpose or meaning if they cease to be judges.

I never felt that way. For me, being a judge was just a job — an important job, to be sure, but still just a job. When I put on my robe, I became "Mr. Justice Brownstone," a representative of a fundamentally important societal institution, and people called me "Your Honour." But when the robe came off, I was "Harvey" and was happy to have people call me by my first name. I never allowed the job to define me as a person because I didn't think that was healthy.

In early 2021 I began thinking about retirement. I knew I would be eligible to retire with a full pension upon my sixty-fifth birthday in July 2021. But the big question was, what would I do to keep busy after retiring? I was much too active and energetic to simply do nothing.

And then the answer came to me.

CHAPTER 17

THE ULTIMATE REINVENTION

Ever since I can remember, I've been a talk-show junkie. I grew up watching Johnny Carson, Merv Griffin, Dinah Shore, Mike Douglas, David Frost, Barbara Walters, Brian Linehan, Larry King, Oprah Winfrey, and my idol, Dick Cavett. Being enamoured of Hollywood and pop culture, I wanted to know as much about my favourite stars as I could. I would watch celebrity interviews and think to myself, "I can do it better. I can ask more profound questions. I know more than the interviewer about the guest's life and career. Why isn't the interviewer following up on what the guest just said?" The dream of being a celebrity interviewer never left my consciousness.

I'm frequently asked, "If you loved talk shows so much as a kid, why didn't you pursue a career as an interviewer instead of going to law school?" Believe me, I wanted to. But I'd already disappointed my parents enormously by telling them I was gay. I just couldn't bring myself to devastate them further by going to Hollywood to take my chances in show business. Besides, after coming out to them, I was ferociously determined to become a successful professional of whom they could be proud. Pursuing a career in the entertainment world was far too uncertain and unpredictable for my liking. There was no guarantee of success in show business, whereas if I pursued a legal career, there was a much better chance that I'd make something of myself. So, I suppressed my lifelong dream of being an interviewer.

One day in February 2021, as I was presiding in court over Zoom, it suddenly occurred to me that if I could see, hear, and speak with lawyers and accused persons on my computer screen, why couldn't I do the same thing with celebrities? Zoom provided all the technology I would need to give it a try. And YouTube provided a worldwide platform allowing people to easily post videos. All I needed now was to find some way to convince famous people to speak with me. And that's how *Harvey Brownstone Interviews* was born.

I started by contacting Jim Keaton, the president of the Helen Reddy Fan Club, with whom I had connected on Facebook. I'm a lifelong Helen Reddy fan and wanted to interview Jim about his friendship with this iconic singer. Within days of posting the interview on YouTube, it went viral. Fans were clamouring for more. Jim and I ended up filming a four-part series about Helen's life and career. The fans ate it up, and I was on my way.

Before attempting to attract major celebrities, I decided to contact authors, hoping they would be happy to grant interviews promoting their books. And it worked. My first author was Ella Burakowski, whose book *Hidden Gold* is one of the most important and compelling pieces of Holocaust literature I've ever read. Since then, I've interviewed numerous authors of books about the Holocaust, which, given my mother's history, is a topic near and dear to my heart.

One of my favourite authors who've appeared on the show is Lee Tannen, whose book *I Loved Lucy* chronicles his close friendship with Lucille Ball. I also had the privilege of interviewing Kathryn Sermak, whose book *Miss D and Me* recounts her experiences as the personal assistant of Bette Davis. Renowned celebrity biographer J. Randy Taraborrelli, bestselling author of books about Frank Sinatra, Marilyn Monroe, Elizabeth Taylor, Diana Ross, Michael Jackson, and the Kennedys, is a terrific and frequent guest. Patti Davis, daughter of President Ronald Reagan, gave an eye-opening interview about her parents. Stewart Pearce, author of *Diana: The Voice of Change*, who was Princess Diana's vocal coach and dear friend, spoke poignantly and with great affection about her. Nelson Mandela's personal secretary Zelda La Grange came on our show to discuss her book *Good Morning, Mr. Mandela.*

So far, one of my viewers' favourite guest authors has been Martin McKenna, whose international bestseller *The Boy Who Talked to Dogs* chronicled his horrific youth as an abused child in Ireland. He'd run away from home when he was thirteen years old and, for three years, lived with a pack of wild dogs in the streets of Dublin. During that time, he learned many secrets about how to communicate effectively with dogs. His appearance on our show stands out as one of the most heart-wrenching and emotionally powerful interviews I've ever conducted.

Once I had a few interviews with authors under my belt, I began writing to the managers, agents, and publicists of my favourite celebrities asking to interview their clients. I explained my love of interviewing and told them I believed my forty years' experience in the courtroom as a lawyer and judge had equipped me with a unique skill set that distinguished me from other interviewers. I mentioned my thorough research skills and promised to make the interviews interesting for their clients by asking them questions they'd never been asked before. Little by little, I started to secure interviews.

The first celebrity to grant me an interview was Olympic diver Greg Louganis, who spoke candidly about his struggles coming out in the homophobic sports world of the 1980s. Then Oscar nominee Lesley Ann Warren agreed to take a chance on me. I'll never forget her heartfelt reaction when I told her how much her performance of "In My Own Little Corner" in the 1965 television production of *Cinderella* impacted me back when I was a severely bullied child. I will always be grateful to Greg and Lesley for taking a chance on me. They opened the door to getting me many more interviews because I was able to show industry executives what I was capable of.

The first legendary star to appear on my show was Robert Wagner, who is well known for being highly reluctant to grant interviews. It took many months of begging and pleading with his publicist to consider my request. One day, out of the blue, my phone rang and I heard that unmistakable voice asking, "Hello, is that Harvey?"

I answered, "Yes, it is."

He replied, "Well, hello there Harvey. This is Robert Wagner. I understand you want to interview me. What would you like to talk about?"

I felt like Jackie Gleason when he portrayed Ralph Kramden on *The Honeymooners* and would say, "Humma humma humma." I was completely tongue-tied, yet managed somehow to croak out a few topics of conversation about his career that I would love to ask him about. He was impressed when I told him I'd read all three of his books and that I wanted to promote them on my show. We hit it off right from the get-go, and that interview was one of the great highlights of my life. He insisted from the outset that I call him "R.J.," and we became fast friends. As I write this, R.J. is ninety-five years old, still going strong, and we speak frequently. I love hearing his many stories about the golden age of Hollywood.

My interview with R.J. was a major turning point in the show. The circles are small in the entertainment industry. Once the big stars and their management teams saw that Robert Wagner had appeared on our show, it became easier to convince more major celebrities to do the same. In quick succession a whole slew of stars granted me interviews, including Pat Boone, Ann-Margret, George Chakiris, Brenda Vaccaro, Stacy Keach, William H. Macy, F. Murray Abraham, Rich Little, Diane Ladd, Linda Evans, Michele Lee, Morgan Fairchild, and dozens more.

By the end of 2021, the show had already amassed hundreds of thousands of viewers and listeners and appeared on every major audio and video podcast platform. I realized that my hobby had now morphed into a full-blown career. And so, much to the shock of my colleagues, who couldn't believe that a judge would leave such a prestigious position to become a mere podcaster, I unceremoniously retired from the judiciary and have never looked back. I've never been happier.

I believe the key to my success as an interviewer is that I found a way to incorporate my courtroom skills into my questioning style, starting with intensive preparation. I spend many hours researching my guests' lives and careers well beyond their Wikipedia pages, websites, and social media posts. I watch as many of their movies and TV shows as I can. If they've written books, I read them. If they've given other interviews, I watch them. When a guest says, "Oh Harvey, you know more about my life than I do" or "I've never been asked that question before" or "This is the best interview I've ever had," those comments are the biggest reward an interviewer can ever receive from a guest.

My interviews always begin with a lengthy introduction detailing the major highlights of my guests' careers, including not only their bodies of work but the most important awards and accolades bestowed upon them. Many viewers have asked why my introductions are so long. Here's the answer: Those introductions perfectly convey to my guests, before I've asked even one question, that they're in the hands of a pro who's done his homework.

That was very important in the early days when no one had ever heard of me. Frequently the celebrities who'd been booked on my show would start the conversation by snapping, "How long is this gonna take?" Not even a hello. They were clearly annoyed with their representatives for subjecting them to yet another likely robotic interviewer who knew nothing about them and would ask formulaic questions they'd already answered hundreds of times before. But when they heard my carefully crafted introductions, reminding them of projects they hadn't thought about in years, they immediately realized they were in for a conversation with someone who knew as much about their careers as they did, and maybe even more.

My trademark introductions quickly became a hallmark of the show. Viewers love the celebrities' reactions, which are always amusing. Lucie Arnaz (singer-actress, daughter of Lucille Ball and Desi Arnaz) responded, "Harvey, I want you to write my biographies for every program from now until the end of time." Michael Learned (co-star of the beloved TV show *The Waltons*) said, "That's the most incredible introduction I have ever had in my entire life." Loretta Swit (co-star of the classic sitcom *M*A*S*H*) replied, "You've taken my breath away." Sharon Gless (co-star of the iconic TV series *Cagney and Lacey*) laughed, "Harvey, my God, I've never heard a resumé like that. I'm exhausted! I didn't realize I did all that!" Linda Evans (co-star of the blockbuster TV drama *Dallas*) gushed, "Oh my goodness! I can't believe all the things you just said about my life!" Renée Taylor (actress and Oscar-nominated co-writer of *Lovers and Other Strangers*) choked out, "You made me cry. I can't even talk." And more than one star has joked, "Harvey, when I die, I want you to write my obituary!"

Once a celebrity guest, having heard their introduction, realizes they're in good hands, they relax and start opening up. My goal is to pierce beneath the protective veils with which famous people cloak themselves to protect their public images. I want to elicit responses that go much deeper than the canned answers celebrities have churned out hundreds of times before. That desire to delve into a guest's soul stems directly from my cross-examination technique as a lawyer. I never interrogated people in the witness stand; I interviewed them. Everything I did in my career prepared me for what I'm doing now as a talk show host.

In order to prompt my guests to bare their souls, I have to devise probing questions aimed at discovering who these people really are, what makes them tick, and how they overcame the many rejections, betrayals, and disappointments that inevitably occur in any show business career. I want to know how they developed their resilience, how they handled fame, and whether they're satisfied with the lives and careers they've had. I put myself in the place of a fan, asking questions they would ask if they could. My goal is to turn every interview into a memorable event for my guests and viewers.

A big part of interviewing is listening — really paying attention to what a guest is saying. By responding with kindness, compassion, and empathy, I create an atmosphere of comfort and safety, which inspires my guests to bare their souls and reveal aspects of their lives they've never publicly discussed before. Loni Anderson (co-star of the popular sitcom *WKRP in Cincinnati*) disclosed details of her turbulent marriage to Burt Reynolds. Soap opera star Susan Seaforth Hayes (*Days of Our Lives*) tearfully explained the impact of losing her beloved husband of fifty years, actor and co-star Bill Hayes. Film star Steve Guttenberg movingly described how he'd cared for his beloved and very ill father during the last few years of his life. Movie star Robby Benson related his experiences of having undergone life-threatening open heart surgery four times. Singing sensation Jackie Evancho shared her struggles with body dysmorphia and eating disorders. Actor Stacy Keach candidly addressed his experiences in jail following his conviction for drug smuggling. Acclaimed director Waris Hussein talked heartbreakingly about living as a closeted gay man in the 1980s and directing a movie about AIDS while, unbeknownst to the cast and crew, he was simultaneously watching his partner die of that awful disease. Actress Karen Grassle (*Little House on the Prairie*) revealed the hardships of enduring workplace harassment from Michael Landon. Gary Lewis (of the pop group Gary Lewis and the Playboys and son of legendary comedian Jerry Lewis) heart-wrenchingly spoke about his father's callous parenting style. Acclaimed folk singer Judy Collins spoke about her struggles with alcoholism. Three-time Oscar nominee Dyan Cannon talked about her troubled marriage to cinematic legend Cary Grant. The list goes on and on.

And sometimes a guest will reveal something so jaw-dropping that I'm gobsmacked. Fifties blonde bombshell Mamie Van Doren's story about her one and only date with screen idol Rock Hudson, which ended up on her kitchen floor, has to be heard to be believed. No spoilers here.

In 2023, I was honoured to be chosen by Louis Gossett Jr. to conduct his final in-depth interview. He was in very poor health, and on the day we spoke, he was feeling pensive and contemplative about his legacy and the impact of his life. Just before we started filming, he said, "Harvey, let's not talk a lot about my career. I've spoken enough about my work. This is my chance to talk about what's in my heart." I threw away my list of prepared questions and decided to simply let him take the lead and see where it went. The result was profoundly moving.

I've had the privilege of interviewing many great musical stars, including Little Anthony of Little Anthony and the Imperials; Peter Noone of Herman's Hermits; Bill Medley of the Righteous Brothers; Marie Osmond; Toni Tennille of the Captain and Tennille; Marilyn McCoo, Billy Davis Jr., and Florence LaRue of the Fifth Dimension; Graham Russell of Air Supply; John Illsley of Dire Straits; Alan Paul of the Manhattan Transfer; and Gilbert O'Sullivan, Sheena Easton, Taylor Dayne, Peabo Bryson, and dozens more who have entertained, enlightened, and comforted us through their artistry. Their music has provided the soundtrack to our lives.

Among my most distinguished guests from the world of musical theatre was Sir Tim Rice, the legendary lyricist who brought us such iconic shows as

Jesus Christ Superstar, *Joseph and the Amazing Technicolor Dreamcoat*, *Evita*, *The Lion King*, and many others. His interview was a master class in the art of writing lyrics, as he generously shared the secrets of his genius in bringing such unforgettable entertainment and joy to the world. And I was elated when he said to me at the end of the interview, "Thank you for being such a brilliantly researched interviewer. You know more about me than I do." When I expressed my hope that I could interview him again one day, he laughingly replied, "I'm free tomorrow at half past three." Unforgettable moments like that make all my hard work so worthwhile.

I'm often asked which interview has been my favourite so far. As of the date of writing, the answer is Tony Orlando of the popular '70s music group Tony Orlando and Dawn. During the interview, as I was mentioning many of Tony's career achievements, he broke down and cried. He was completely blown away that an interviewer had taken the time to do so much research about his life. We actually had to pause the interview so he could compose himself. I was completely taken aback. Although I've had many guests shed a tear or two during an interview, Tony's emotionality turned this interview into pure magic. The interview went viral, so much so that Tony returned to the show three weeks later by popular demand to continue the conversation, which was equally memorable.

When I can establish an emotional connection with a guest, as happened with Tony, my viewers are actually watching a friendship being created in real time. This also happened with esteemed songwriter Paul Williams, who lives an intensely private life and notoriously shuns interviews. He was persuaded to appear on our show by his friend and colleague, musician Dan Foliart, who was impressed by my therapeutic interviewing style when he appeared on the show.

Having watched the 2011 documentary about Paul Williams called *Still Alive*, I knew he was living with emotional demons emanating from his struggles to cope with fame. And in an effort to make him feel better about himself, I told him I understood why, as a young star, he'd used self-deprecating humour to overcompensate for the insecurity he felt in Hollywood. Smiling, he said, "You have wisdom worthy of the Bench, sir."

I then told him I thought the reason he always wanted to hang around the biggest stars was because he needed to feel like "a member of the club." Paul replied, "You know, I spend a lot of money on therapists, but you're doing a really good job."

I went on to say that one of the reasons his fans loved him so much was because he always presented as being on the outside looking in, and that was exactly how his fans felt. Paul chuckled and said, "You know what? I don't know what I paid my last therapist, but do you mind if I send you a cheque?"

At the end of this remarkably touching conversation, Paul called me "a classic representative of kindness" and went on to say, "We will stay friends. You're an exceptional man and it's an honour to talk to you." Believe me, the honour was all mine.

Over the years, I've been privileged to interview the children of some of the greatest cinematic icons in the history of show business, including Errol Flynn, Orson Welles, Boris Karloff, Frank Sinatra, Hedy Lamarr, Audrey Hepburn, John Garfield, Jack Lemmon, Lucille Ball, Leonard Bernstein, Peggy Lee, Mel Tormé, Don Knotts, Tim Conway, Glen Campbell, and many more. The children of great stars are extremely protective of their parents' legacies, and it's an enormous privilege to be entrusted by them to celebrate their parents' careers and bodies of work on my show.

One of the greatest thrills I've ever received was to have Grammy-nominated, multi-platinum singer-songwriter Harriet Schock write a song inspired by my life struggles, entitled "I Am Yours." This beautiful ballad resulted from a conversation Harriet and I had after one of her appearances on my show. She asked me to tell her about my life, so I briefly told her about the difficulties I endured to gain parental acceptance. The song, recorded by popular singer Gary Lynn Floyd, is also included on Harriet's album *Paintings*, and she performed it on her highly acclaimed documentary concert film *Hollywood Town: The Harriet Schock Story*. "I Am Yours" never fails to bring tears to my eyes because Harriet's haunting melody and brilliant lyrics perfectly express my anguish, heartache, and longing.

Another immensely important person who came into my life, first as a guest on my show and then as a beloved friend, is celebrated producer, interviewer, and author Julian Schlossberg. His fascinating, compelling, and entertaining memoirs *Try Not to Hold It Against Me: A Producer's Life* and *My First Book — Part 2* are must-reads for every show-business lover. Julian is a brilliant raconteur (he hilariously credits Marilyn Monroe with making him ambidextrous), and he's also a cherished mentor, both personally and professionally. His support and love have contributed much to my life and to the success of the show.

Harvey Brownstone Interviews was initially intended to be nothing more than a post-retirement hobby, but as you can see, it took on a life of its own. In 2022, as the show continued to attract legendary stars and the audience was compounding exponentially, I was approached by a fledgling cable TV network in the United Kingdom — XPTV1, run by the magnanimous Darren Jay — who asked for permission to broadcast the show. Of course I agreed, and that turned what had been available only on YouTube into a television show as well. Since then, XPTV1 has grown into a successful broadcasting company that airs *Harvey Brownstone Interviews* throughout the U.K., Europe, North Africa, and the Caribbean. As of the date of writing, the show attracts an audience of over ten million viewers per week.

That same year, I was approached by Dominique Benedict, owner of Breakfast at Dominique's, a company producing exclusive, artisanal signature coffee blends licensed by the estates of many illustrious stars including Joan Crawford, Bette Davis, Ava Gardner, Ella Fitzgerald, and Boris Karloff. She wanted to produce a signature coffee in my honour and sent me a sample — a bold and balanced medium roast produced from fair trade, organic coffee beans. I loved it, and voilà, the "Harvey Brownstone Talk Show Blend" coffee was born! People tell me all the time that it's the best coffee they've ever tasted, which is very gratifying.

In 2022, I was approached by the wonderful management team of Rick Marcelli and Robin Bragg-Marcelli of the Marcelli Company in Hollywood. They persuaded me to "dream big," and with their invaluable leadership and guidance, the show has risen to heights I never could have imagined. In 2023, *Harvey Brownstone Interviews* was listed at number twelve on the "Hollywood 411 List of the Top 50 Talk Shows in the World." And in 2024, *Daily Hollywood News* called my show "one of the most epic and popular television extravaganzas to have risen in a long time" and described me as "a superstar almost overnight." Later that same year, the *Los Angeles Weekly Times* ranked *Harvey Brownstone Interviews* at number three on its "Best of the Best" list of the top internet shows in the world. It's truly a dream come true.

But of all the special moments I've had since launching my show, the number one spot belongs to my idol, talk show superstar host Dick Cavett, who came out of retirement at the age of eighty-seven to grant me an interview. I had written to him many times saying he was my hero and that his talk show inspired me to launch my own interview program. Finally, with the help of his former program coordinator, Joan Kramer, who appeared on our show with director David Healey to promote their wonderful book *In the Company of Legends*, Dick agreed to watch a few episodes of my show. He was hooked, and immediately agreed to grant me an interview.

Dick was everything I had hoped he'd be: brilliant, witty, erudite, and endlessly charming. We talked about many memorable moments on his long-running TV show. And at the end of our conversation, he knocked my socks off by saying, "Harvey, I want you to admit right now that you are *really good.* And if anyone tries to tell you that you don't have what it takes, they're wrong. You're one of the people who has learned how to do a very difficult and tricky thing. You're very good at it and your show is well worth watching." I'm still floating on cloud nine. Hearing those words from a person I've idolized my entire life meant the world to me.

Writing this book, and looking back at my journey and the series of roller-coaster surprises, obstacles, heartbreaks, and triumphs that have brought me to this point, I now have attained the clarity to finally realize I wouldn't change a thing. Your past doesn't have to define you, but it shapes the person you become and equips you with the life lessons you need to be the best person you can be and reach your highest potential.

There were many times when, as a young man, I felt pressure to suppress and even repress who I am. The most significant instance occurred soon after I began working at the Ministry of the Attorney General in 1989. The Attorney General, Ian Scott, was a brilliant lawyer and a highly respected cabinet minister. He also happened to be gay. It was an open secret. Everyone at the ministry and in the political world knew it, but he never talked about it. He always attended public events accompanied by a female friend who was happy to serve as his "beard." I'm quite certain the media knew he was gay, but they respected his privacy and never "outed" him.

One day, a senior member of the Attorney General's political staff invited me to a dinner party at Mr. Scott's home. He explained there was a tight-knit network of high-powered gay men in Toronto, often referred to as the "gay mafia," and Mr. Scott enjoyed hosting dinner parties several times a year to foster that network. Someone had told him there was a new, young gay lawyer working at the support enforcement agency, and he instructed one of his assistants to invite me to the party.

I couldn't believe it. I'd never met the Attorney General and was beyond excited to be included in his inner circle. Upon entering the rarefied atmosphere of his beautifully decorated mansion on Castle Frank Avenue, a ruggedly handsome twenty-something blond Adonis with the look of a California surfer boy greeted me at the door and introduced himself as Ian Scott's partner, Kim Yakabuski. We stepped into a voluminous space replete with plush bluish-grey Persian carpeting, pale peach walls lined with paintings that appeared to be worth more than my annual salary, and antique Chippendale chairs upon which were perched some of the country's well-known and powerful glitterati — lawyers, politicians, businessmen, and real estate tycoons — all of whom were gay, but closeted.

Kim then brought me over to meet Mr. Scott, an attractive, fit-looking, grey-haired man in his mid-fifties with a wide, warm smile and a firm handshake, wearing a navy-blue turtleneck sweater under a grey-blue Harris tweed sports jacket and grey, plush velvet corduroy pants. His black Gucci tassel loafers were the shiniest shoes I'd ever seen. He looked like a model out of *Gentlemen's Quarterly* magazine.

As Mr. Scott shook my hand, he placed his other hand on my shoulder and said, "Nice to meet you, Harvey. I've heard great things about you. Welcome to the club." He then introduced me to many of his other guests, all of whom I'd heard of but none of whom I'd ever met. I felt like I had truly arrived.

During the sumptuous roast beef dinner served by exquisitely tailored staff, who looked even more delicious than the food, the conversation inevitably turned to the subject of the pros and cons of coming out, which gay people talked about ad nauseam in those days. The consensus among my tablemates was that anyone wishing to attain success should remain closeted. Ian Scott led the pack, saying, "Take it from me, gentlemen. Coming out is professional suicide. Consider my situation. Would I ever have been elected to public office, let alone be named Attorney General, if I had come out?" Everyone heartily agreed with him.

Taking a deep breath and hoping for the best, I meekly offered, "But Mr. Scott, surely you're aware that your sexual orientation is well known within the ministry and even beyond. I heard you were gay long before I started working there. What would you say if a journalist asked you if you were gay? Would you deny it?"

A palpable silence permeated the room and all eyes turned to Mr. Scott. He clenched his jaw, aimed his steely blue eyes directly at me, and bristled, "I don't care what people think they know about me. They can *say* whatever they want, but I will never confirm it. And as for the media, if a reporter ever *dared* to ask me such a question, I'd remind him that our government amended the Human Rights Code to include sexual orientation *precisely* so that no one would ever have to answer a question like that. And here's my advice to *you*. Work hard at your job, live your life discreetly, and never give *anyone* the satisfaction of knowing for sure that you're a pariah."

That was the best advice I *never* took. And that was the last time I saw Ian Scott. His term as Attorney General came to an end the next year, in 1990, when his government was defeated. Sadly, his partner Kim Yakabuski died of AIDS in 1993, and Mr. Scott finally acknowledged his sexual orientation in the eulogy he delivered at Kim's funeral. The next year, Mr. Scott suffered a debilitating stroke, and he passed away in 2006 at the age of seventy-two. Although I strongly disagreed with his stance on coming out, his professional accomplishments are worthy of the greatest admiration and respect.

As I reflect on the adventure that's unfolded into the life I've lived, I'm filled with gratitude to have experienced a world that has become increasingly "without prejudice." There is still much work to be done to achieve true equality for LGBTQ+ people in many places, particularly in Africa and the Middle East. But I'm immensely appreciative to have lived through a monumentally positive evolution in the civil rights of gays and lesbians in North America, and in much of the rest of the world. These changes were totally unimaginable when I was a young man struggling to build a positive future.

Despite the obstacles I faced, I'm proud to have trusted my destiny by always staying true to myself and listening to the ever-constant voice inside my head telling me what's right for *me*. I take pride that, notwithstanding the many pressures imposed upon me by family, friends, and colleagues to conform to so-called societal norms, I persevered in maintaining my authenticity. As rock star Janis Joplin said, "Don't compromise yourself. You're all you've got." I'm glad I took those words to heart.

When I was growing up, and during my time in law school and as a young lawyer, it was entirely inconceivable that an openly gay person could ever be appointed to the judiciary, the very summit of the legal profession. It happened not only because societal attitudes towards homosexuality improved, but because a trailblazing Attorney General, Marion Boyd, had the courage to make a landmark appointment that changed the course of history. I'm fortunate that, by becoming Canada's first openly gay judge, I had a role in helping to make society more tolerant, inclusive, and just. I'm grateful to have helped make the judiciary more reflective of the society it serves, and to have opened doors for future generations of lawyers and judges. Now, dozens of gay and lesbian lawyers throughout North America have been appointed to the judiciary.

I'm deeply honoured to have participated in making marriage equality a reality in our lifetime. Although one cannot predict with certainty what future governments might do, I pray that never again will a gay or lesbian person attend a wedding feeling like they're on the outside looking in, excluded from one of the most fundamental institutions in our society.

I'm grateful that my parents lived long enough to see the son they were so ashamed of become a respected member of society and someone they could be proud of. By coming to terms with their antiquated bigotry and learning to love and accept their son with all their hearts, their attitude towards homosexuality most definitely evolved into being without prejudice, in the best sense of the term.

I'm filled with gratitude to the many guardian angels who came into my life over the years when I needed them most and blessed me with kindness, generosity, and guidance. I'm also profoundly thankful for the opportunities life has given me to keep reinventing myself and finding new ways to keep growing and hopefully make a positive difference in the world. I hope my story will inspire and embolden you to remember that no one but you gets to decide whether you're good enough. And if you look hard, life will always present you with opportunities to keep fighting to make your biggest dreams come true. Yes, dare to dream big, to embrace your own uniqueness, to keep believing in yourself, to never give up.

And most of all, to anyone who has ever been bullied, rejected, or told that you'd never amount to anything, I hope you'll harness all the hurt, anger, and negativity triggered by being spurned and channel all of that energy into relentless ambition, drive, and a determination to achieve all your goals and aspirations, without prejudice.

And please never forget: Success is the best revenge!

Entertainment. Writing. Culture.

ECW is a proudly independent, Canadian-owned book publisher. We know great writing can improve people's lives, and we're passionate about sharing original, exciting, and insightful writing across genres.

Thanks for reading along!

We want our books not just to sustain our imaginations, but to help construct a healthier, more just world, and so we've become a certified B Corporation, meaning we meet a high standard of social and environmental responsibility — and we're going to keep aiming higher. We believe books can drive change, but the way we make them can too.

Being a B Corp means that the act of publishing this book should be a force for good — for the planet, for our communities, and for the people that worked to make this book. For example, everyone who worked on this book was paid at least a living wage. You can learn more at the Ontario Living Wage Network.

This book is also available as a Global Certified Accessible™ (GCA) ebook. ECW Press's ebooks are screen reader friendly and are built to meet the needs of those who are unable to read standard print due to blindness, low vision, dyslexia, or a physical disability.

This book is printed on FSC®-certified paper. It contains recycled materials, and other controlled sources, is processed chlorine free, and is manufactured using biogas energy.

ECW's office is situated on land that was the traditional territory of many nations, including the Wendat, the Anishinaabeg, Haudenosaunee, Chippewa, Métis, and current treaty holders the Mississaugas of the Credit. In the 1880s, the land was developed as part of a growing community around St. Matthew's Anglican and other churches. Starting in the 1950s, our neighbourhood was transformed by immigrants fleeing the Vietnam War and Chinese Canadians dispossessed by the building of Nathan Phillips Square and the subsequent rise in real estate value in other Chinatowns. We are grateful to those who cared for the land before us and are proud to be working amidst this mix of cultures.

ecwpress.com